THE AA GUIDE TO

Lake District
& Cumbria

About the authors

Hugh Taylor and Moira McCrossan are travel writers and musicians who live for most of the year in a small, picturesque village in southwest Scotland, and spend their winters in a historic hill town just north of Rome. Although they have travelled extensively they now limit their escapades abroad and spend a large part of each year exploring nearer home. With the Lake District being just over an hour's drive away they are frequent visitors.

As well as writing for a variety of publications ranging from *The Times* to *The Glencairn Gazette* and producing radio programmes for the BBC, they have written or contributed to over 40 travel and outdoors guidebooks including *Essential Scotland, Spiral Scotland, Exploring Britain, Book of Britain's Walks, Walks Through Britain's History* and *50 Walks in the Lake District,* all published by the AA.

Published by AA Publishing (a trading name of AA Media Limited, whose registered office is Fanum House, Basing View, Basingstoke, Hampshire RG21 4EA; registered number 06112600)

© AA Media Limited 2016
First published 2014
Second edition 2016. Reprinted 2017
Third edition 2018

Maps contain data from openstreetmap.org
© OpenStreetMap contributors
Ordnance Survey data © Crown copyright and database right 2018

A CIP catalogue record for this book is available from the British Library.

ISBN: 978-0-7495-7943-2

A05591

Cartography provided by the Mapping Services Department of AA Publishing.

Printed and bound in Italy by Printer Trento Srl.

Every effort has been made to trace the copyright holders, and we apologise in advance for any accidental errors. We would be happy to apply the corrections in the following edition of this publication.

The contents of this book are believed correct at the time of printing. Nevertheless, the publishers cannot be held responsible for any errors or omissions or for changes in the details given in this book or for the consequences of any reliance on the information it provides. This does not affect your statutory rights. We have tried to ensure accuracy in this book, but things do change and we would be grateful if readers would advise us of any inaccuracies they may encounter by emailing us at travelguides@theaa.com.

THE AA GUIDE TO

Lake District & Cumbria

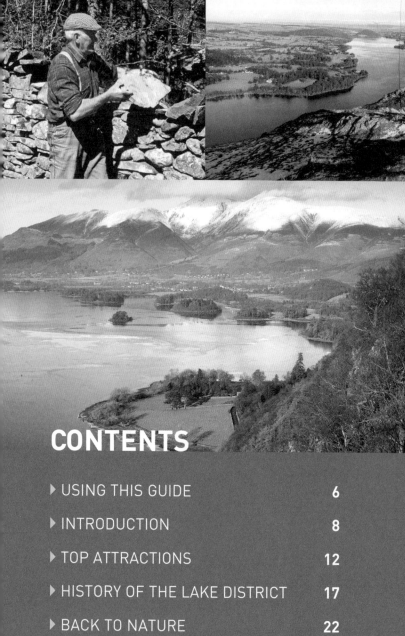

CONTENTS

USING THIS GUIDE

Introduction – has plenty of fascinating background reading, including articles on the landscape and local mythology.

Top attractions – pick out the very best places to visit in the area. You'll spot these later in the A–Z by the flashes of yellow.

Before you go – tells you the things to read, watch, know and pack to get the most from your trip.

Campsites – recommends a number of caravan sites and campsites, which carry the AA's Pennant rating, with the very best receiving the coveted gold Pennant award. Visit theAA.com/self-catering-and-campsites, theAA.com/hotels and theAA.com/bed-and-breakfasts for more places to stay.

A–Z of Lake District & Cumbria – lists all the best of the region, with recommended attractions, activities and places to eat or drink. Places Nearby lists more to see and do.

Eat and drink – contains restaurants that carry an AA Rosette rating, which acknowledges the very best in cooking. Pubs have been selected for their great atmosphere and good food. Visit theAA.com/restaurants and theAA.com/pubs for more food and drink suggestions.

Index – gives you the option to search by theme, grouping the same type of place together, or alphabetically.

Atlas – will help you find your way around, as every main location has a map reference, as do the town plans throughout the book.

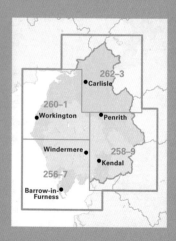

INTRODUCTION

Close your eyes and try to imagine a landscape so piercingly lovely that it takes your breath away. Now visualise yourself standing on a high fell top, looking out over a lush green valley with sunlight shimmering on the surface of the lake running along its length.

You see a shadow on the water, as an osprey swoops from the sky and snatches a plump fish in its talons before soaring skywards again. If you can visualise that you're halfway there but, in reality, the Lake District is far more beautiful than anything you could possibly imagine.

The Lake District, a World Heritage Site, is part of the County of Cumbria, an area stretching from the Scottish Border in the north to Lancashire and North Yorkshire in the south – from the Irish Sea in the west to Northumberland and County Durham in the east. It's a mountainous region containing the highest peaks in England, two National Parks and Hadrian's Wall, also a World Heritage Site.

Cumbria has the second lowest population of any of the English counties yet the Lake District is the most populated of

all the National Parks. Even so, the 41,000 people who live in the National Park make little impact. Cumbria is largely rural, with only one city and only five towns with a population of more than 20,000, so there is plenty of space for visitors.

There are lots of reasons for visiting the Lake District. You may be interested in its historic sites, outdoor areas or tourist attractions. Or you may simply be looking to get away from it all, a place where you can hide away in a remote cottage with a pile of books, a bottle or three of wine and a roaring log fire. If you are keen on archaeology then there are enough ancient sites and remains to spend the rest of your life poking around, and still not cover a fraction of them.

Naturally, it's the best place in England for hill walking with so many routes to choose from. Peace and quiet are popular and, contrary to popular belief, always easy to find. Even at the height of summer, with congested roads and hordes bustling round the main beauty spots, it is still possible to find solitude. On the Northern Fells, in an area known as the Back o' Skiddaw, you can spend days walking and not meet another soul. These fells lie north of Blencathra and Skiddaw, separated from them by a marshy area shown on maps as Skiddaw Forest – although you'd be hard pushed to find much in the way of trees there. Beyond the highest point, Knott is a wonderful circular walk that goes through Trusmadoor – a mountain pass between Meal Fell and the amusingly named Great Cockup – before flanking Little Cockup to return to the road. Spend an afternoon there and you might start to believe that you are the last person left on Earth.

Then there's the area's reputation for fine food and drink. Nothing tastes quite as good as a few slices of freshly cut Cumberland ham. Another mouth-watering experience is Tattie Pot, a rich, lamb-based stew, which is greatly enhanced by the addition of black pudding.

Cumbria has been described as a 'foodie heaven' with good reason. You'll easily find locally grown and produced delicacies, such as Cumberland sausage, Herdwick mutton, the famous Kendal Mint Cake and Grasmere Gingerbread as well as many different products made from damsons, which have been grown in Westmorland since the early 18th century.

There's a very popular food festival held in Cockermouth every September and that's the best place to sample and buy Cumbrian fare. At other times, you can arrange your own tours around the various artisan producers. Or, if you prefer a more hands-on approach to food, you can sign up for a variety of courses where you can learn to cook, bake, cure hams, preserve food in traditional ways or even acquire the skills and knowledge needed to forage for food in the wild.

If you would prefer an activity holiday then look no further. It's hardly surprising that fell walking is one of the most popular outdoor activities in the Lakes, or that there are abundant opportunities for sailing, kayaking, canoeing, waterboarding, windsurfing and waterskiing.

Why not try your hand at quad bike riding, abseiling, scrambling, rock climbing, caving, aquaseiling or even ghyll and gorge scrambling – that's if you don't mind getting wet. There are opportunities to try skydiving, paragliding or learning to fly a fixed-wing aircraft and glider. Or you could try outdoor survival skills, and learn to cook with a Kellie Kettle, trap animals and build a survival shelter. And don't forget that this is also an amazing place to go cycle touring or mountain biking.

▶ Ashness Bridge
◀ Derwentwater (previous page)

TOP ATTRACTIONS

▲ Derwentwater

Derwentwater (see page 118) is over a mile wide, making it the Lake District's widest lake. It also has a number of charming islands, and some amazing waterfalls on its eastern side. The lake and its surrounds are accessible by ferries, running from seven landing stages, making this an ideal area for climbing, walking, sight-seeing and relaxing.

▼ Cumberland Pencil Museum

Bizarre yet fascinating, this unusual museum (see page 163) looks at the history and technology of the humble pencil. This was, apparently, first made locally in the 16th century, after graphite was discovered in nearby Borrowdale. It's ideal for kids, with an on-site giant, puzzle trails and other exciting stuff.

◄ Theatre by the Lake

Described as 'the most beautifully located and friendly theatre in Britain' (see page 164), this venue is just a short stroll from Derwentwater. The 400-seat main house and 100-seat studio host up to nine productions a year. There are also a variety of festivals, visiting companies and musicians, and the theatre is open all year.

► Brantwood

Brantwood (see page 106) is one of the most beautiful houses in the Lake District. It was home to writer, artist and thinker John Ruskin from 1871 until his death in 1900. There is a museum on Ruskin, and the estate's grounds are also well worth a visit, encompassing ancient woodland, lakeshore meadows, open fell and eight landscaped gardens.

◄ Brockhole

Brockhole (see page 246), on the shore of Windermere, is set in 32 acres of grounds. Opened in 1969, it was England's first National Park Visitor Centre. You'll find all the info on the Lake District you could want, as well as details on lake cruises and canoe hire. There's an adventure playground, indoor play area and an extensive events programme, including exhibitions.

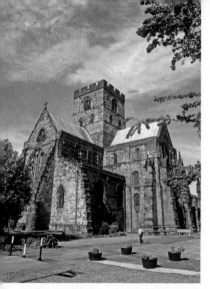

◀ Carlisle Cathedral

Carlisle Cathedral (see page 91) was founded in 1122 as a priory, but became a cathedral in 1132 and has held a daily service for almost 900 years. It has a magnificent high ceiling, with a beautiful blue background and gold painted stars; stained-glass windows dating from the 14th to the 20th centuries; and a 16th-century Brougham Tryptich altarpiece made in Amsterdam.

▶ Honister Slate Mine

Honister (see page 72) is the last working slate mine in England. You can explore the caverns hacked out by Victorian miners, learn the history of the famous Honister green slate, find out how to rive slates and see local skills in action. The tour is both underground and overground and involves some clambering.

◀ Rydal Mount

Rydal Mount (see page 206) was poet William Wordsworth's home from 1813 until his death in 1850. He lived here with his wife, three children, his sister and his sister-in-law; and wrote more than half of his published poetry here. The house was originally a farm, built in 1550, and enlarged around the middle of the 18th century. The garden here is still much as he left it.

▲ The World of Beatrix Potter

The World of Beatrix Potter (see page 245) is like stepping into the books and meeting old friends. The exhibition features 3D scenes from Potter's tales, complete with sounds and smells which transport you to the bustle of Mrs Tiggy-Winkle's kitchen and help you savour the ripe tomatoes in Mr McGregor's greenhouse. Walk through Jemima's woodland glade, the Peter Rabbit Garden, and see the gooseberry bush where Peter got caught in a net. There's also an interactive timeline, which tells the author's life story.

▼ Hill Top

This small 17th-century house (see page 193) is where Beatrix Potter wrote many of her famous children's stories. It's just as she left it, and in each room you can recognise something that appears in one of her books. Her will decreed that Hill Top should remain exactly as she had known it, and it is chock full of Beatrix Potter memorabilia, including her original drawings.

◄ Lake Windermere

Windermere (see page 240) is England's longest lake, and it's very easy to get onto, either by hiring a dinghy, or on a cruise via Waterhead and Lakeside. Belle Isle, the largest of the lake's islands, still has the romantic roundhouse built there in 1774. There's plenty of lakeside walking on the western shore, much of which belongs to the National Trust.

▶ Ullswater 'Steamers'

See some of England's most magnificent mountain scenery from the water. The diesel-powered Ullswater 'Steamers' (see page 223) call at Pooley Bridge, remote Howtown and Glenridding, at the foot of the Helvellyn mountain range, with flexible ticket options.

◄ Muncaster Castle

The view from the terrace of Muncaster Castle (see page 190) is quite something, but there's much more to this charming Victorian castle. Lord Muncaster remodelled both the medieval remains and the 18th-century house to create a castle complete with towers, carved chimneypieces, an octagonal library and a collection of silverware.

HISTORY OF
THE LAKE DISTRICT

Prior to 1974, Cumbria didn't exist. That is, in the political sense; the land and everything it contains, of course, has been around much longer – several millennia in fact.

Politicians created this 'new' place with an Act of Parliament, which took the ancient areas of Westmorland, Cumberland, Carlisle, North Lonsdale, Lancashire North of the Sands and part of the West Riding of Yorkshire and stuck them all together. However, it's good to know that this ceremonial name changing had little effect on the locals and you'll still hear them using the old names and find newspapers with such subversive titles as the *Westmorland Gazette* and the *Cumberland and Westmorland Herald*.

So much for Cumbria's recent history, but if you were to go back to the very early Stone Age, you would find a large community of people living and working here. They've left few signs, but if you wander about the southern slope of Pike of Stickle in Langdale and look for the small cave near the summit you'll be exploring one of the most important stone axe factories in Europe.

▲ Castlerigg stone circle

Life advanced slowly through the Mesolithic period before entering the Neolithic or New Stone Age. However, by the early Bronze Age (4,500–1,500 BC) folk were getting the hang of building stone circles, lots of them. About 25 per cent of all the stone circles in England are here. These range from the spectacular and easily accessible – such as Castlerigg (see page 101) and Long Meg and her Daughters (see page 138) – to the obscure, remote and partially buried remains that you're likely to spot only while exploring the remote moorland on foot.

The builders of these ancient monuments made and worked with bronze, turning it into axes, spearheads and luxury goods. They developed trading networks, via the main valleys, plains and along the coast, which connected the various settlements. Unfortunately, only a few isolated examples of their bronze works have been found in the area.

Next the Celts arrived and with them the Iron Age. The Celts were a tribal people and it was the Carvetii tribe who settled in North Cumbria. They lived in roundhouses, enclosed by a ditch and bank or, in some cases, a drystone wall. They probably spoke a version of *Brythonic*, the great-great-grandfather of modern Welsh. Ancient names, such as Blencathra, hold echoes from that time. Go tramping across the fields and fells and you'll find plenty of evidence of settlements, field systems and their network of hill forts. Those at Swarthy Hill and Carrock Fell have been dated to around 500 BC.

Around AD 43, the Romans – intent on world domination – arrived in England. But it took them the next 30 years to sort out the troublesome southerners and make it to the Lakes. The impact of these invading legions is still highly visible in the region in the roads and forts they left behind. For example, the Stangate was an ancient road that was built to link forts in modern-day Carlisle with Corbridge in Northumberland.

However, the Romans never really got to grips with the tribes north of the Solway, so Emperor Hadrian had a huge wall built to keep them out – and you'll find the longest visible stretch of it in Cumbria. You can trace the line of the Roman road from Brough (see page 78) – via the fort of *Galava* at Ambleside (see page 55) – to Ravenglass (see page 200), where you'll find the tallest surviving Roman structure in the UK. The bathhouse that served the nearby fort of *Glannaventa* dates from the second century.

If you drive up the narrow, twisting road that climbs the impossibly steep Hardknott Pass (see page 144), you'll find the remains of another fort founded by Hadrian. Built between 120 and 138 AD, the outline of the commandant's house, parade grounds, bathhouse and barracks are visible. The fort was abandoned during the Antonine advance into Scotland during the mid-second century.

The Romans hung around for several centuries but by AD 410 they'd gone home and Britain entered the Dark Ages – so-called because few records remain, yet a number of myths and legends date from this time. One such tale is that King Arthur, for example, actually roamed around Cumbria and not Cornwall, as historians would have you believe. Arthur's father, Uther Pendragon, allegedly lived in a castle in the Eden Valley. In his book, *The Quest for Merlin*, Nikolai Tolstoy firmly places the tribe of Arthur in modern northwest England/southwest Scotland.

Warlords quickly filled the power vacuum left by the Romans and while they were busy doing what warlords the world over do, Christianity arrived. St Patrick may be the patron saint of Ireland, but before he went there to interfere with the snake population, he lived in Cumbria. He was probably born near Ravenglass or somewhere on the Solway. St Ninian was another local holy chap who crossed the Solway, and introduced Christianity to the Scots. St Mungo, alias St Kentigern, was another. He headed north into Strathclyde to do a spot of missionary work but they threw him out. Fortunately, he was a persistent soul and went back to eventually found a little place called Glasgow.

▼ Hardknott Roman Fort, Hardknott Pass

▲ Herdwick sheep

By the seventh century, it was the turn of the Anglo Saxons to invade and they set about Anglicising the Celts with a spot of applied genocide, ably assisted by periodic outbreaks of pestilence and famine. Meanwhile, royal patronage considerably boosted the power of the church when, in AD 685, a bishop called Cuthbert was given 'Cartmel and all the Britons therein'.

As the power of the bishops increased and their estates expanded, they built fabulous abbeys, monasteries and churches. Life was good, if you were a bishop. Until, of course, the pesky Vikings came along and spoiled everything. Unlike the royals, the bishops' ineffective military meant they were unable to defend their estates against the invading hordes.

These Vikings, or Norsemen, were no respecters of the locals, and raped, pillaged and laid the countryside to waste, reducing Carlisle to rubble. They had so much fun they decided to stay in the region for a while. Today, many descriptive names introduced by the Norsemen – including dale, howe, thwaite, fell and the famous Herdwick sheep – are still in common usage.

Cumbria also shares a border with Scotland and there are periods in its history when it was part of Scotland. The Normans took it from the Scots in 1072 and built Carlisle Castle to stop them from taking it back again. Despite this, the Scots returned in 1136 and stayed until they were kicked out again in 1157.

Many of Cumbria's square stone towers, or peles, date from the 15th and 16th centuries when they were built to defend the local landowners against the border reivers, who made frequent raids – carrying off livestock and any human beings they thought worthy of a ransom. Raids went in the opposite direction too and you'll find a similar network of towers on the Scottish side of the border.

Cumbria is rich in minerals, and they've been mined here since the 12th century. This activity peaked during the Industrial Revolution, when new communication networks were needed to transport minerals, raw materials and goods manufactured in the Cumbrian factories and mills. As a result, three canals were built at Kendal (see page 154), Ulverston (see page 225) and Carlisle (see page 88). Then the railways came and the canals declined. In turn, the motorcar brought about the decline of the railways, but by then the era of the tourist had dawned.

The Romantic poet William Wordsworth was instrumental in encouraging the upper classes and literati to visit by writing his *Guide to the Lakes* in 1835, even though he was against the general masses spoiling his Lakeland idyll. Later, Wainwright's *Pictorial Guides to the Lakeland Fells* encouraged increasing numbers to visit as fell walking became fashionable. The railways also enabled rich industrialists from Lancashire to reach the lakes easily, and so they built their great mansions round Windermere (see page 240).

It wasn't long, however, before the rising visitor numbers started to have an adverse effect on the environment and so the Lake District National Park was formed in 1951. Its aim was to preserve the countryside from commercial and residential expansion. Tourism continued to increase with the building of the M6, which allowed easier access to the northwest, but you'll find the old narrow roads get congested during peak periods.

Until the end of the 20th century, Cumbria's industries included shipbuilding, gypsum, bakeries and nuclear power – Calder Hall at Sellafield was the world's first commercial nuclear power station. Now, in the 21st century, agriculture and forestry are both major industries and, more recently, renewable energy and water have also started playing their parts.

Tourism, however, remains the Lakeland's most vital industry and every year thousands of visitors flock here to walk, to take in the scenery or to simply enjoy the fine air, good food and convivial company. So perhaps it's not surprising that in 2015 a controversial decision was taken to extend the National Park by 3 per cent – effectively joining it up with its neighbour, the Yorkshire Dales. The new extended boundary in the Lake District includes an area in the east from Birkbeck Fells Common to Whinfell Common; in the south from Helsington Barrows to Sizergh Fell; and an area north of Sizergh Castle and part of the Lyth Valley.

BACK TO NATURE

Did you know that the collective noun for a group of toads is a knot? Or that those wonderful, furry, flying mammals called bats are each capable of devouring over 3,000 midges in a single night?

With so few people actually living in this largely rural area, there's plenty of room for a huge variety of creatures. This is the best place to visit if you want to get up close to nature or see creatures you won't see in other parts of the country.

You'll also stand a good chance of spotting Britain's indigenous red squirrel here. While they have been all but wiped out in southern Britain owing to the advance of the North American tree rats (grey squirrels), red squirrels are still hanging on in the Lake District where they make their homes in the abundant conifer woods. Seek them out in the woodland round Thirlmere (see page 219).

Another rare sight is the osprey. With a wingspan of nearly 5 feet, this massive raptor is very popular owing to its spectacular hunting techniques. Swooping down to the water's surface with talons outstretched and wings swept back, it snatches an unlucky fish from under the surface before taking off again. Once a common sight in Britain, ospreys were hunted nearly to extinction

◀ Rare red squirrel ▲ Osprey

by 1916. A breeding pair returned to Scotland in 1954 and with conservation protection their population has grown. They reappeared in England in 2001 when a pair nested in the Lake District. They spend the winter months in Africa so you'll only see them here between early spring and mid-autumn. Ospreys nest in pine forests near lakes and rivers where they can find food. If you head to the osprey observation point (see page 232), a 10-minute walk uphill from the Mirehouse car park, north of Keswick, you'll enjoy a wonderful view over Bassenthwaite Lake. You'll need to hang about a while to catch a glimpse of one though. If you don't fancy the trek or can't manage it, the Whinlatter Forest Visitor Centre (see page 232) has a video link to an osprey's nest.

Natterjack toads are probably the noisiest of the amphibians and during their mating season can be heard for miles. You can tell them apart from the common toad by a yellow line which runs down the middle of their backs and their shorter legs, which make them appear to run rather than hop.

Although this is not the most northerly colony (that's on the Scottish side of the Solway) Cumbria has two of the country's largest colonies in England and about 65 per cent of the total natterjack toad population. During the breeding season from April to June, the National Trust Nature Reserve at Sandscale Haws near Barrow-in-Furness (see page 65) runs guided tours.

Like natterjack toads, bats are nocturnal and the best way to see them is on an organised tour. Eight distinct species can be found in Cumbria, including the pipistrelle, Soprano pipistrelle, Daubenton's, Brown long-eared, Brandts's, Natterer's, Whiskered and Noctule. The National Trust runs organised bat walks at Fell Foot Park, Newby Bridge, Windermere, at Acorn Bank, Temple Sowerby near Penrith and at Sizergh Castle south of Kendal (visit nationaltrust.org.uk for details).

Cumbria is home to some pretty rare butterflies too. Bring a field guide with you and see how many you can spot. The National Nature Reserve at Finglandrigg Wood (see page 95) on the Solway Plain is a large area of semi-natural woodland where you'll sight some toppers – including the marsh fritillary. This butterfly was extinct in Cumbria by 2005 but was reintroduced in 2007 and is doing very well. Mid-May through to the first half of June is when you should look for it. You may also come across the purple hairstreak, pearl-bordered fritillary and ringlet butterflies during the summer, as well as the forester and silver hook moth. This reserve also contains peat bog, heathland and rough pasture, providing homes for shy creatures such as the otter and badger, roe deer, brown hare and tiny wood mouse. Keen twitchers can spot over 40 species of birds, including long-tailed tits, tawny owls, buzzards, reed buntings, grasshopper warblers, garden warblers and willow tits.

A rare gem of an insect can also be found here. The mining bee is a solitary beastie unlike the sociable honey or bumblebees. The female lays her eggs in a series of underground chambers along with some nectar and pollen. This keeps the larvae going until they become adults and head for the surface in the spring. Don't worry about getting stung as these bees are not at all aggressive.

The reserve is well served with interpretation boards covering the history and the wildlife of this spectacular landscape and how it is managed.

▼ Tawny mining bee

LORE OF THE LAND

In the wild, dramatic landscape of the Lake District, it was believed that the caverns and fissures in the rocks were the entrances to fairyland, while elves dwelt in the hills and inhabited burial mounds where they feasted at night. An old tale tells of a man who was thrust off his horse by the elves and, had he not had a Bible in his pocket for protection, would have been dragged into their den, never to be seen again. Travellers also traditionally carried iron or steel crosses and rosaries as charms against the evil powers of fairies, and made sure that they crossed over running water to dispel the fairy influences. Elves, it was thought, could also use minute arrows or 'elf shot', given to them by the fairies, to kill cattle in the dead of night.

Massive in the memory

Giants loom extra large in Lakeland lore and evidence of their presence is all around, from the tumulus at Standing Stones in Cumbria – marking the grave of a giant killed in battle – to Kentmere Hall, built with the aid of the Troutbeck Giant – a man

◀ Thirlmere to Helvellyn Mountain; Castlerigg Stone Circle (page 25)

of huge strength and appetites who, unaided, lifted a beam that had defied the muscle of 10 ordinary mortals.

Most spectacular of all is the Giant's Grave in a Penrith churchyard, a pair of 11-foot-tall mutilated stone crosses and four hogback stones – said to symbolise wild boar killed in nearby Inglewood Forest – and a cross known as the Giant's Thumb. What's intriguing is that the grave, said to be the resting place of Sir Hugh (or Ewain) Cesario, may commemorate two heroes conjoined in folk memory – Owain, son of Urien of Rheged from the late sixth century, and 10th- or 11th-century King Owain of Strathclyde. Near Edenhall, a pair of Giants' Caves, or Isis Parlis, sited on the face of a perpendicular rock, were the refuge of Sir Hugh – and the alleged abode of the Giant Isis who seized men and cattle, then drew them into his den to devour them.

Lakeland spirits

Today, you can waterski across Lake Windermere, but in the past you would have always needed a ferryman to row you over. Legend has it that one stormy night, the ferryman was called from Rawlinson's Nab on the eastern bank, but returned from his mission alone and 'ghastly and dumb with horror' having been summoned by a mysterious spirit – the Crier of Claife. A few days later the ferryman died and for weeks afterwards shouts and yells could be heard from the Nab, particularly when storms were raging. People were so afraid that a monk was called to confine the troublesome ghost to a quarry on Claife Heights above the lake. He's believed to be there still, wailing with the wind.

Haunting Thirlmere Lake is a black dog, seen swimming across the lake in a ghostly replay of the marriage of a murdered bride, half-strangled and then thrown into the water to drown. Armboth House, where the wedding was to have taken place, is now beneath the waters of the reservoir created in 1894. But it's said that on the anniversary of the tragedy, which happens to be Hallowe'en, the wedding feast is laid out and the sound of church bells, eerie music and breaking plates echoes up from the deep.

Nature lore

Trees in the Lake District have special powers. Owing to its ability to overcome the malign influence of witches and evil spirits, sprigs of rowan (mountain ash) were hung in shippons and stables to protect valuable animals, and in dairies to make butter solidify or 'come'. In order to see the 'dead light' or spirit form of someone who had recently passed away, a branch of yew was cut with a large V-shaped notch in one end then lowered to the ground, while its bearer knelt with his right eye closed and peered through the V.

Individual trees stand out too. At Satterthwaite a massive oak tree was regularly decorated with rags and crockery on Maundy Thursday in a ceremony inherited from pagan tree worship, while at Hesket-in-the-Forest and near Anthorn hawthorn trees mark out the locations of ancient courts. To commemorate the death of a hound named Hercules, who expired after chasing a stag from Whinfell to Redkirks in Scotland and back again, the Hartshorn Tree on the Clifford Estate was decorated with the stag's horns. Equally legendary were the Capon Trees, like the one now marked with a memorial near Brampton. Lovers kept their trysts beneath the Brampton Tree until 1746, when six Jacobite rebels were hanged from it, then drawn and quartered – transforming the tree into a place of dread haunting. Many a Brampton mother has threatened naughty children with punishment by the Capon Tree Boggles.

Beneath the branches of the oak trees that they held sacred, Lakeland Druids lived and worked their charms with the help of mistletoe gathered from nearby. At the centre of Castlerigg Stone Circle – a place of pagan worship – it's said that the beautiful virgin Ella, her neck garlanded with oak leaves, was sacrificed as a sop to the 'Great Spirit'. But although she was set on fire after the Arch Druid rubbed two pieces of wood together in strong sunlight, she was miraculously saved by the sudden upsurge of floodwaters.

Witches and wizards

Cumbria's famous witches include Mary Baynes, whose cottage reeked of brimstone – the 'Devil's perfume' – and who cursed a man who was later blinded in an accident. Like other witches, she could, at will, turn herself into a hare. The Eskdale Witch could do the same, and could only be killed with a silver bullet.

For extreme spookiness, few places beat the old coffin path in Wasdale over which bodies were carried by pony and cart to St Catherine's Church in Eskdale. One day, when a young man's body was being taken on its final journey, the pony bolted and both horse and corpse disappeared. A few months later, the same thing happened with the body of the man's mother. The villagers ran after the pony and found it – and the young man's coffin but not the mother's. Today it's said that the ghost of a horse can still be seen galloping over the moor at night, pulling a coffin behind it.

Cumbria lays claim to wizards too. Michael Scot, who lived in the 13th century, is said to have built a church in a single night, thrown rocks onto Carrock Fell, and turned a coven of witches to stone, thereby creating Long Meg Stone Circle, as a punishment for dancing on a Sunday. He could summon demons and command

▲ Rowan tree

the sea. He cured the illnesses of the Holy Roman Emperor, and measured the distance to the stars.

A matter of luck

Even if fitted with the latest electronic security devices, many prestigious Lake District homes are still 'protected' by drinking vessels known as 'Lucks'. Most famous is the Luck of Edenhall, near Langworthy, a glass beaker enamelled and gilded in green, red and white, and allegedly left by the fairies after they had been sorely interrupted by human intrusions while drinking. 'If that glass should break or fall/Farewell the luck of Edenhall', sang the fairies as they departed and, although the house was demolished, the glass – which was almost certainly brought from Syria at the time of the first Crusade in the 13th century – is preserved today in the V&A in London.

At Haresceugh Castle near Renwick, the Luck, now vanished, was a silver-rimmed wooden bowl, imbued with the power of a guardian spirit. Different again is the Luck of Burrell Green, a brass dish with a central spiral-shaped boss in the form of a rose, and assigned occult powers. In 1417, so the story goes, at the wedding between a daughter of the resident Lamb family and a king of Mardale, a servant was sent to the well for water. As he did so, hobgoblins appeared saying 'Bring us food and wine and we will bless the wedding.' The servant did as he was told and was given the dish as a reward.

The idea that luck can change hands is still prevalent among Lake District farmers. When cattle are sold, the vendor traditionally gives back a portion of the money received to the purchaser. If this is not done, the animals will fail to thrive and could even die. On receipt of a knife, scissors or other cutting tool as a gift, then a penny is given in exchange, the coin symbolising the fact that the gift will not sever the friendship.

LITERARY LAKES: RABBITS, DAFFODILS, CATS AND ROGUES

A walk in the Lake District inspired one of the best-known poems in the English language. William Wordsworth and his sister, Dorothy, were returning to their home in Grasmere (see page 133) in 1802 when, according to Dorothy, they 'saw a few daffodils close to the water side... as we went along there were more & yet more & at last under the boughs of the trees, we saw that there was a long belt of them along the shore, about the breadth of a country turnpike road.' Much later William sat down and wrote:

> *I wandered lonely as a cloud,*
> *That floats on high o'er vales and hills,*
> *When all at once I saw a crowd,*
> *A host, of golden daffodils;*
> *Beside the lake, beneath the trees,*
> *Fluttering and dancing in the breeze.*

◄ Lake Coniston and the Old Man of Coniston

If you visit in spring, you can still walk around Ullswater (see page 222) to Rydal Bay and see the bright yellow blooms.

Although the first English writer to mention the Lake District was Thomas Gray in 1769, its literary associations really began with Wordsworth. You can visit the large Georgian town house in Cockermouth (see page 102), where Wordsworth was born in 1770. He lived his entire life in the Lakes, moving first to Hawkshead to attend school, then travelling through Europe for a spell before taking up residence with his sister at Dove Cottage in Grasmere.

Other poet friends came to live nearby: Robert Southey, who would later become Poet Laureate, and Samuel Taylor Coleridge. They became known as the Lakes Poets. Wordsworth, his sister and family moved to Rydal Mount (see page 206) near Ambleside in 1813 and this is where he died on 23 April 1850. He was buried at the Church of St Oswald, Grasmere (see page 134).

Some of the best-known children's books have strong Lake District connections too. You may not come across Postman Pat and Jess, his black and white cat, on your travels round the sparsely populated valley of Longsleddale near Kendal but that is the setting of fictitious 'Greendale'. John Cunliffe, the creator of the *Postman Pat* children's books, lived in Kendal. Pat's Post Office was based on the one at 10 Greenside in Kendal, near where Cunliffe lived. Sadly, this Kendal branch office closed in 1993.

Beatrix Potter's delightful *The Tale of Peter Rabbit* and other stories may have had their genesis in Scotland but the success of that book and a small legacy enabled her to buy Hill Top at Near Sawrey (see page 193) where she moved in 1905.

Potter's charming fictional characters Jemima Puddleduck and Tom Kitten sprang from her experiences of living and farming there. As well as writing and illustrating, she became an acknowledged breeder of Herdwicks, the very hardy breed of fell sheep indigenous to the Lake District. She also bought up neighbouring farms and land in an attempt to preserve traditional fell farming. When Potter died, she left most of her estate to the National Trust. Today you can visit her farm at Hill Top, ramble across large parts of the countryside and view her illustrations at the Beatrix Potter Gallery (see page 147), located in her husband's former law offices in Hawkshead.

When you outgrew Peter Rabbit you may have enjoyed *Swallows and Amazons* and later followed Rogue Herries as he tramped the Lakeland fells. You can relive your childhood by joining the Swallows, or the Amazons, in their adventures. The stories involve a lot of sailing and while the author, Arthur Ransome, set them in actual Lake District locations he moved things round a bit. The Lake described is Windermere (see page 240) but the land around about is actually Coniston (see page 105). A 1974 film, available on DVD, used Ransome's actual locations.

In 1924, Hugh Walpole bought Brackenburn, a traditional Cumbrian stone cottage on the west bank of Derwentwater. The superb views across the water to Skiddaw, and Castlerigg Fell were the inspiration for his series *The Herries Chronicles*. They're fiction but the landscape and buildings are real.

On a windy night in 1730 Francis 'Rogue' Herries brings his family to their ancestral home in remote Borrowdale:

'Under the black hills it seemed so very small, and in the white moonlight so cold and desolate... there were two little attic windows like eyebrows...'

The Hazelbank Hotel occupies the very spot where Walpole created this home of the 'Rogue' and was the birthplace of his daughter Judith Paris. Take the bridleway from Rosthwaite, past the hotel and over the fells to the picturesque hamlet of Watendlath and seek out Judith Paris's House. A plaque on the corner is a clue.

You can see a lot of grand Lake District scenery by visiting the locations in *The Herries Chronicles*. Read the books and study maps, or cut corners by watching *Herries Lakeland – The World of Hugh Walpole and the Herries Chronicles*.

▾ Derwentwater

MINING THE LAKELAND'S RICH INDUSTRIAL HERITAGE

Seeing so many mountains and valleys with vast expanses of water and just a few, scattered, small towns, you could be forgiven for assuming that the Industrial Revolution bypassed the Lake District. However, you soon find lots of evidence to the contrary if you gently scrape the surface. While this area may not have been crammed full of the smoke and the fire-belching 'dark satanic mills', which characterised much of Lancashire and The Black Country, it did play its part.

Cumbria is blessed with lots of natural resources, including minerals, rocks, slate and limestone. Add lots of water, a coastline, river estuaries, mountains and dense woodland and you have the raw materials that sustained the industrialised society of the 18th and 19th centuries.

The origins of Cumbrian industry go much further back though. During the Neolithic age, this was a major centre for making stone axes. When the Romans arrived they burned lime to provide building mortar. Later, during the Agrarian Revolution, lime was used to make the soil less acidic. Large-scale commercial kilns produced the lime but many farmers and

▲ Mining bucket, Coniston

builders built their own, smaller kilns. Look for the remains of one on the pier at Whitehaven harbour. Walk the fells and the valleys and you'll soon come across more. At Greenside Lime Kiln in Kendal there's a large-scale commercial kiln with interpretation boards that tell you everything you need to know about the lime-burning industry.

Cumbria is one of the most extensively mined areas in England and you'll find old workings throughout the county. Evidence of mining exists as far back as the 12th century, and no doubt was carried out by the Romans before that. Through the ages men have burrowed deep underground to extract lead, coal, copper, zinc, tungsten, barite, graphite and iron ore. Cumbria had, until recently, the last working iron ore mine in Europe. The Florence Mine closed in 2007 when it was no longer viable to keep pumping out the water. Its Heritage Centre is now an arts centre but there are many similar sites that tell the story of mining in Cumbria.

On Whinlatter Pass, above Braithwaite, you'll find Force Crag, the last working metal mine in the region. It operated from 1839 to 1991, producing lead, zinc and barites. The buildings are early 20th century but it's the only site still containing most of its processing equipment. The National Trust runs periodic guided tours, which must be booked in advance.

At the top of the steep and narrow Honister Pass, connecting Borrowdale and Buttermere, is Honister Slate Mine (see page 72), which is still working and produces Westmorland green slate – it is a fascinating place to visit as you can see the slate being mined and worked. If you want a more detailed insight into this industry then sign up for their Industrial Heritage tour.

Borrowdale (see page 71) is also the place where graphite was first discovered in the 16th century, the only deposit of solid graphite ever found in such a quantity. At first shepherds used it to mark their sheep, then the government took over and used it to line cannonball moulds. Later, in nearby Keswick, it was used to make the first pencils. They are still made there and the original factory now houses the Cumberland Pencil Museum (see page 163), which is more interesting than it sounds.

You'll find the last traces of a vanished copper mining industry up a mile-long unsurfaced track behind Coniston village. Most of the mine buildings in Coppermines Valley have now been converted into holiday homes and a youth hostel but you may still come across shaft entrances. Don't under any circumstances venture inside. Many are highly unstable, some with rotten wooden floors, which you could fall through into the deep voids below. You'll get more enjoyment from your visit here if you check out the mining display in The Ruskin Museum (see page 107) in Coniston beforehand.

Locally mined ore was processed at Duddon Iron Works, near Broughton-in-Furness. What's left is one of the most complete charcoal-fired blast furnaces in Britain and a must-see. It opened in 1736 and produced iron for 130 years. Water powered, the bellows and locally produced charcoal fuelled the furnace. The remains have been partially restored and the interpretation boards provide a good overview of iron production.

Charcoal burners working in the Cumbrian woods were responsible for producing the fuel for this mighty furnace. Foresters ensured that there would be a constant supply of wood to feed the mills that produced the bobbins essential to the Lancashire spinning and weaving mills. Stott Park Bobbin Mill (see page 177) was making a quarter of a million bobbins every week at its peak. It's one of the finest surviving examples and the mill's new exhibition covers the production from tree to bobbin on the original belt-driven machinery.

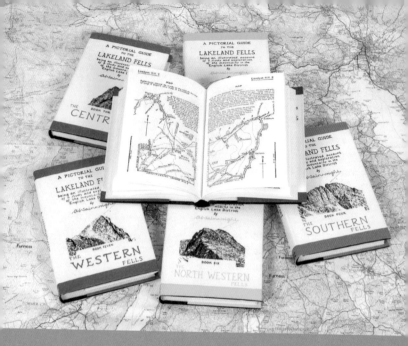

WAINWRIGHT'S LOVE LETTERS TO THE LANDSCAPE

There is a wonderful series of small, handwritten and illustrated books by Alfred Wainwright, which have been aptly described as 'love letters to the landscape'. There are seven of them, each with the title *A Pictorial Guide to the Lakeland Fells*. Published between 1955 and 1966, they have been described by the author Mark Richards as being '– on a par with the songs of Lennon and McCartney, both innovative in their time and now classics of their genre.'

With the aid of these guides, you can explore the fells and remote places of Lakeland in the company of one who knew them best. They are the *de facto* reference manuals to 214 fells but can be read as much as a philosophical work than a series of dry instructions. Each guide contains observations, history, advice, opinions and some of the author's dry humour, such as the comment on his final resting place, 'And if you, dear reader, should get a bit of grit in your boot as you are crossing Haystacks in the years to come, please treat it with respect. It might be me.'

Even if you don't use them as guides you will want to own them. Mark Richards, who has 'adored their tiniest detail since first discovering them at the age of 12', confesses to never having used them on the fells.

Alfred Wainwright is known to millions, but how did he come to write these little books and why are they still so popular?

Wainwright was born into a poor Lancashire family in 1907. He left school when he was 13 but, having done well, secured an office job with Blackburn Borough Engineers department. He studied hard at night school and eventually gained a qualification in accountancy, advancing his career in local government. Outside of work he had three main interests – walking, drawing and supporting Blackburn Rovers.

When Wainwright was 23, he went on a walking holiday to the Lake District and fell in love with the place. Eleven years later he moved to the Lakes, got a job in the Borough Treasurer's Office in Kendal, eventually becoming Borough Treasurer. He spent the rest of his life in the Lakes.

He had a very unhappy marriage and it was probably seeking escape from the problems at home that drove him to spend all his spare time walking on the fells, or in his small study working on his books.

He started the first book, *The Eastern Fells*, in November 1952 and it was completed by Christmas 1954. In its conclusion he wrote that other than climbing he would be 'happy to sit idly and dream of them...' However, he also realised that he should put something back so started to write about them, and to draw pictures. He went on walking trips at weekends, writing notes, sketching and taking photographs. Then he painstakingly prepared the pen-and-ink drawings and wrote the text in his neat handwriting. One page was an evening's work and it took him 13 long years to complete all seven books. In the final volume he concludes, 'When I came down from Starling Dodd... I had just succeeded in obtaining a complete view from the summit before the mist descended.' He'd been trying to get this view for weeks but managed just before the end of the summer bus service. He didn't drive and failure would have put the book back a year.

Wainwright self-published his first volume; it's a facsimile of the manuscript but his handwriting is so neat it looks typeset. Further volumes were produced by various publishers and are now available from Frances Lincoln. Obviously, if you plan to use Wainwright's guides for walking you'll also need an up-to-date OS Outdoor Leisure map.

In the 1970s, Wainwright's friend and fellow outdoor writer Mark Richards 'spent many weekends in his company, watching him craft his final guidebooks'. It was that close contact and influence that led Richards to produce *The Lakeland Fellranger* series. Published by Cicerone, these guides contain Harvey specialist walking maps but are illustrated by Mark's pen-and-ink drawings.

Wainwright divorced his first wife, Ruth, in 1967 and married the much younger Betty McNally, his walking companion, with whom he'd been having an affair. When he died on 20 January 1991, Betty, following his wishes, scattered his ashes on his favourite fell.

'All I ask for, at the end, is a last long resting place by the side of Innominate Tarn, on Haystacks, where the water gently laps the gravelly shore and the heather blooms and Pillar and Gable keep unfailing watch. A quiet place, a lonely place. I shall go to it, for the last time, and be carried: someone who knew me all my life will take me there and empty me out of a little box and leave me there alone.'

In Buttermere Church there's a monument to the memory of this remarkable man and you'll find more information about the great man's life and works at Kendal Museum (see page 157) in Kendal.

▼ The summit of Haystacks

LOCAL SPECIALITIES

Cumbria is foodie heaven and many of the delicacies you'll find here are based on traditional, often secret, recipes that have been carefully handed down through the generations.

Cumbrian people are fortunate in having plenty of good quality local ingredients with which to work, including meat from Herdwick sheep and hand-reared pigs and produce from well-husbanded dairy cattle. Add to that wild game from the moors and forests and locally caught trout and salmon, char, shrimp and herring, and it's hardly surprising that Cumbria produces some mouth-watering dishes.

One of the most distinctive of all the Cumbrian delicacies is the long, flat, coiled sausage. It's made from pork, chopped not minced, so it's chunkier than standard sausages. It now has protected geographical status, so you know anything labelled 'Traditional Cumberland sausage' was made here. Buy them from a local butcher and you can guarantee that the sausages on your plate won't contain any preservatives or artificial colouring.

Cumberland hams are dry-cured in salt for a month and sometimes also rubbed with brown sugar. Then they are washed, dried and hung in a cool place for a few months to finish. You'll need to soak the ham overnight to remove a lot of the salt content before boiling it. It's mouth-wateringly delicious when sliced and served with pickle, fresh bread and salad. Or try it with the Cumberland sauce that's made from redcurrant jelly mixed with mustard, ginger, port and the juices of oranges and lemons. The sauce is also the perfect accompaniment for lamb and other meat dishes.

Stews and hotpots used to be staple food for most working people and you'll still find regional variations throughout Britain, from Irish stew to Lancashire Hotpot and Scottish Stovies. In Cumbria the finest dish of them all is Cumberland Tattie Pot. It's made from diced lamb with layers of carrots, swede and black pudding, topped with sliced potatoes, then baked in the oven until the meat is tender and juicy. Pickled red cabbage is a great accompaniment.

Then there's cottage pie. Similar to Tattie Pot, but with mushrooms and tomatoes instead of black pudding, it is stewed then topped with mashed potatoes and cheese. If you've read this far, your mouth is probably watering, and you'll find these dishes served in village pubs and small, family restaurants throughout the Lake District.

Another Lakeland speciality is the delightful flavoured bread called A Whig which you'll come across in artisan bakers and village stores. There are different variations depending on the particular village. In Hawkshead they favour adding caraway seeds.

Grasmere Gingerbread is another Lakeland treat and can only be bought from one shop – yes, you've guessed, The Gingerbread Shop in Grasmere (see page 135). The shop's bakery is housed in the old village school and the gingerbread is still made from a secret recipe devised by Sarah Nelson, who died in 1904. You'll find it very different from most other gingerbreads.

Cartmel Sticky Toffee Pudding, while originating in the village of the same name in the south Lakes, is widely available throughout the county as well as in Cartmel Village Shop.

If you get a chance, do sample Cumberland Nicky Rum. It's a flan made from rum, ginger, dates, molasses and

▼ Herdwick sheep

various spices. The pudding originated in Whitehaven, which was once England's second biggest port. During the time of the East Indies trading routes, these ingredients were among the cargoes unloaded here and small quantities were 'acquired' by returning seamen to take home to their wives.

Hillary and Tensing ate Kendal Mint Cake on the summit of Everest in 1953, and it's still made in Kendal by three different companies. However, its creation was apparently an accident. A confectioner, while making a batch of clear mint, had a lapse of concentration and the product ended up cloudy. But it tasted nice and so Mint Cake was born. It is widely sold in camping shops throughout the Lake District.

Having eaten your way through some of this stuff, you'll be looking for something to wash it down with and there are lots of local beers to fit the bill. Keswick Brewery is a small, recently established craft brewer producing a variety of very tasty ales and beers. Jennings Brewery in Cockermouth (see page 102) was established in 1828 but is now part of a much larger brewing empire. However, it still makes exceedingly fine ales using pure Lakeland water. You can also seek out the many microbreweries that have sprung up over the last few years.

In more remote Ennerdale there's the excellent Ennerdale Brewery at Croasdale Farm, and Old Hall Brewery is south of Hawkshead. There are many more. Some offer guided tasting tours and most have on-site shops.

▼ Jennings Brewery, Cockermouth

BEFORE YOU GO

THINGS TO READ

There are a few books you might like to start reading to whet your appetite before you pack your case and head off to the Lake District.

Hugh Walpole's *Herries Chronicles* (1930–33) would be a very good first choice (see also page 32), and if you don't want to read the entire series start with *Rogue Herries*, which has excellent descriptions of Borrowdale.

Surprisingly few crime novels have been set in the Lakes. Or so novelist Martin Edwards discovered when he started looking at Cumbria as the backdrop for his novels, and so set his two main characters, DCI Hannah Scarlet, of the Cumbria Constabulary Cold Case Team and the historian Daniel Kind in the county. Try the first novel in the series, *The Coffin Trail* (2005) and you'll probably want to read the rest.

The true story of local lass Mary Robinson (1778–1837), known as the Maid of Buttermere, is one which Wordsworth and Melvyn Bragg used in different ways. The poet mentions her in *The Prelude* (1850) while Bragg turned the tale into a novel (*The Maid of Buttermere*, 1987). Bragg was born and raised in the region and has written other books which are set here. *The Cumbrian Trilogy* (1969–80) is based mostly on Wigton and follows the lives of a family from the 1920s through to the 1970s. They may be works of fiction but *The Hired Man* (1969), *A Place in England* (1970) and *Kingdom Come* (1980) are all firmly rooted in the landscape and the history of the Lake District.

Ernest Hemingway featured the region in his novella *The Torrents of Spring* (1926), and Ian McEwan in his Booker Prize winning *Amsterdam* (1998). *The Plague Dogs* (1977), by Richard Adams, has lots of excellent and very accurate descriptions of the countryside, while Hunter Davies' *Wainwright: the Biography* (2007) is a must-read if you are interested in fell walking. Davies' biography, *William Wordsworth* (2009), deals with the poet's relationship with his sister, his marriage and his affair with a French girl that produced a child. Davies has also written several non-fiction books that are now over 30 years old but still worth reading. *A Walk Along the Wall* (2000) and *A Walk Around The Lakes* (2000) are invaluable resources of information if you plan on walking here or along Britain's most important Roman monument, Hadrian's Wall. For a more-up-to date walking guide you can't beat *50 Walks in the Lake District* (2013) by AA Publishing.

THINGS TO WATCH

You shouldn't be surprised to learn that the Lake District is a major star of television and film. The great director, Alfred Hitchcock, used Langdale Chase Hotel near Windermere as his location for *The Paradine Case* (1947). And, although it sits at 1,000 feet above sea level, the market town of Alston (see page 54) was transformed into the fishing village of Bruntmarsh for the ITV dramatisation of *Oliver Twist* (1999).

Fictional Belgian detective, Hercule Poirot, moved with his characteristic 'rapid mincing gait' along the cobbled streets of Kirkby Lonsdale's (see page 169) Main Street and Market Square in the TV episode *Double Sin* (1990). But the rather elegant Art Deco hotel featured in the series is actually the Midland Hotel in Morecambe, just over the Cumbrian border in Lancashire. In October 2013, Kirkby Lonsdale was again transformed to play the part of early 19th-century Launceston for a BBC adaptation of Daphne Du Maurier's smuggling tale, *Jamaica Inn* (2013).

The BBC also made two series of *Wainwright Walks* (2007), with Julia Bradbury following many of the writer's walks. But it's the scenery that steals the show. Both series are regularly broadcast on a number of satellite channels.

Lots of films have Lake District locations or are based on Lakeland stories. Ennerdale (see page 124) is instantly recognisable in the final scenes of Danny Boyle's, post-apocalyptic horror, *28 Days Later* (2002), and the final scenes of Harold Pinter's interpretation of John Fowles' novel *The French Lieutenant's Woman* (1981) were shot around Windermere.

Pandaemonium (2000) is also worth watching as it tells the story of the early years of the Lakeland poets, William Wordsworth and Samuel Taylor Coleridge.

Although *Miss Potter* (2006) was mainly filmed in Italy and the Peak District, it's nevertheless a smashing introduction to Beatrix Potter's years in the Lake District.

Probably the best Lake District film of them all is *Withnail and I* (1987), a black comedy set in the 1960s. When the protagonists escape from London to Uncle Monty's cottage in the countryside it's the landscape around Shap and Bampton that you're seeing. Sleddale Hall, near Shap's Wet Sleddale Reservoir was used as the cottage. You'll find the telephone box that Withnail uses to phone his agent on the main road in Bampton, and the bridge – where he and Marwood go fishing – at the bottom of the hill from Sleddale Hall.

THINGS TO KNOW

Cumbria has the longest lake in England (Windermere), the deepest (Wast Water) but confusingly only one real lake. Other than Bassenthwaite Lake the rest are all meres or waters.

You'll find England's smallest church, St Olaf's, at Wasdale Head, Europe's second smallest cathedral in Carlisle (see page 88), and England's highest peak, Scafell Pike, which reaches 3,210 feet.

In an area noted for its steep mountain passes, it's really not surprising that the Lake District has England's steepest road. Hardknott Pass (see page 144) has an overall gradient of 1 in 3 but parts of it are 1 in 2.5. It is also narrow and twisting, so don't try towing a caravan up or down here. It's so steep you might feel that your car is toppling backwards.

Ulverston (see page 225) was the birthplace of comedian Stan Laurel, the sport of pole vaulting and the cradle of the

Quaker movement – their first headquarters were at 16th-century Swarthmoor Hall (see page 225).

In the Pennine Hills, Alston (see page 54) claims to be the highest market town in England. Keswick has the world's longest pencil (over 26 feet) and Hadrian's Wall is Britain's most important Roman monument. Long Meg (see page 138) is the second largest stone circle in Europe, and at Muncaster Castle (see page 190) you'll find one of the finest collections of captive owls in the world.

The most scenic railway line in Britain has to be the 72-mile stretch of the Settle–Carlisle line (see page 61), which runs through the Eden Valley and over the Pennines into the Yorkshire Dales. And, finally, a 2013 YouGov survey gave the accolade of 'Britain's Best Road' to the A591 between Windermere and Keswick.

THINGS TO PACK

OK, now you've made the decision to head to the Lake District. Do you go prepared and loaded for Arctic conditions or travel exceedingly light?

Which option you choose will depend on a number of factors, such as the time of year, what you want to do and your personal preferences. Even in the summer months you'll need wet-weather gear, unless you're very lucky, as well as sandals, sunscreen and swimwear. In winter, take plenty of warm clothing. Here are a few suggestions.

Fell walkers will need a sturdy, and preferably waterproof, pair of walking boots, a small rucksack, several layers of clothing – to regulate body temperature – and a waterproof outer shell. You'll also need a compass and the relevant OS Outdoor Leisure maps. You could take a GPS but don't rely on it for navigating. Batteries flatten and equipment malfunctions in more remote areas and could leave you stranded. Pack spare clothing, a flask for hot drinks, a water bottle, enough food to keep you going – and don't forget the obligatory Kendal Mint Cake. You'll also need a decent walking guide so you might want to take a copy of the AA's *50 Walks in The Lake District*.

If you prefer water sports then you'll want a good quality neoprene wetsuit. Even in the height of summer the water is perishingly cold. Do take a camera or video and don't forget to pack the charger. The scenery is so spectacular that you'll want to have lots of images to help you remember your trip.

Everyday clothes should be casual but comfortable. Swimwear, shirts, tops and shorts for during the day in summer, with long sleeves and trousers at night. There are some fancy restaurants in the Lakes so you might want to think about taking something you can dress up a bit in if necessary.

You will need a warm jumper or fleece in the evening, even in the summer months. In

▼ Scafell Pike

winter, you'll probably want to keep one on during the day too.

There are plenty of clothing stores in the Lake District. Keswick, in particular, is a shopper's paradise as its many outdoor equipment shops seem to have permanent sales. If your idea of a grand holiday in the Lakes is just to go clothes shopping then the bare essentials are all you'll need.

BASIC INFORMATION

Before rushing headlong towards the Lake District, spare a few minutes to read this section – your wealth and sanity may depend on it. Here are a few suggestions to keep you out of trouble, help preserve your bank balance and make the most of your trip.

Don't use a satnav

The very first thing you should know about visiting Cumbria is that in these parts, your satnav is not your friend. Lakeland has several, breathtakingly gorgeous but exceedingly steep, narrow, winding mountain roads that are a tad challenging. If you're not used to driving on roads like this, then you don't want your first experience of them to possibly be on a dark, wild, rainy night, trying to find your accommodation. If you are pulling a caravan as well, then you could be in trouble.

One local business went as far as to say that if potential visitors used a satnav to find them they would 'end up on top

of a fell', while another reported that most of their satnav-igating customers ended up at a remote farmhouse.

If you must use your satnav, then don't rely on it. Plan your routes on a map sticking to main roads and then programme the beast to stick to them. But don't avoid the Hardknott and Wrynose passes altogether or you'll be missing out on a great free Cumbrian attraction. You should try them during the day, however, when you can at least see what you're getting into.

Think about when you want to visit

You may not have any choice about when to take your holidays but if you do, think first about why you want to come to the Lake District. During the summer months the main beauty spots and attractions get crowded with visitors and the roads leading to them become very congested. If you're heading to the fells it's not so bad but you'll still come across a crowd of other walkers. Going off-season you'll likely to find the Lakes much quieter and over the winter months the fell walking is superb – particularly on a crisp, frosty day with a clear blue sky. The downside is that many of the attractions will shut.

Head out onto the fells for a picnic

If you hate waiting in a queue for a table or can't afford to eat out all the time consider buying some of the fresh Cumbrian goodies that you will find on sale everywhere. Freshly baked artisan bread, a slice or three of Cumberland ham, some local cheeses, farmhouse pickles, some locally made gingerbread or cake and a bottle of locally brewed beer is all you'll need. Then have yourself a picnic on the fells, by a lake or even in your car, if it's raining.

Things to do with kids when it's raining

Nothing can ruin a family holiday quite as effectively as a few days of incessant rain. And, yes, it has been known to happen in the Lake District – even in August. Add a car full of bored restless children and your sanity might well be on a shaky peg indeed. Bundling them into paid attractions is a sure-fire way of burning a week's budget in a couple of days. There's the admission fee, a small gift from the shop ('Aw, pleeeease, can I just have a pencil or a rubber'), then lunch or afternoon tea. Even your bank manager will be weeping.

One solution might be to take out a family membership to the National Trust and use it to gain admittance to all of their properties whenever you want. Even when it is wet the children will have a great time sailing on the restored Victorian steam yacht *Gondola* on Coniston Water, or visiting Wordsworth's Birthplace in Cockermouth, Beatrix Potter's farmhouse or Sizergh Castle.

Many brownie points will be earned if you take them on the Lakeside Railway from Haverthwaite to Windermere. It's only a short route, but the train is exceedingly slow. You might also want to visit the Aquarium of the Lakes before the return journey.

The World of Beatrix Potter is also a great treat, particularly if it is on a day when they are serving Peter Rabbit Teas – which means they'll get fed.

Alternatively head to Rheged near Penrith, which, as well as being indoors, has an IMAX cinema and a shop selling paper and art materials – perfect for keeping fidgety fingers busy.

▼ The World of Beatrix Potter

FESTIVALS & EVENTS

From the sensible to the downright bizarre, Cumbria has lots of festivals and events. Here's a selection of the best.

▶ FEBRUARY

Keswick Film Festival
Held in several venues including the Alhambra Cinema, Theatre by the Lake and the IMAX at Rheged.

▶ MARCH

Words by The Water
Celebrating books and words, this festival is held over 10 days in Keswick.

▶ LATE MARCH/EARLY APRIL

Bowness Bay Blues
Held in a picturesque setting on the eastern shore of Lake Windermere, this event specialises in acoustic music and rhythm and blues.

▶ MID-APRIL TO AUGUST

Peter Rabbit Tea Parties
A great event for kids at The World of Beatrix Potter in Bowness-on-Windermere. The tea parties always have lots of cake. Beatrix Potter reads *The Tale of Peter Rabbit* then the kids get a small gift and a balloon. The ticket also includes entry to The World of Beatrix Potter, where you'll find the rabbit in question and more of Potter's characters, including Mrs Tiggy-Winkle.

▶ MAY

Ireby Festival
The small, rural village runs a superb music festival featuring guests such as Eddi Reader and Kate Rusby.

▶ JUNE

Appleby Horse Fair
One of the longest running Cumbrian events is Appleby Horse Fair, which has been held in Appleby since 1685 when it was granted a Royal Charter by James II. This is a major tourist attraction for the town.

Dentdale Music and Beer Festival
A great opportunity to try 25 real ales and enjoy live music. There's a separate area on the field for younger festival goers, too.

Stepping Stones
Folkies will love this small music festival, launched by Steeleye Span's Maddy Prior in 2012. It's held in the attractive grounds of Kirklinton Hall, near Longtown.

Ulverston Music Festival
This week-long music-fest has evolved over the years from its classical roots to become a hugely popular concert series featuring something for everyone – think classical, chamber, jazz, family, choral as well as comedy.

▶ JULY

The Cumbria Steam Gathering
Held at Cark Airfield in Flookburgh, near Grange-over-Sands, steam enthusiasts will enjoy admiring the huge variety of engines, vintage commercial vehicles and classic cars, military vehicles, cars, motorbikes and bicycles on show.

Elephant Festival
Kids will be delighted by this colourful event, which takes place in the attractive small village of Tebay. Everybody makes their own Elephant, and these are then displayed all over town.

Cock Rock
This three-day festival, held in busy Cockermouth, was established in 2006 to promote musicians and raise funds for the hard-working Cumbria's Air Ambulance and the town's Mountain Rescue Team.

Kendal Calling
A mixture of traditional rural entertainment, contemporary music and art in Lowther Castle Gardens, this is a small intimate event with a limited number of tickets. But with eight stages there's still enough variety to satisfy most people.

Maryport Blues Festival
This well-established weekend event takes place in Maryport, the most southern town on the Solway Firth.

▶ AUGUST

Solfest
If you want to take your children to a music festival then your first choice should be Solfest. This popular, eclectic gathering started in 2003. The emphasis is on providing a safe, family-friendly atmosphere with superb music. It's run as a not-for-profit venture by volunteers. As well as the music, there's world shopping, kids' activities and healing therapies and a variety of other workshops.

Lake District Summer Music Festival
If your taste in music is more towards the classical then this festival in Kendal will appeal.

▶ SEPTEMBER

Taste Cumbria Food Festival
Head to Cockermouth to see the county's best produce all in one place and sample the best that Cumbria has to offer.

Egremont Crab Apple Fair
This is the oldest fair in the world and offers a host of attractions, including the annual 'gurning' competition. Aspatria resident Tommy Mattinson won it 15 years in a row and is in the *Guinness Book of Records* as the World Champion. His father was 10 times winner before him.

▶ OCTOBER

Borderlines
Carlisle hosts this week-long celebration of the written and spoken word. Speakers have included Val McDermid, Sir Chris Bonington and Alistair Campbell.

▶ NOVEMBER

The World's Biggest Liar Competition
This popular competition is held each year at the Bridge Inn, Santon Bridge (see page 203). It's a memorial to a Wasdale publican called Will Ritson, famed for his tall tales. These tales have included that Cumbrians are, genetically, two per cent badger and that a chip shop had opened on the summit of Scafell Pike.

CAMPSITES

For more information on these and other campsites, visit theAA.com/self-catering-and-campsites

Castlerigg Hall Caravan & Camping Park ▶▶▶▶▶
castlerigg.co.uk
Castlerigg Hall, Keswick, CA12 4TE | 017687 74499
Open mid-Mar to 7 Nov
Spectacular views over the Derwent Water add to the many attractions of this lovely Lakeland park. Old farm buildings have been converted to offer excellent toilet facilities (with private washing cubicles and a family bathroom), a reception and a well-equipped shop. There's also a kitchen/dining area for campers, and a restaurant/takeaway for when you don't want to cook.

Dandy Dinmont Caravan & Camping Park ▶▶▶
caravan-camping-carlisle.co.uk
Blackford, Carlisle, CA6 4EA
01228 674611 | Open Mar–Oct
The grass pitches are immaculately kept and there are larger hardstandings for motor homes. This park attracts mainly adults; cycling and ball games are not allowed.

Lakeland Leisure Park ▶▶▶▶
HOLIDAY CENTRE
haven.com/lakeland
Flookburgh, LA11 7LT | 0800 1972080 | Open mid-Mar to Oct
This flat, grassy site is ideal for families. The touring area is quietly situated away from the main amenities, but the swimming pools, all-weather bowling green and evening entertainment are just a short stroll away. There is a lake for water sports enthusiasts.

Wild Rose Park ▶▶▶▶▶
wildrose.co.uk
Ormside, Appleby-in-Westmorland, CA16 6EJ | 017683 51077
Open all year
Situated in the Eden Valley, this large, leisure group-run park offers superb facilities including four wooden wigwams for hire. Traditional stone walls and the planting of lots of indigenous trees help it to blend into the environment, and wildlife is actively encouraged. There is a stylish reception with adjacent internet cafe. There's

a bar and a choice of adults-only rooms, as well as family entertainment rooms. Note: tents are not accepted.

Lowther Holiday Park ▶▶▶▶▶

lowther-holidaypark.co.uk
Eamont Bridge, Penrith, CA10 2JB
01768 863631 | Open mid-Mar to mid-Nov

Lowther Holiday Park is a secluded natural woodland site with lovely riverside walks. The park is home to a rare colony of red squirrels, and trout fishing is available on the 2-mile stretch of the River Lowther that runs through the park.

Park Cliffe Camping & Caravan Estate ▶▶▶▶▶

parkcliffe.co.uk
Birks Rd, Tower Wood, Windermere, LA23 3PG | 015395 31344
Open Mar–8 Nov

A lovely hillside park set in 25 secluded acres. The camping area is sloping and uneven in places, but well drained and sheltered; some pitches have spectacular views. The park is well equipped for families, and an attractive bar and brasserie restaurant serves quality food.

The Quiet Site ▶▶▶▶▶

Ullswater, Watermillock, CA11 0LS
07768 727016 | Open all year

A well-maintained site in a lovely, peaceful location, with good terraced pitches that offer great fell views; the very good toilet facilities include family bathrooms, and there's a charming 'olde-worlde' bar. There are wooden camping pods, seasonal bell tents and 10 superb heated 'Hobbit Holes' (underground accommodation for six people), each with an en-suite toilet and wash basin.

Skelwith Fold Caravan Park ▶▶▶▶▶

skelwith.com
Ambleside, LA22 0HX
015394 32277 | Open Mar–15 Nov

In the grounds of a former mansion, Skelwith Fold is in a beautiful setting. A real plus is the five-acre family recreation area, which has spectacular views of Loughrigg Fell.

South End Caravan Park ▶▶▶▶

walneyislandcaravanpark.co.uk
Walney Island, Barrow-in-Furness, LA14 3YQ | 01229 472823 | Open Mar–Oct

A friendly family-owned park next to the sea and close to a nature reserve, on the southern end of Walney Island. It offers an extensive range of quality amenities including an adult lounge, and continues to uphold high standards of cleanliness and maintenance.

Woodclose Caravan Park ▶▶▶▶▶

woodclosepark.com
High Casterton, Kirkby Lonsdale, LA6 2SE | 015242 71597 | Open Mar–Oct

Woodclose is set in idyllic countryside within the Lune Valley. Ideal for a 'back to nature' kind of experience, with riverside and woodland walks, top notch amenities blocks and a 'Wigwam' pod village.

A–Z of
Lake District
& Cumbria

VISIT THE MUSEUMS | GET OUTDOORS | EXPLORE BY BIKE | GO BACK IN TIME | TAKE A TRAIN RIDE | MEET THE WILDLIFE

TAKE IN SOME HISTORY | HIT THE BEACH | EAT AND DRINK | GET INDUSTRIAL | VISIT THE GALLERIES | GO CANOEING

TRY HORSE-RIDING | PLACES NEARBY | CATCH A PERFORMANCE | GO ROUND THE GARDENS | TAKE A BOAT TRIP

▶ Alston   MAP REF 263 E5

An isolated North Pennine town, Alston is set in the middle of spectacular moorland and shares the title of 'highest market town in England' with Buxton in Derbyshire. With its cobbled streets, ancient buildings and railway station, it seems that little has changed in the last 100 years. The C2C cycle path and the Pennine Way long-distance path intersect here. The surrounding countryside is home to a rich variety of wildlife.

TAKE IN SOME HISTORY
Whitley Castle
epiacumheritage.org
Castle Nook Farm, Kirkhaugh,
CA9 3BG | 01434 382080
Open access all year
With fun trails to keep the kids entertained, this Roman fort lies just off the A689, 2 miles north of Alston. Also known as Epiacum, it was built in the early second century and has unusually complex defensive earthworks.

WALK THE NORTH PENNINES
Pull on your hiking boots and an anorak, and head out into the rugged landscape of the North Pennines to discover the region's unusual but characteristic rock formations, peat bogs, moorland and waterfalls. If you are a nature lover, take to the moors to see black grouse, golden plover, merlin and many more rare bird species; or stroll through woodlands where red squirrel and deer still roam.

You will pass by rivers alive with otters, herons, salmon and brown trout. There are several short walks around the town, such as from the Gossipgate Bridge to the Seven Sisters waterfall. For something more adventurous, you can walk part of the historic Pennine Way.

TAKE A TRAIN RIDE
South Tynedale Railway
south-tynedale-railway.org.uk
The Railway Station, Hexham Road,
CA9 3JB | 01434 338214
If you love steam trains, take a trip on this narrow-gauge railway through the beautiful South Tyne Valley. The line runs between Alston and Slaggyford via Kirkhaugh. The timetable and the type of locomotive vary according to the season. Check before you visit to find out which trains are running and when. In general, trains run daily during the summer and weekends only at other times. In December, there are regular Santa specials and the trains may be off completely in January and February. Check the website for other special events.

PLAY A ROUND
Alston Moor Golf Club
alstonmoorgolfclub.org.uk
The Hermitage, Middleton-in-Teesdale Road, CA9 3DB
01434 381675 | Open daily
This is the highest golf course in England and has stunning views of the North Pennines.

EAT AND DRINK

Alston House ⑳⑳

alstonhousehotel.co.uk

Townfoot, Alston

CA9 3RN | 01434 382200

Located at the lower end of Alston, the recently refurbished Alston House offers bright, individually decorated rooms, many with views over the attractive gardens. Food forms an important part of the service here and the owner-chef cooks up a variety of traditional dishes as well as an extensive pizza/pasta menu. They'll even deliver a pizza to your room if you can't be bothered to dress for dinner. Manicures, pedicures, waxing and tanning are all available in the Beauty Room.

Ambleside MAP REF 257 E2

Right at the top of Lake Windermere, Ambleside is a perfect base for touring the central Lakes, with Grasmere and the Langdale valleys just a short drive away. Like many Lake District towns, it seems that every other shop sells walking boots and outdoor clothing.

The Romans built a fort they called *Galava* close to where the rivers Brathay and Rothay combine and flow into Windermere. Now called Waterhead, the remains of the fort are still visible; while in the Armitt Museum you can see many of the artefacts unearthed here over the years. A few hundred years after the Romans, the Vikings overran the area, supposedly bringing with them the hardy local Herdwick sheep. Although Ambleside won its market charter in 1650, it still remained fairly isolated and remote from the rest of Britain. However, this all began to change during Queen Victoria's reign as the Industrial Revolution brought charcoal production and woollen mills, and at the same time the town gained fame and prosperity through the steady growth of tourism.

Traditional Lakeland sports are held at Ambleside on the Thursday before the first Monday in August. Events on display include fell racing, hound trails, and Cumberland and Westmorland wrestling.

TAKE IN SOME HISTORY

Bridge House

Rydal Road, LA22 9AN

015394 32617

The most photographed building in Ambleside is also the smallest. It won't take long to view it, but it's definitely not one to miss. It is 300 years old, built on a little bridge across the beck of Stock Ghyll, and thought to have been an apple store for Ambleside House. Supposedly a family with six children once lived in this small space, but now it must be one of the tiniest National Trust shops in the land.

VISIT THE MUSEUM
The Armitt Museum
armitt.com
The Armitt Museum & Library,
Rydal Road, LA22 9BL
015394 31212 | Open Tue–Sat
10–4.30 (last entry)
If you want to get an overview
of Lake District history, this
fascinating and entertaining
collection celebrates the land
and the people, spanning 2,000
years from the Roman
occupation to the 20th century.
There are facts, artefacts,
historic photographs and
renowned works by the area's
better-known former
inhabitants such as Beatrix
Potter, Kurt Schwitters and
John Ruskin, as well as
displays about the daily lives
of Ambleside's hard-working
townspeople in past times.
The collection includes most
of Beatrix Potter's scientific
illustrations as well as pictures
by artists such as William
Green and J B Pyne. Originally
founded as a library by the

▼ Bridge House, Ambleside

Armitt sisters in 1909, it still
has over 11,000 books in its
reference library.

SEE A LOCAL CHURCH
St Mary the Virgin
Vicarage Road, LA22 9DH
Designed by Sir George Gilbert
Scott and built between 1850
and 1854, this large, early
Gothic-style church is worth a
visit to see the many stained-
glass windows – particularly
the Children's Windows
designed by Henry Holiday, in
commemoration of the 1870
Education Act. The 26-foot-long
Rushbearing Mural is perhaps
the highlight of the church. It
was painted in 1944 by Gordon
Ransom and depicts the
Rushbearing Ceremony, which
still takes place on the first
Saturday in June, when the old
rushes on the church floor are
thrown out and replaced with
new ones. The mural includes
more than 60 figures
representing local people.

GET ON THE WATER
Waterhead
Just a short walk from the
centre of Ambleside is the
lake at Waterhead. Just
imagine Bowness Bay in
miniature, with a short stretch
of beach, rowing boats for hire
and ever-hungry ducks, and
you've got the picture. You can
board the steamers *Swan*, *Tern*
and *Teal* here on their round-
the-lake cruises. Just cruise
round the lake or get off at
Wray Castle and take the gentle
lakeside walk to Ferry House

▲ Stock Ghyll Force, Ambleside

and then continue round the lake by boat to Ambleside. A walk in the opposite direction, following Stock Ghyll through lovely woodland, will bring you to the entrancing Stock Ghyll Force waterfall. 'Force' is a corruption of 'foss', the old Norse word for waterfall. Or combine a cruise with a visit to the Lakeland Motor Museum (see page 63) or the Lakes Aquarium (see page 176).

EXPLORE BY BIKE
Ghyllside Cycles
ghyllside.co.uk
The Slack, LA22 9DQ
015394 33592

If you fancy a spin on the open road, you can hire everything you need here, from bikes to helmets, and a puncture repair kit just in case. There are bikes of all sizes and tag-alongs for children. The friendly and knowledgeable staff will advise you on the best options for your family, including routes to suit your abilities.

PLAY IN A CASTLE

Wray Castle

nationaltrust.org.uk/wray-castle
Low Wray, Ambleside, LA22 0JA
01539 433250 | Open daily Apr–Oct 10–5, Nov Sat–Sun 10–4, closed Dec and Jan, daily Feb–March 10–4

Great for children, this Gothic-style castle, complete with turrets, is home to a range of children's activities. There's a Peter Rabbit adventure for the youngest, while older children can dress up, help build a castle, take a tour and learn the castle's history or go outside to swing on ropes, build dens and explore the trails and gardens.

EAT AND DRINK

The Apple Pie Eating House and Bakery

applepieambleside.co.uk
Rydal Road, LA22 9AN
015394 33679

As well as their famous (and eponymous) apple pie, you could try the Lakeland gingerbread or a Bath bun here. With views over Bridge House and the hills, it's the ideal spot to enjoy the delicious treats, baked dishes or just a coffee.

The Old Stamp House Restaurant ❀❀

oldstamphouse.com
Church Street LA22 0BU
015394 32775

It's not widely known that William Wordsworth was Cumbria's 'Distributor of Stamps' back in the first half of the 19th century, and this is where he plied his trade. Ryan Blackburn has turned this historic building into a restaurant that reflects the great poet's love of the county, with evident passion for regional produce on show. A warren of subterranean spaces, with whitewashed walls and slate floors, simple wooden tables and artworks depicting the local landscape, make for a charmingly rustic setting. The organic and foraged ingredients on show, plus a fondness for contemporary cooking techniques, make this a thoroughly modern sort of restaurant. Prices are fair given the craft and creativity, with the fixed-price lunch a veritable bargain.

Wateredge Inn

wateredgeinn.co.uk
Waterhead Bay, LA22 0EP
015394 32332

The popular Wateredge Inn was converted into a bar and restaurant from two 17th-century fishermen's cottages complete with large gardens, so there's plenty of seating running down to the attractive lakeshore. The same family has run the inn for nearly 30 years and provide a warm welcome. The lunch menu offers sandwiches, salads, pub classics and slates – platters of smoked fish, charcuterie or cheese and antipasti, while the dinner menu has a wider choice of equally good food.

Waterhead Hotel ❀

englishlakes.co.uk
Lake Road, LA22 0ER
015394 32566

The poems of Alfred, Lord Tennyson and the paintings of and Joseph Mallard Turner have immortalised the splendid Lakeland landscapes framing Windermere, and, just a half-mile stroll from the bustle of Ambleside, the Waterhead Hotel is fortunate to have a ringside seat to take it all in. The view from the Bar and Grill restaurant is timeless. The venue itself sports a thoroughly modern boutique look with funky purple LED lighting to go with its up-to-date brasserie dishes. With Lake Windemere on your doorstop, this is a great place to base your holiday.

▶ **PLACES NEARBY**

South of Ambleside, and overlooking Lake Windermere, you'll find Stagshaw Gardens (NT), an 8-acre wild garden created in 1957. Featuring over 300 flowering shrubs and trees, it's at its best in spring and early summer when the camellias and rhododendrons are out, and the woodland floor is a sheet of bluebells. En route here you'll pass the substantial remains of *Galava* Roman Fort (EH), built on the road to Ravenglass under the Emperor Hadrian in the second century (see The Armitt Museum, page 56), or head north towards Grasmere (see page 133), taking in Wordsworth's home at Rydal Mount (see page 206) on the way.

▶ Appleby-in-Westmorland MAP REF 259 D2

Appleby sits in a loop of the tree-lined River Eden, with its Norman castle standing protectively above. Although much of Appleby Castle dates from the 17th century, when it was restored by the redoubtable Lady Anne Clifford, Appleby still has an impressive 11th-century keep. Once the county town of Westmorland, with a royal charter dating from 1174, it has a typical medieval layout, with the castle at the top of the hill and the church at the bottom.

At either end of its main street, Boroughgate, one of the widest in England and also one of the finest, the High Cross and the Low Cross mark what were once the boundaries of Appleby market. The lime trees lining the avenue were planted in the 17th century. The attractive almshouses, known as Lady Anne's Hospital, are still maintained by a trust fund set up by Lady Anne Clifford to provide homes for 13 widows. Lady Anne is buried in Appleby, in St Lawrence's Church, which also has one of the oldest working church organs in the country.

Each June the town hosts the famous Appleby Horse Fair, the largest horse trading fair in the world.

TAKE IN SOME HISTORY
Appleby Castle
applebycastle.co.uk
CA16 6XH | Book a tour online or telephone the tourist information office in Appleby (017683 51177)
This is one of the oldest and most interesting castles in Cumbria (now open again after being closed for over a decade). You need to book a castle tour in advance and they are limited to 20 visitors at a time, but you will get the undivided attention of your guide. The keep is over 900 years old and there would have been wooden keeps and forts here even before that, going back to Roman times. The stories of Lady Anne Clifford – in her own words – are fascinating. You can see her chair, her bed and her accounts; climb the spiral staircase to the top of the tower and hear all about the ghosts.

SEE A LOCAL CHURCH
Church of St Lawrence
Low Wiend, CA16 6QN
Although it might be said to be a bit of a hotchpotch of styles, this building is still impressive. The oldest part of the church is 12th century, the porch is early 14th century but the arch, with its impressive dogtooth moulding, was built 100 years earlier. The interior is largely in the Decorated style. Enter through the imposing arch of the Gothic-style cloisters and don't miss the Clifford Chapel with its fascinating memorials to the formidable Lady Anne Clifford and her mother. You can also see the oldest (c.1542) working church organ in Britain, which was transported here from Carlisle Cathedral in 1683. The organ case woodwork dates from the 1540s, 1680s and 1830s.

▼ Church of St Lawrence

TAKE A TRAIN RIDE
Settle–Carlisle Railway
settle-carlisle.co.uk
Appleby Station | Check the website for tickets and timetables

Whether you love trains, just love travelling through beautiful countryside or have children who haven't experienced train travel, go for a ride on the highest railway line in England. Trains leave every two hours and the 40-minute trip from Appleby to Ribblehead will take you through the wild and remote countryside of the Westmorland Dales, over spectacular viaducts and into Yorkshire at Ribblehead. You can download audio guides from the website and there are often volunteer guides on the trains. At Ribblehead there is an information centre for the line as well as views of the massive 24-arch Ribblehead viaduct. Appleby Station also has a gift shop.

EXPLORE THE TOWN
You can easily explore Appleby-in-Westmorland and its surroundings either by picking up one of the self-guided walking leaflets at the Tourist Information Centre or going on one of the guided walks, which usually start from the Cloisters every Tuesday at around 11am, except in the winter months (check with Tourist Information Centre, 017683 51177). Whatever your level of fitness you will find a walk to suit – from an easy stroll around the historic centre to tackling part

5 castles

of the long-distance Pennine Journey, which passes through the town.

PLAY A ROUND
Appleby Golf Club
applebygolfclub.co.uk
Brackenber Moor, CA16 6LP
017683 51432

This remotely situated heather and moorland course offers interesting golf with the rewarding bonus of several long par 4 holes that will be remembered, and challenging par 3s. There are superb views of the Pennines and the Lakeland hills, and it's renowned for the excellent greens and very good drainage.

EAT AND DRINK
Appleby Manor Hotel & Garden Spa ◉
applebymanor.co.uk
Roman Road, CA16 6JB
017683 51571

The outlook over Appleby Castle and the Eden Valley towards the fells of the Lake District is a real pastoral treat, and this

Victorian sandstone house was put up by someone with an eye for a view. The hotel's newest addition is the 1871 Bistro, named in honour of the year the house went up, and it delivers some breezy feel-good dishes in a charming rustic room with French windows opening on to a charming garden. The main restaurant takes a more refined approach, white linen on the tables, and oak panels on the walls. There's regional produce on the menu and the kitchen delivers some smart, upscale food.

Tastes of Eden Teashop

tastesofeden.co.uk
1 Low Wiend, CA16 6QP
017683 51999

You'll find an all-day range of tasty, home-made food at this friendly delicatessen, cake and tea shop, where there are plenty of gluten-free choices. There are hot and cold dishes available at lunchtime, with vegetarian and vegan options.

Tufton Arms Hotel

tuftonarmshotel.co.uk
Market Square, CA16 6XA
017683 51593

This imposing, gabled building sits at the foot of Appleby's main street, close to the River Eden below the curvaceous fells of the wild North Pennines. There's an elegant, country house feel to the public rooms, with astonishing attention to detail producing classic atmosphere and contemporary comforts. At the heart of the hotel, overlooking a cobbled courtyard, is the Conservatory Fish Restaurant. The menu covers all bases, but it's for fresh fish dishes that the Tufton has a particular reputation, with daily deliveries of the best of the catch from Fleetwood. Beer connoisseurs may enjoy the hotel's own popular house ale.

▸ **PLACES NEARBY**

St Margaret and St James Church

Long Marton, CA16 6JP

Long Marton is just 3 miles north of Appleby on the B6542. The Grade I listed church predates the Norman Conquest. The tower was added around the 12th century and, although it has been much altered and restored over the centuries, the original Saxon stone carvings and Norman additions are well worth a visit.

▸ Askam-in-Furness MAP REF 257 D5

Askam-in-Furness is a Victorian town, which grew up around the iron ore industry. Few signs now remain of its industrial past, apart from a pier, consisting of slag from the works, that juts out into the bay towards Millom, and numerous streets names such as Steel Street and Furnace Street. The iron ore ran out in 1918 and the industrial buildings were gone by 1933. There is still a railway station in the town.

GET OUTDOORS
The Duddon Estuary
There are great views from the long beach across the Irish Sea and the old slag heaps are a haven for wildlife. In particular, there's a colony of rare natterjack toads; even if you don't see one, you can't miss their very loud mating calls between the end of April and July. The beach is a Site of Special Scientific Interest (SSSI).

Askam Pier
The pier, built out of slag from the ironworks, is quite a sight, stretching right out into the sea.

PLAY A ROUND
Dunnerholme Golf Club
atantalus.com/dunnerholme
Duddon Road, LA16 7AW
01229 462675
A unique 10-hole (18-tee) links course with views of the Cumbrian mountains and the Duddon Estuary. Two streams run through and around the course, providing water hazards on the 1st, 2nd, 3rd and 9th holes. The par 3 6th is the feature hole on the course, playing to an elevated green on Dunnerholme Rock, an imposing limestone outcrop jutting out into the estuary.

▶ PLACES NEARBY
The South Lakes Safari Zoo (see page 114) is roughly halfway between Askham and Dalton-in-Furness (see page 114), while just to the southwest you'll find the nature reserve at Sandscale Haws (see page 65). Besides the magnificent views from its dunes, the reserve also hosts plenty of child-friendly activities during the summer months. Over the course of the winter you may see over 20,000 wildfowl flying into this area, making it a birder's paradise.

▶ Backbarrow MAP REF 257 E4
Backbarrow lies on the River Leven just south of Windermere. In the past there were corn mills on the river, an iron furnace and a dye works, but now people visit for the views of the river, the walking and the motor museum.

VISIT THE MUSEUM
Lakeland Motor Museum
lakelandmotormuseum.co.uk
Old Blue Mill, LA12 8TA
015395 30400 | Open daily
9.30–5.30
This is the perfect wet-weather day out in the Lake District. Whether you are particularly interested in cars or not, the whole family will find plenty to interest them here. As well as the 30,000 exhibits, there is a range of motoring memorabilia, bringing back a bygone age in petrol pumps, adverts and ornaments. For adults, memories will be invoked of a beloved first car, while children will find the quaint old cars

fascinating. There are pedal cars – every boy's most memorable Christmas present – and at the opposite extreme, the story of Donald Campbell's daring exploits in *Bluebird*. This British speed record breaker broke eight absolute world speed records in the 1950s and 1960s, and remains the only person to set both world land and water speed records in the same year (1964). But even if you are completely unmoved by cars in any shape or form, there are bicycles and motorbikes, replica shops, fashions and the story of the Women's Land Army. The one thing you can be sure of is that you'll never get round everything.

GET ON THE WATER

Sail down to Lakeside from either Bowness (see page 240) or Ambleside (see page 55), then jump on the connecting bus and head off to the Lakeland Motor Museum (see page 63). Alternatively, start and finish at the Lakeland Motor Museum and spend some time mooching around the shops in Bowness in between. The service operates daily in summer and winter at weekends.

EAT AND DRINK
Café Ambio
lakelandmotormuseum.co.uk
Old Blue Mill, LA12 8TA
015395 30448
The cafe at the Lakeland Motor Museum is a lovely airy space with views to the river and the trains. The food is good and fresh, and the service fast and friendly. Couldn't do better really.

▶ Barrow-in-Furness   MAP REF 256 C5

Barrow might not be the most beautiful of Cumbrian towns, but there's plenty to see. Until the mid-19th century there was just a tiny fishing village here, on the tip of the Furness Peninsula. What made it grow at an astonishing rate were the iron- and steel-making industries, closely followed, logically, by the construction of ships. The shipbuilding company of Vickers became almost synonymous with Barrow and, even today, long after the great days of British shipbuilding have gone, the docks and shipyards are an impressive sight.

TAKE IN SOME HISTORY
Furness Abbey
english-heritage.org.uk
LA13 0PJ | 01229 823420
Open daily Apr–Sep 10–6, Oct 10–5, Nov–Mar Sat–Sun 10–4
The majestic red sandstone remains of this beautiful 12th-century abbey lie in a peaceful valley, which poet William Wordsworth called the 'vale of nightshade'. View the fine stone carvings and visit the exhibition to find out more about the powerful religious community that was once based

Barrow-in-Furness

0   200 m

here. You can get some idea of the size of the community from the monks' dormitory, which is 200 feet long.

VISIT THE MUSEUM
Dock Museum
dockmuseum.org.uk
North Road, LA14 2PW
01229 876400
Open all year Wed–Sun 11–4
You'll get a fascinating overview of shipbuilding, past and present, at this fantastic little museum. Sitting astride a deep dry dock, the exhibition tells how, in the space of a generation, Barrow became a major force in maritime engineering. Barrow's past,

however, concerns much more than ships. You'll find exhibits telling tales of the Vikings, the Romans and even the story of the oldest known northerner from 10,000 years ago.

GET OUTDOORS
National Trust Nature Reserve at Sandscale Haws
Barrow-in-Furness, LA14 4QJ
01229 462855
The estuary of the River Duddon is just 4 miles north of Barrow-in-Furness. Its sandy grassland dunes are home to a variety of wildlife including migratory birds such as red knot, common redshank and pintail. You'll also find some

interesting flora including the rare dune helleborine. Look out for natterjack toads – one fifth of the entire UK population lives here.

SEE A LOCAL CHURCH
Church of St Mary
Duke Street, LA14 3QU | Open daily

St Mary's was the first Catholic church to be built in Barrow. Designed by Edward Welby Pugin in 1866, building was completed in 1888 with its landmark tower and spire. Edward's father, A W N Pugin, who designed parts of the Houses of Parliament, was a leading figure in the Gothic Revival and the arcaded interior is richly decorated in that style with carvings and different-coloured marbles.

WALK THE CISTERCIAN WAY

Enjoy the sands of the Furness Peninsula, the wildlife and the abbey by following part of this 33-mile walk from Grange-over-Sands to Roa Island. It is an ancient trail that crosses the low limestone fells on the shores of Morecambe Bay and the sands of the Furness and Cartmel peninsulas. The trail takes two to three days to complete.

CATCH A PERFORMANCE
The Forum Theatre and Arts Centre
theforumbarrow.co.uk
28 Duke Street, LA14 1HH
01229 820000

Have a look at the varied activities and performances in this small theatre. There are exhibitions, lectures, workshops and all sorts of performances, from dance to amateur dramatics as well as music concerts by performers on tour.

PLAY A ROUND
Barrow Golf Club
barrowgolfclub.co.uk
Rakesmoor Lane, Hawcoat,
LA14 4QB | 01229 825444
Open daily

This pleasant course is laid out on two levels of meadowland, with views of the nearby Lakeland fells and west to the Irish Sea. The upper level is affected by easterly winds.

EAT AND DRINK
Abbey House Hotel ◉
abbeyhousehotel.com
Abbey Road, LA13 0PA
01229 838282

The grand red-brick house stands in 14 acres of countryside and gardens not too far from all the Lakeland action. It's also home to the rather charming and gently contemporary Oscar's restaurant. The house was originally built for a bigwig at Vickers shipyard and much of the period character remains, not least in the restaurant, where the grandeur of the space is matched with tasteful contemporary colour tones and modern designer fittings. There's nothing stuffy about the place, with a relaxed (but professional) approach. The kitchen turns out modern dishes based on a good amount of regional produce. There's a stylish cocktail bar, too.

The Last Resort
141–143 Cavendish Street, LA14 1DJ
01229 813518
Tucked away off Dalton Road, this laid-back cafe serves excellent coffee and delicious home-made cakes, scones and biscuits, and light lunches with a daily changing menu. This might include watercress and spinach soup, lasagne, chicken and pesto mayonnaise sandwiches and a good range of vegetarian choices. There are delicious iced coffees, frappés and smoothies for the summer months. Service is friendly and there is a children's menu.

▶ Bassenthwaite Lake   MAP REF 261 D4

Owned by the National Park, only quiet activities are permitted on the lake. It is important as a home for a rare fish, the vendace, as well as for wintering wildfowl, and is designated as a Site of Special Scientific Interest and a National Nature Reserve. It is an inspiring setting, with Skiddaw (3,054 feet, 931m) rising in the east and it certainly inspired Tennyson, who described, in his poem *Morte d'Arthur*, the dying King Arthur being carried across the waters of the lake on a barge, thus making Bassenthwaite Lake the last resting place of Excalibur. Take some time to pop into the pre-Norman Church of St Bega. There must have been a problem with lengthy sermons here because there is a wrought-iron hourglass used for timing them, although there is no information about what happened if the sands ran out. St Bega's Church inspired the opening lines of Tennyson's *Morte d'Arthur*, which he wrote while staying at Mirehouse (see page 67) in 1835.

> *...to a chapel nigh the field,*
> *A broken chancel with a broken cross,*
> *That stood on a dark straight of barren land.*

Just a short distance from the shores of the lake is Bassenthwaite, an archetypal English village with its green and pub at the heart of community life. It is primarily an agricultural community with limited, but nevertheless charming, amenities.

TAKE IN SOME HISTORY
Mirehouse and Gardens
mirehouse.co.uk
Keswick, CA12 4QE | 017687 72287
House open 30 Mar–Oct Wed, Sat–Sun (also Fri in Aug) 1.30–4.30; gardens, lakeside walk and tea room open 30 Mar–Oct daily 10–5
Beside the A591 are the grounds of this 17th-century

▲ Skiddaw, Bassenthwaite Lake

house, leading down to the eastern shores of the lake. Mirehouse was first built for the eighth Earl of Derby in 1666 and was sold by him to the Greggs 22 years later. Since then, it has been in the same family. It was left in 1802 by the last of the Greggs to John Spedding of Armathwaite Hall, who sat at the same school desk as William Wordsworth. You can easily spend a whole day here enjoying the heather maze, a rhododendron tunnel and a poetry walk for children and grown-ups alike. There are four adventure playgrounds in the gardens, which stretch from Dodd Wood to Bassenthwaite Lake. You can wander leisurely through the wildflower meadow and the walled garden, or explore inside the house with its fine furniture, portraits and manuscripts reflecting the family friendships with Tennyson, Wordsworth, artist Francis Bacon and many more. Or take the waymarked walk to enjoy the lakeside scenery.

MEET THE ANIMALS
Lake District Wildlife Park
lakedistrictwildlifepark.co.uk
Bassenthwaite Lake, CA12 4RD
017687 76239 | Open daily
Mar–Oct 10–5, Nov–Feb 10–4
Enjoy a fun and educational day out amid breathtaking scenery,

– whisky, gin and vodka. There's a well-stocked shop and the Bistro for anything from coffee and afternoon tea to a full supper menu.

GO FISHING
Bassenthwaite Lake
Permits available from Keswick TIC (Moot Hall, Keswick, Cumbria, CA12 5JR | 0845 9010845; keswick. org) Youdales Newsagents, Keswick (017687 72259) or The Castle Inn (017687 776401)
You will find mainly pike here although there are also roach, perch and eels, and there is some salmon fishing at the outflow by Ouse Bridge.

EAT AND DRINK
Armathwaite Hall Hotel and Spa ⓦⓦ
armathwaite-hall.com
CA12 4RE | 017687 76551
Bordering Bassenthwaite Lake and standing in 400 acres of grounds, Armathwaite boasts all of the hoped-for open fires, rich fabrics and acres of oak panelling, and a facelift has brought all the mod cons expected in a 21st-century hotel, including a spa. The Lake View Restaurant is a lovely high-ceilinged room with oak panelling, rich golds and reds and comfortable chairs at formally set tables. Attentive staff are sprucely turned out – as you'd expect of a restaurant with a smart dress code. The kitchen steers a careful course to satisfy both traditionalist and modernist dining tastes.

at this award-winning wildlife park. From antelopes to zebras, you can see over 100 species from every corner of the world, ranging from cheeky mandrills and meerkats to endangered species, such as gibbons and Asian fishing cats.

TASTE A TIPPLE
The Lakes Distillery
lakesdistillery.com
Setmurthy, CA13 9SJ
01768 788850
Take a tour of this distillery, set below Skiddaw. Things kick off with a 25-mile visual journey from the source of the River Derwent to the sea, before a guide helps you explore the distillery itself and sample the three spirits distilled here

The Old Sawmill Tearoom

theoldsawmill.co.uk

Mirehouse, Under Skiddaw,
CA12 4QE | 017687 74317

At the foot of Dodd, just off
the A591 and handy for both
Mirehouse and the osprey
observation points in Dodd
Wood, this lovely woodland tea
room serves hot and cold
snacks, as well as home-made
cakes and scones.

Ravenstone Lodge ◉

ravenstonelodge.co.uk

CA12 4QG | 01768 776629

A country-house hotel on a
human scale, the buildings that
make up Ravenstone used to be
the mews and coach house for
the big house across the way.
This place has plenty going on,
including a bar and bistro in the
former stables. There's some
good cooking on show.

▶ Birdoswald Roman Fort   MAP REF 263 D3

english-heritage.org.uk

Birdoswald, CA8 7DD | 016977 47602 | Open Apr–Oct and Feb half-term
daily 10–5, Nov–Mar Sat–Sun 10–4

The perfect place for a family day out, Birdoswald Roman Fort
is set above the dramatic Irthing Gorge, with a picnic area now
looking out over it. The remote 5-acre remains of the Roman
fort and settlement at Birdoswald is the most interesting spot
in this western expanse of Hadrian's Wall. It was built in about
AD 125 when its Roman name was *Banna*, and at its busiest
would have housed up to 500 foot soldiers. They were there to
protect the wall and, in particular, the bridge across the River
Irthing, from the Scots. The part of the wall that runs
eastwards from Birdoswald towards Harrow's Scar is the
longest visible remaining stretch. You can explore the
perimeter wall of the fort with its entrance gates and part of
one turret, while the interactive visitor centre brings to life a
vivid picture of Birdoswald in Roman times. Excavations have
unearthed the granaries, added in about AD 200, and other finds
have included an arm purse, containing 28 silver coins, and
some delicate gold jewellery now on display in Carlisle's Tullie
House Museum (see page 92).

▶ Blackwell, the Arts & Crafts House   MAP REF 257 E3

blackwell.org.uk

Bowness-on-Windermere, LA23 3JT | 015394 46139 | Open 18 Jan–Dec
daily 10.30–5 (closes at 4 Nov–Feb)

This is a most impressive house. Designed by the architect
Mackay Hugh Baillie Scott and completed in 1900, Blackwell
still retains almost all of its original details in pristine
condition. It is undoubtedly one of the most important

examples of an Arts and Crafts house in Britain and after a restoration project, costing a staggering £3.25 million, it was opened to the public in 2001.

William Morris and John Ruskin both influenced Baillie Scott and the Arts and Crafts' rural motifs are evident everywhere – in the stained-glass windows, tiles and decorative friezes of wild flowers, berries and animals. In room after room you'll find delightful details and interplays of light, all with the majestic backdrop of lake and distant fells. The White Drawing Room is considered to be one of the finest interiors of its period. The overall impression of the interior is strikingly modern, spacious and minimalist.

Blackwell is also an important exhibition space for innovative ceramics, textiles, jewellery and furniture by contemporary artists.

EAT AND DRINK
Macdonald Old England Hotel & Spa ❀
macdonaldhotels.co.uk
23 Church Street, Bowness, LA23 3DF | 015394 87890
There is something rather wonderful about dining with a view over water, and with its lakeside setting, the Number 23 Church Street Restaurant at the Macdonald Old England serves up a very nice one indeed. It is Lake Windermere, of course, that you'll see through the floor-to-ceiling windows (or better still the terrace), but there are plenty of other good reasons to come here. The Victorian mansion is much extended these days and includes a spa among its many attractions. The comfortable restaurant has a good deal to offer apart from the views, from steaks cooked on the grill, through to some gently contemporary dishes.

▶ Borrowdale   MAP REF 261 D5

The so-called Jaws of Borrowdale, where the high crags on either side of the valley almost meet, squeeze the road – the B5289 – and the River Derwent together in the tight space. The road then swings round to the west, through the village of Seatoller, to climb through the equally dramatic Honister Pass – where you can tour the Honister Slate Mine (see page 72). This wooded valley then runs south from Derwentwater and splits into three tranquil valleys – Watendlath, Stonethwaite and Seathwaite.

Some time prior to 1565, an enormous deposit of pure, solid graphite was discovered near Seathwaite, and so the pencil industry was born nearby in Keswick (see page 161); it remains the only deposit of graphite ever found in this form.

▶ Honister Slate Mine MAP REF 261 D5

honister.com

Honister Pass, CA12 5XN | 01768 777230 | Open all year daily 9–5

Although slate has been used as a building material for centuries the first records of slate mining in Honister do not appear until the early 1700s. The Romantic poet, William Wordsworth, even mentions slate quarrying in his diaries. Here at Honister you can tour the last working slate mine in England and explore the caverns hacked out by Victorian miners. You can learn the history of the famous Honister green slate, find out how to rive slates and see local skills in action. Be warned: the tour includes both underground and surface sites and involves some scrambling.

If the ultimate underground experience beckons, you could join the Climb the Mine tour. Not for the faint-hearted, this tour sees visitors led by a guide through the original mine workings and includes vertical climbs, rope-bridge crossings and scrambles up rock-face rungs. You'll finish on the roof of the mine for a unique Lake District adventure. If that whets your appetite, you can try the Via Ferrata, a fixed route over 2,000 feet above the valley floor.

▼ Honister Slate Mine

▲ Borrowdale from Castle Crag

GET OUTDOORS
The Bowder Stone
Signposted along a path east of the B5289 Borrowdale road, south of Grange

Why stop to look at a stone? Well, this particular one weighs about 2,000 tons and appears to be precariously balanced, ready to topple over. A set of steps leads up to the top of its 36 feet, and, despite the attempts of almost everyone who visits to give it a push, it hasn't fallen yet. It was put into place by a glacier, which later melted around it.

GO FISHING
Watendlath Tarn and Borrowdale Fisheries
lakedistrictfishing.com
017687 77362

This beautiful little tarn, along the narrow minor road to Watendlath, off the B5289, is stocked with rainbow trout to add to the small wild brown trout. Day permit options are available from the tea rooms and farm at Watendlath.

GO WALKING
Whether you want to stroll gently through the valley or hit the high fells, there are plenty of routes to choose from in Borrowdale. From Grange, follow the River Derwent upstream for 3 miles to Seatoller, winding your way through oak woods as you go. Catch the bus back or head up to the base of the fells to stride out along an excellent bridleway clinging to the western side of the valley. The summit of little Castle Crag (950feet/290m), with its amazing views of the valley and surrounding fells, is

▲ Stone bridge in Borrowdale

a short, steep climb from the village of Rosthwaite. For a greater challenge, climb the 2,569feet/783m Glaramara or head on to the Newlands fells, including Dale Head (2,470feet/753m). Many hikers also start their Scafell Pike adventures from Borrowdale.

EAT AND DRINK

Caffle House Tearoom
Watendlath, CA12 5UW
This cosy National Trust tea room serves soup, sandwiches and home-made bakes. The location in the tiny hamlet of Watendlath, overlooking the tarn, is very beautiful.

Grange Bridge Cottage Tea Shop
Grange in Borrowdale,
CA12 5UQ | 017687 77201
Just a few yards from the famous double bridges and close to the river, this 400-year-old cottage is a favourite on the Borrowdale tea-shop trail. There's a cosy, cottage-like interior but the beautiful riverside tea garden has real wow factor, dropping steeply down to the river. Home-baked cakes, cream teas and light lunches are served all day.

Hazel Bank Country House ◉
hazelbankhotel.co.uk
Rosthwaite, CA12 5XB
017687 77248
If you are aiming to get away from it all, it may be comforting to know that it's very hard to get a mobile signal in the village of Rosthwaite, where this classic stone-built Lakeland house sits amid 4 acres. A beck-side walk is one attraction, and the dining room looks out over grounds where red squirrels are known to scamper. The drill is a daily-changing four-course menu.

The Langstrath Country Inn
thelangstrath.co.uk
Stonethwaite, CA12 5XG
017687 77239
If you want to get slightly off the beaten track, you'll find this lovely family-run inn in the little village of Stonethwaite is just perfect. The 16th-century inn, originally a miner's cottage, is

located close to England's highest peak, Scafell Pike, and also sits on the coast–to–coast and Cumbrian Way walks. There are spectacular views from the restaurant, while the food is local and fresh with a range of cask conditioned beers and a thoughtful wine selection.

Leathes Head Hotel ●●
leatheshead.co.uk
CA12 5UY | 017687 77247
The Leathes Head was built in Edwardian times as a gentleman's residence, and remains full of original character. It's a lovely spot set in its own 3 acres of gardens and is surrounded by rolling fells and meandering rivers. A new head chef has reinvigorated the kitchen's output. Dishes showcase a real passion for locally grown and reared produce in the daily-changing menus full of smartly presented contemporary fare that simply lets the quality ingredients shine.

▷ Bowness-on-Solway   MAP REF 261 D1

Part of the Solway Coast Area of Outstanding Natural Beauty, Bowness-on-Solway's main claim to fame is that Hadrian's Wall (see page 141) starts here. It stretches 73 miles from here to Wallsend near Newcastle, across the neck of England. If you are doing the Hadrian's Wall walk it is worth spending some time in Bowness at either the start or end of your walk. The sand dunes, salt marsh, shingle beds and peat mosses make this a favourite spot with a number of species of birds. And there are viewpoints and laybys for spotting the waders: oystercatcher, curlew, golden and grey plover, lapwing, knot, dunlin, bar-tailed and black-tailed godwit, redshank and turnstone – all in all, it's a twitcher's paradise.

▷ Bowness-on-Windermere

see **Windermere & Bowness-on-Windermere**, page 240

▷ Brampton   MAP REF 262 C3

One of Cumbria's many attractive market towns, Brampton has held its charter since 1252. Today, the cobbled town square bustles on market day each Wednesday. Off the square is Moot Hall, an octagonal structure built in 1817 with an external staircase for access to its upper floor. The building is now home to Brampton's Tourist Information Centre. In 1745, Brampton was the headquarters of Bonnie Prince Charlie's army while the troops laid siege to Carlisle Castle. On a motte, just out of town, stands a statue of the seventh Earl of Carlisle.

TAKE IN SOME HISTORY

Lanercost Priory

english-heritage.org.uk

CA8 2HQ | 016977 3030

Open daily Apr–Sep 10–6, Oct 10–5,
Nov–Mar Sat–Sun 10–4

This Augustinian priory, founded in the 12th century, is worth a visit for its atmospheric ruins and sense of history. Part of the medieval settlement is in use as the village hall, part is cared for by English Heritage and can be visited, part has been converted to private dwellings, and the interior of the nave is intact and still in use as a parish church. Set in a tranquil rural landscape, surrounded by fields and close to Hadrian's Wall, Lanercost is a magnificent and fascinating complex of historic buildings. It has been a place of worship for almost 850 years. But things have not always been as peaceful as they are now. Owing to its proximity to the Scottish border, the priory suffered during the Anglo-Scottish wars of the 14th century – in 1311 Robert Bruce himself raided it. The thick walls of the tower were possibly used for defence.

SEE SOME LOCAL CHURCHES

**The Priory Church
of St Mary Magdalene**

The most important thing to see in the church is the huge, 24-foot-by-4-foot embroidered woollen cloth designed by William Morris, which is now restored and hangs on the wall. Known as the Lanercost Dossal, it was embroidered by the ladies of the Parish including Mrs Bulkeley, Mrs Chapman and Mrs Dodgson, wives of past vicars. It was hung behind the altar on Easter Day 1887 and rehung after its restoration on Easter Day, 2013. There are also some fine stained-glass windows, designed by the Pre-Raphaelite artist Edward Burne-Jones and made by William Morris & Co. Look out too for the inscribed Roman centurial stone in the priory's fabric; it shows that stone used to build the original structure came from Hadrian's Wall. You can clearly see the stone, but it was incorporated into the stonework upside down.

Church of St Martin

stmartinsbrampton.org.uk

Front Street, CA8 1SH

A Pre-Raphaelite masterpiece and the only church designed by architect Philip Webb, the Church of St Martin is completely different in style from the elaborate Gothic style of the time, as it opens from a small entrance into a simple space of light and dazzling colour. It contains one of the finest collections of stained-glass windows in England, designed by Edward Burne-Jones and made in William Morris's studio. The east window is a blaze of colour depicting Christ the Good Shepherd and a pelican. Known as the Pelican Window, it marks the beginning of the art nouveau movement.

GO FISHING

New Mills Trout Farm

newmillstroutfishingpark.co.uk
CA8 2QS | 016977 41115

Whether you are a regular and experienced fisher, would just like to try the sport out, or have kids who would like to have a go, this is a great place to launch a line. You can take your own rod and buy a ticket to fish or you can hire a rod. The one-acre lake, set in lovely grounds around an old corn mill, is regularly stocked with trout. The ticket price includes keeping the first fish caught but then throwing back the rest – if you're that successful. There is special fun fishing for children and helpful members of staff are on hand to help.

GO WALKING

Atmospheric woodland and hidden gorges provide great walking opportunities in and around Brampton. Climb to the Moat above town and then stride out along the beech-lined ridge with its far-reaching views into Scotland, or enjoy the lively company of the River Gelt on a nearby woodland hike.

PLAY A ROUND

Brampton Golf Club

bramptongolfclub.com
Tarn Road, CA8 1HN
016977 2255

This is a challenging heathland course in rolling fell country. A number of particularly fine holes include the lengthy 3rd and 11th. However, even if you are struggling with the course there are panoramic views of the Lake District, Pennines and southern Scotland that more than compensate.

EAT AND DRINK

The Golden Fleece ◉

thegoldenfleececumbria.co.uk
Rule Holme, Irthington, CA6 4NF
01228 573686

Refurbishment has transformed this white two-storey inn into the eye-catching combination of bar and restaurant with rooms it is today. Log fires and beams in low ceilings remain in place, and the three dining areas have more of a feeling of an inn than a formal restaurant, although tables are smartly set and kindly staff wear their own livery. The menu neatly encapsulates both pub elements and more refined offerings.

Off the Wall Coffee Shop

4 Front Street, CA8 1NG
016977 41600

There's free WiFi and original art for sale at this cosy and friendly all-day cafe, which welcomes dogs as well as humans. Coffee is Italian, baking the best of British, and there are soups, delicious tarts and baked potatoes at lunchtime.

▶ PLACES NEARBY

A tiny hamlet in a remote corner of Cumbria, Bewcastle is less than 7 miles from the Scottish border and just north of Hadrian's Wall.

Bewcastle Cross
bewcastle.com
CA6 6PS

One of the oldest stone crosses in Europe, this is a cross without its cross, as the top fell off and no one knows what happened to it. However, it is still a magnificent sight, standing over 13 feet high and made of yellow sandstone. Its weathered surface is patterned with early Celtic scrolls and intricate designs, and decorated with carvings first made some 1,300 years ago.

Church of St Cuthbert
CA6 6PS

The present church was rebuilt in 1792 and is a simple building with a west tower and bellcote, while inside there is a tapestry depicting St Cuthbert. Past rectors have included successful reivers, border raiders that operated along the Anglo-Scottish border from the late 13th century through to the 16th century. This may account for the local legend that only women were buried in Bewcastle – the local men were all hanged in Carlisle! Though only the east end remains, the earliest recorded church here dates from 1277, with building material being taken directly from the remains of the Roman fort previously on the site.

Bew Castle

Located within a short walk of Bewcastle, the castle was built in about 1092 on the site of a former Roman fort. The south wall is still standing, to almost its full height, but it is a castle to be appreciated for its setting rather than its present state.

▶ Brantwood
see **Coniston,** page 106

▶ Brough   MAP REF 259 E2

Brough is a small town in the Eden Valley, at the foot of the North Pennines a few miles north of Kirkby Stephen. It is a twin village, and the southern part, Church Brough, has a ruined Norman castle and a Roman fort once stood here. The northern Market Brough is on a medieval road, and in the 18th and 19th centuries was an important stop on the road to Scotland.

TAKE IN SOME HISTORY
Brough Castle
english-heritage.org.uk
CA17 4EJ | 0370 333 1181 | Open daily Apr–Sep 10–5, Oct–Mar 10–4

Dating from Roman times, the atmospheric 12th-century keep at Brough Castle replaced an earlier stronghold which was destroyed by the Scots in 1174. The structure was carefully restored by the indomitable Lady Anne Clifford in the 17th century.

▶ Brougham Castle   MAP REF 258 B1

english-heritage.org.uk

CA10 2AA | 01768 862488 | Open daily Apr–Sep 10–6,
Oct–Mar Sat–Sun 10–4

There is a lot to explore in this castle with its winding stairs and passages. A good place to start is the exhibition, which tells the story of the rich and powerful Anne Clifford, who died here in 1678, when she was almost 90 years old. As well as Brougham, she arranged the restoration of Appleby and Brough castles, with no expense spared so that all three of her castles would be habitable.

The Great Tower was built in the 12th century of sandstone rubble, with more expensive, decorative cut stone at the corners and on windows and doors. People have added and restored the buildings over the centuries, most notably Anne Clifford. However, the Great Tower remains Brougham's most impressive feature, still standing almost to its original height. Climb to the top of the keep if you want to soak up the fabulous panoramic views over the Eden Valley.

TAKE IN SOME HISTORY
Brougham Hall

broughamhall.co.uk

CA10 2DE | 01768 868184

Open daily 9–6. Cafe, closed Mon, closes at 4

This inspired project, housing a range of small businesses, includes a cafe housed in a 15th-century ruin. It is well worth a visit to view the building, as the exterior of the hall is in a gradual process of restoration. Inside you'll find a variety of crafts including a gallery, jewellers and potters.

▼ The River Eamont and Brougham Castle

▶ Broughton-in-Furness   MAP REF 257 D4

A lovely little town in Dunnerdale (see page 122), Broughton-in-Furness stands back from the Duddon Estuary. The market square is dominated by a huge chestnut tree and has a stepped obelisk and a pair of stone tables that were once used to sell fish caught in the River Duddon.

GO WALKING

The Lickle Valley

You will find walks to suit all ages and abilities, from gentle riverside walks and forestry rambles to more strenuous fell walks and hikes. Footpaths cross over the fells into the Duddon Valley, or up onto Stickle, Caw, White Pike and on to Coniston Old Man. Guides to walks in the Lickle Valley, Duddon Valley and Woodland Valley are available to buy at the Blacksmiths Arms (see below).

EAT AND DRINK

Blacksmiths Arms

theblacksmithsarms.com
Broughton Mills, LA20 6AX
01229 716824

Originally a farmhouse and then an inn and blacksmith's (hence the name), this whitewashed pub dates from 1577 and stands in the secluded Lickle Valley, with miles of glorious walks radiating from the front door. The interior remains largely unchanged, with oak-panelled corridors, slate floors, oak-beamed ceilings and log fires. The Lanes own and run the Blacksmiths, Michael dividing his time between the kitchen and the bar, and Sophie running front of house. The bar is reserved for drinking only, with local ales and Westons Old Rosie cider. The sheltered, flower-filled front patio garden is great for alfresco dining.

Broughton Village Bakery

broughtonvillagebakery.com
Princes Street, LA20 6HQ
01229 716284

This is a splendid little retreat to enjoy a tall latte or a snappy espresso. You can get a light lunch or snack or try one of the tempting home-baked cakes.

The Square Café

thesquarecafe.biz
The Square, LA20 6JA
01229 716388

Overlooking the village square, with a few outside tables, this traditional cafe is popular with walkers, cyclists and motorcyclists. Afternoon teas with home-made scones are a favourite.

▶ PLACES NEARBY

Duddon Iron Works

Near Broughton-in-Furness

This is the restored remains of one of the most impressive, charcoal-fired Iron Works from the Industrial Revolution. It lies just north of Broughton-in-Furness on the A595. Park in the lay-by just beyond the bridge and walk from there. Open site.

▶ Buttermere & Crummock Water   MAP REF 260 C5

These two neighbouring lakes in the Buttermere Valley, separated only by a half-mile strip of meadowland, were probably one lake originally. Buttermere is perhaps the more beautiful, although Crummock Water is twice its size with one of the most impressive waterfalls in the Lakes. Scale Force, on its western side, plunges 172 feet into the lake.

GO WALKING

Walking is the top activity around here and there are loads of fantastic routes to choose from. The rough walk to Scale Force begins in Buttermere village through a tree-lined gorge where the Scale Beck plummets to the lake. Another path leads all the way along Crummock Water's western shore, to join up with the B5289 along the eastern shore. This road links Lorton Vale to the north of Buttermere, with the steep Honister Pass to the east before continuing on to Borrowdale. If you want a testing climb, Buttermere is surrounded by high hills, such as the 2,126-foot Fleetwith Pike, guarding the Honister Pass, and the 1,959-foot Haystacks. Or there is an easy two-hour walk around Buttermere with superb views in all directions. To the northwest are the Derwent Fells, crossed by the Newlands and Whinlatter passes, while to the west, above Burtness Wood, stands another range of dramatic crags and fells.

▼ A view across Buttermere

GO FISHING

You can get fishing and boating permits for Buttermere, Crummock Water and Loweswater from the ticket machine in the National Trust car park in Buttermere (CA13 9UZ). Trout, char, pike and perch can all be found in these waters. No motorised craft allowed.

SEE A LOCAL CHURCH

St James, Buttermere
CA13 9XA

There's been a church above the village of Buttermere since 1507, though the present church dates from the 1840s. It's chiefly worth a visit to see the memorial to Alfred Wainwright, the famous hill-walker and author of many

▲ The lake at Buttermere

iconic guidebooks about the Lakes. The memorial is set on a windowsill on the church's south side, from where you can see his favourite walking site, Haystacks, where his ashes were scattered after his death. Look out for the east window by Henry Holiday.

5 top lakes

EAT AND DRINK

Croft House Farm Café
crofthousefarmcafe.co.uk
Buttermere, CA13 9XA
017687 70235
This award-winning cafe prides itself on looking after walkers, who can either buy sandwiches, snacks and drinks to take away or sit in. There's free WiFi, and they sell basic groceries and a range of maps and guides.

Syke Farm
Buttermere, CA13 9XA
017687 70277
Don't leave without trying the ice cream here, it's home-made with milk from the farm's resident herd of Ayrshire cattle. But this tiny tea room just below the church is also great for home-made bakes, and there's a little craft shop too.

▶ PLACES NEARBY

Seathwaite
From here you can get onto well-known mountains such as Scafell Pike, Great Gable and Glaramara. So not surprisingly, this little hamlet in Borrowdale is now a popular starting point for walkers. Alfred Wainwright said of it, 'Seathwaite, once in a little world of its own with few visitors, has become a pedestrian metropolis. Great days on the fells begin and end here.'

Newfield Inn
newfieldinn.co.uk
Seathwaite, LA20 6ED
01229 716208
Tucked away in the peaceful Duddon Valley – Wordsworth's favourite – is Paul Batten's 16th-century cottage-style pub. Hugely popular with walkers and climbers, the slate-floored bar regularly throngs with parched outdoor types quaffing pints of local ales. Served all day, food is hearty and traditional and uses local meats. There is a beer festival here in October.

▶ Caldbeck MAP REF 261 E3

It's well worth a visit to this traditional fell village, preserved as a conservation area. It's not as busy as some of the better-known parts of the Lake District, but it is equally lovely. The walking and cycling routes are as likely to have ponies, sheep or ducks wandering along them as people. The Cald Beck provided the water for the 17th- and 18th-century woollen mills, bobbin mills, corn mills, a paper mill and a brewery. Many of the old mill buildings are still in use and it is easy to imagine the hive of industry that existed here in the 18th century. Caldbeck is also a good stopping point if you happen to be traversing The Cumbria Way (see page 94) long-distance footpath.

▶ Cald Beck runs through Caldbeck

TAKE IN SOME HISTORY
Priest's Mill
watermillcafe.co.uk
Priest's Mill, CA7 8DR
016974 78267 | Open Feb–Dec daily 9–5, Jan Fri–Sun 9–4

Built by a former rector in 1702, this mill wheel has been restored to full working order. There's also an 18th-century watermill, a cafe (see also Eat and Drink, The Watermill Café) and craft shops.

SEE A LOCAL CHURCH
St Kentigern's Church
CA7 8DP

You can really get a flavour of the past by visiting the churchyard of this 12th-century church. Here you can find the final resting place of the famous local huntsman, John Peel, immortalised in the song *D'Ye Ken John Peel,* and the grave of Mary Robinson Harrison, the Maid of Buttermere.

GET OUTDOORS
'A delicious spot in which to breathe out a summer's day – limestone rocks, hanging trees, pools and waterbreaks – caves and cauldrons which have been honoured with fairy names...' So wrote Dorothy Wordsworth after visiting The Howk with her poet brother William. After passing the romantic ruins of an old bobbin mill that once had a 42-foot waterwheel, the well-trodden path from the village enters a narrow, densely vegetated limestone gorge that is home to a deafening waterfall. Leaflets for this and other walks can be bought from the Kirkland Stores and Post Office (016974 78252, open Mon–Sat 9–5, Sun 9–12) in the village centre.

EAT AND DRINK
Oddfellows Arms
oddfellows-caldbeck.co.uk
CA7 8EA | 016974 78227

Located opposite the church, this 17th-century coaching inn serves Jennings real ales, lunchtime snacks and simple pub grub. You can admire the dramatic northern fells from the garden and the Cumbria Way goes right past the door.

The Watermill Café
watermillcafe.co.uk
Priest's Mill, CA7 8DR
016974 78267

You can easily spend a relaxing hour or two here, eating and browsing. This beautifully restored monastic mill, overlooking the Cald Beck, has craft shops as well as the Watermill Café. Fair Trade and vegetarian options are a speciality, and on warmer days you can sit on the terrace which also overlooks the village cricket pitch.

▶ PLACES NEARBY
Nearby the picturesque village of Hesket Newmarket is the birthplace of Eddie Stobart, the man who established the well-known haulage firm. His lorries each boast a female name on the front – fun for kids to look out for on car journeys.

Ireby is an unspoiled village in the peaceful fells of the northern Lake District, in the area to the north of Keswick, known as 'Back o' Skiddaw'. It was once a thriving market town, with a market cross, believed to date from 1200.

Not far from here too, is lovely Bassenthwaite (see page 67), home to the lakeside gardens at Mirehouse and the Lake District Wildlife Park (see page 68).

EAT AND DRINK
The Old Crown

theoldcrownpub.co.uk
Hesket Newmarket, CA7 8JG
01697 478288

This pub is a very good reason for a visit to the pretty village of Hesket Newmarket. Owned co-operatively by the locals, the exceptionally fine ale is produced in the brewery at the back. They also serve decent pub grub and the craic is mighty too.

▼ St Kentigern's Church, Caldbeck

▶ **Carlisle** MAP REF 262 B4

There is plenty to see and do in Carlisle and if you are making an extended visit to Cumbria don't miss its only city. Carlisle is the main shopping centre for the English border area and much of southern Scotland. The capital of Cumbria has been an important centre of population since before the Roman occupation. You can tell that it was an important town from the size of the castle and the cathedral and the extent of the city walls – built, some 1,000 years after Hadrian's Wall, around the remains of the Roman town and fort. The 12th-century West Walls, which run behind St Cuthbert's and around the cathedral, are the best surviving examples.

Located so close to the border with Scotland, perhaps it's not surprising that the Scots and the English fought over the town many times and, over the centuries, both the Scots and English held it at different periods. William II, the son of William the Conqueror, built a castle in Carlisle around 1,000 years ago, after he took the town from the Scots. It was originally wooden but soon replaced by a stone castle. It has been much attacked, but some of the 14th-century buildings remain. Carlisle is steeped in history, as you'll see from a walk

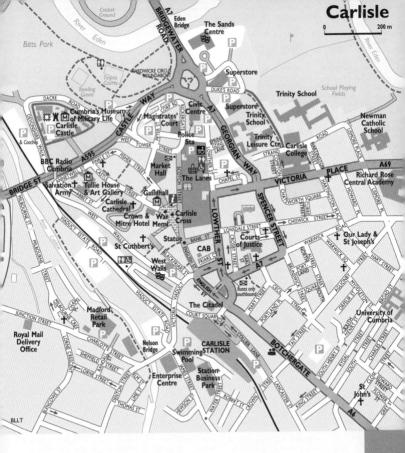

Carlisle

0   200 m

around its historic centre, but it is also a vibrant town with modern shops, cafes and leisure facilities. In the wide Green Market you'll find street entertainers, a farmers' market and seasonal celebrations, while not far away is a modern shopping mall, the Lanes.

If you want to find out about the history of Carlisle, visit the award-winning Tullie House Museum and Art Gallery in Castle Street. The magnificent 12th-century Carlisle Cathedral is also well worth a visit, emphasising again Carlisle's importance in medieval times. The 14th-century timber-framed Guildhall now houses the Guildhall Museum. Other notable buildings include the Citadel, with its 19th-century towers dominating Henry VIII's 16th-century entrance to the city, and the 18th-century Town Hall, which is now used as a visitor centre.

Carlisle offers plenty of entertainment too; head for the Sands Centre, for everything from a gym and climbing wall to live entertainment, or take in a movie at the multiplex cinema. Alternatively, you could have a flutter at one of the regular meetings held at Carlisle Racecourse.

◀ The Citadel

TAKE IN SOME HISTORY
Carlisle Cathedral
see highlight panel opposite

Carlisle Castle
english-heritage.org.uk
Castle Way, CA3 8UR
01228 591922 | Open Apr–Oct daily
10–5, Nov–Mar Sat–Sun 10–4.
Check website for school holiday
times

A visit to Carlisle Castle is a
great day out for all the family.
Kids will enjoy exploring the
ramparts. Several rooms in the
gatehouse are decorated in
medieval style, while you can
explore the warren of chambers
inside the castle.

Carlisle's location, so close
to the Scottish border, ensured
its importance in history. The
first castle overlooking the
River Eden was nothing more
than a triangular area of land
encircled by a wooden fence.
William Rufus, the son of
William the Conqueror, built it
in 1092. When he was killed in
a hunting accident in the New
Forest, his brother Henry
ordered that a castle and walls
should be built to protect the
town. However, despite the new
fortifications, the castle fell to
the Scots 14 years later. It was
held by David I and Malcolm IV,
kings of Scotland, from 1136
until 1157, and was taken back
into English hands by Henry II.
Another Scottish king, William
the Lion, besieged the castle
from 1173 to 1174. Other
highlights in the castle's history
include the distinctive rounded
battlements – added much later
by Henry VIII. Mary, Queen of
Scots was imprisoned here, and

▼ Main entrance to Carlisle Castle

▶ **Carlisle Cathedral** MAP REF 262 B4

carlislecathedral.org.uk
Cathedral Office, The Abbey, CA3 8TZ | 01228 548151
Open Mon–Sat 7.30–6.15, Sun 7.30–5; Christmas & New Year 9.45–4

In 1122, 30 years after the castle was built, Carlisle Cathedral was founded. It was originally a priory but became a cathedral under Henry I in 1132 and has held a daily service for almost 900 years. Inside, the first thing you notice is its magnificent high ceiling, with its beautiful blue background and gold painted stars. The stained-glass windows date from the 14th to the 20th centuries – the oldest is in the East Window. Look out also for the bishop's throne or 'cathedra'; the 16th-century Brougham Tryptich, a carved wooden altarpiece made in Amsterdam; and two runic inscriptions carved in the 12th century. Don't forget to look up at the stone carvings atop the pillars, where the medieval masons carved their daily lives as decoration – animals, plants and the labours of the year, month by month. Don't miss seeing the buildings opposite the cathedral's main entrance too. The Fratry was a 13th-century monastic common room and now contains the cathedral library and the Prior's Kitchen Restaurant. Across from the Fratry, the 13th-century Prior's Tower was used, among other things, as a place of refuge from reivers and other Scottish raiders.

▼ Carlisle Cathedral

the castle was captured by 'Bonnie' Prince Charlie in 1745. You can also find the Border Regiment Museum here.

VISIT THE MUSEUMS AND GALLERIES

Border Regiment and King's Own Royal Border Regiment Museum

cumbriasmuseumofmilitarylife.org
Alma Block, The Castle, CA3 8UR
01228 532774 | Open daily Apr–Sep 10–6, Oct–Mar Sat–Thu 10–4. Times subject to change, check website

Trophies, models, pictures, weapons, uniforms, medals and silver tell the story of the regiments. There are many tragic and heroic stories from the wars in which the regiments have been involved. The museum has recently relocated to Carlisle Castle's Alma Building from its former home in Queen Mary's Tower.

Guildhall Museum

Green Market, Fisher Street, CA3 8JE
01228 618718 | Open summer Thu 12–4

One of the oldest houses in Carlisle, the Guildhall Museum is a fine Grade I listed building, built in the 14th century. Inside, you'll find a range of displays telling the fascinating story of the medieval guilds with different rooms reflecting the individual trades. The guilds were established for weavers, tailors, tanners, glovers, shoemakers, smiths, butchers and merchants to protect trade. The guildhall was given to the city by Richard de Redeness

and used as the meeting place by the town's Trade Guilds. Four of the Guilds survive today and continue to meet annually in the building on Ascension Day.

Linton Tweeds Visitor Centre

visitcumbria.com
Shaddongate, CA2 5TZ 01228 527569

On a visit here, you can watch the latest designs being woven on the original old hand looms. You can even have a go yourself on another old hand loom. The family-run business is over 100 years old, and was started by William Linton in the Caldewgate area of Carlisle in 1912. William's friend, Captain Molyneaux, introduced him to a young lady known as Coco Chanel. The fashion house is still a customer today and Michelle Obama is among the many well-known people from around the world who wear these fabrics. There's also a shop and coffee shop.

Tullie House Museum & Art Gallery Trust

tulliehouse.co.uk
Castle Street, CA3 8TP
01228 618718 | Open Apr–Oct Mon–Sat 10–5, Sun 11–5; Nov–March Mon–Sat 10–4, Sun 12–5

If you want to find out about the history of Carlisle, this is the place to go. The story is told from before the Romans to the railways, via the reivers, Robert the Bruce and the Roundheads with lively displays and lots of activities, which combine education and entertainment.

Children will most definitely not be bored here. You can try writing on Roman wax tablets, have a go with a crossbow, or go through a mine tunnel. The galleries include the Roman Frontier gallery and the Border Galleries, with interactive displays and artefacts bringing these bloodthirsty times to life. It also has natural history displays and art galleries.

Set in beautiful gardens, Old Tullie House is an original Jacobean building from 1689 containing a nationally important collection of Pre-Raphaelite art.

ENTERTAIN THE FAMILY
Sands Centre
thesandscentre.co.uk
CA1 1JQ | 01228 633766
Call or check website for details
This is the major venue for performances of all kinds in Cumbria and beyond. Check the website for its programme, which ranges from touring shows including ballet, opera and theatre productions to big-name bands, solo

▼ Underpass to the Tullie House Museum & Art Gallery

performers, comedy and pantomime. The Centre also has a state-of-the-art gym, climbing wall and sports hall, where all sorts of sports and activities are tailored for all ages. Check the website for the holiday programme for kids, sports on offer regularly and special sessions for seniors.

CATCH A PERFORMANCE
Old Fire Station
oldfirestation.carlisle.city
Peter Street, CA3 8QP | 01228
817358 (tickets 01228 598596,
McGrew's Bistro 01228 817389)
Dating from the late 19th century, Carlisle's old fire station was left devastated by the floods that hit the city during 2005, but has recently been transformed into an entertainment venue that's a more intimate alternative to the Sands Centre. It hosts comedy nights, music events, drama and art exhibitions. It's also home to McGrew's Bistro which serves breakfasts, lunches and light snacks from 10–5.

SEE A LOCAL CHURCH
St Cuthbert's Church
stcuthbertscarlisle.org.uk
Blackfriars Street, West Walls,
CA3 8UF | 01228 521982
Slightly overshadowed by the cathedral is St Cuthbert's Church. Also built in the 12th century, the present buildings date from the 1700s. Its most unusual feature is a moveable pulpit, mounted on rail tracks, while the nearby tithe barn now functions as the church hall.

GO TO THE RACES
Carlisle Racecourse
carlisle.thejockeyclub.co.uk
Durdar Road, CA2 4TS
01228 554700
If you fancy a day at the races, check the website for fixtures. Children are generally admitted free and there are family fun days throughout the year.

WALK A LONG-DISTANCE PATH
The Cumbria Way
This 72-mile long-distance route from Ulverston to Carlisle takes a straight line through the heart of the Lake District, through some of its most beautiful areas. From Ulverston the route traverses the length of Coniston, passes the lovely Tarn Hows and Rosthwaite, goes by Derwentwater to Keswick then Skiddaw and Blencathra to Caldbeck, and then on through gentler pastoral countryside to Carlisle. Unsurprisingly, this is one of the most popular long-distance paths in the country. It takes about a week to complete and there are companies that will organise the entire walk for you, including accommodation and luggage transfer.

PLAY A ROUND
Carlisle Golf Club
carlislegolfclub.org
Aglionby, CA4 8AG | 01228 513029
Open daily
This majestic, long-established parkland course has great appeal, providing a secure habitat for red squirrels and

deer. It's a complete but not too severe test of golf, with fine turf, natural hazards, streams and many beautiful trees. No two holes are similar.

Eden Golf Course

edengolf.co.uk
Crosby-on-Eden, CA6 4RA
01228 573003 | Open daily
This is a championship-length parkland course following the River Eden. There are tight tree-lined fairways and many natural water hazards. The nine-hole Hadrian's course is set in natural undulating surroundings and has a contrasting style to the main 18 holes.

EAT AND DRINK

Foxborough Smokehouse Restaurant

foxboroughrestaurant.com
52 Cecil Street, CA1 1NT
01228 317925
Tucked away down some basement steps in a side street, this lively restaurant is worth seeking out for lunch, dinner and weekend brunch. The emphasis is on American-style smoked and barbecue meats.

Fox's Café Lounge

foxescafelounge.co.uk
18 Abbey Street, CA3 8TX
01228 491836
Perfectly set for visitors between the Cathedral and the Castle, this friendly and relaxed cafe serves delicious coffee, smoothies, local ales and wine. Cakes and cookies are home-made and there are good hot

and cold sandwiches and snacks throughout the day.

Garden Restaurant Tullie House

tulliehouse.co.uk
Castle Street, CA3 8TP
01228 618718
On the ground floor of the museum and art gallery, overlooking the quiet garden, this large refectory-style restaurant is a great meeting place and ideally situated close to Carlisle's city centre. Serving snacks and more substantial lunches, it's also family friendly.

▶ **PLACES NEARBY**

Finglandrigg Wood on the Solway Plain

You'll find this on the B5307 about 8 miles from Carlisle. There's a lay-by with a Natural England sign about a mile after Kirkbampton and as well as picnic tables you'll find waymarked paths onto the reserve. It has a wide variety of wildlife and plant life.

Church of St Mary

stmaryswreay.org
Wreay, CA4 0RL | 016974 73687
If you only have time to visit one church, this is the one to see. Its dramatic and imaginative design is very unusual. Sara Losh (1785–1853), a local landowner, designed St Mary's in 1842, partly in memory of her sister and parents. Influenced by the architecture she had seen on her Grand Tour of Europe, the church is built like a Roman basilica with a large

rectangular area and a semicircular apse. The light stone and white-painted interior walls create a strong contrast with the dark timbered roof, pews and decorative details. The building is alive with symbols of life and death, darkness and light. Gargoyles guard the exterior and, inside, there are many figures. A short walk away, the Sarah Losh Heritage Centre (open daily 10–4) tells the story of the village and the Losh family. It's housed in the Chapel of Rest, another of Sarah's creations.

Crown Hotel ◉

crownhotelwetheral.co.uk
Station Road, Wetheral, CA4 8ES
01228 561888

This white Georgian hotel, updated for the 21st century, is in a pretty village a few miles out of Carlisle close to Hadrian's Wall. Overlooking the landscaped gardens, the Conservatory Restaurant has a striking raftered ceiling, red quarry floor tiles and padded dining chairs at wooden tables. The kitchen favours a largely modern British approach and gives dishes their own distinctive identity.

Solway Aviation Museum

solway-aviation-museum.co.uk
Carlisle Airport, Crosby-on-Eden
CA6 4NW | 01228 573823
Open Apr–Oct Fri–Sun and BHs
10.30–4.15 (last entry)

If you are interested in planes, you will want to spend a good few hours here, admiring the vintage aircraft on display. Even if you're not an enthusiast, this is a highly entertaining museum for the whole family. Children will love climbing into the cockpits of some of the exhibits, in particular the stunning Vulcan bomber. Exhibits include remnants from Blue Streak, the failed missile project from nearby RAF Spadeadam, a Sikorsky helicopter and a 1930s Hawker Hart biplane.

Wreay Woods Nature Reserve

Wreay, CA4 0RL

Centuries ago, the entire valley of the River Petterill was heavily wooded with indigenous trees. These have been cleared over the centuries to make way for farmland, but this nature reserve preserves some of the ancient landscape in a steep-sided narrow gorge. The area is best seen in springtime when the woodland floor is carpeted with bluebells and ransomes, and wagtails and kingfishers can be seen busying themselves on the riverbanks.

The String of Horses Inn

stringofhorses.com
Faugh, CA8 9EG | 01228 670297

Close to Hadrian's Wall in the peaceful village of Faugh, this 17th-century Lakeland inn is tucked away just 10 minutes from busy Carlisle. There are oak beams, wood panelling, old settles and log fires in the restaurant, where imaginative pub food is on offer, and in the bar, stocked with real ales from Brampton Brewery.

▶ Cartmel MAP REF 257 E4

If you wonder why this tiny village in the middle of the South Lakeland District fells and countryside should have such a large and magnificent church, it is because Cartmel grew up around its famous 12th-century Augustinian priory church. Owing to it being stipulated that the local community should always have the right to worship in the Priory Church of St Mary and St Michael, it was saved when the monastery was disbanded.

Much of the stone from the monastery was re-used to build the present village and the only other relic of it that remains is the gatehouse (now a private residence in the care of the National Trust) in the little market square. The stepped market cross still stands but the markets themselves are long gone. Today, Cartmel is a pretty little village, worth exploring in its own right as well as for its gem of a church.

To the south of the village is Holker Hall (see page 152), the home of the Cavendish family; allow plenty of time for your visit because there's a lot to see.

SEE A LOCAL CHURCH

The Priory Church of St Mary and St Michael

cartmelpriory.org.uk

Priest Lane, LA11 6QD

01539 536261

This priory church will make a lasting impression on you, overshadowing the village as it does and giving an idea of how the early priories – with all their attached buildings – must have dominated the surrounding area.

Founded as a priory for Augustinian canons in around 1189, the oldest parts are the chancel, transepts, the south doorway and part of the north wall of the nave, where you can see the plain and massive arches, characteristic of the period. Look for the two blocked-up doorways in the transepts, one of which once connected to the monks' dormitory. The huge east window nearly fills the east wall and some sections hold fragments of medieval glass rescued from earlier works. The south porch has the oldest glass, which dates from the 14th century and depicts angels. There is also some stunning Victorian glass, with rich colours and beautifully detailed drawings.

The Priory Church of St Mary and St Michael also served as a parish church, which saved it from outright destruction during the Dissolution of the Monasteries in the 1530s. The priory was dissolved, and four of the monks were hanged along with 10 villagers who had supported them, but the church survived, as did the precinct gatehouse (see page 98), though other domestic structures were destroyed.

The 15th-century choir stalls, each with a misericord, bear many carvings of animals, including a unicorn, mermaid, ape and peacock, as well as the Green Man. The delicate 17th-century stall backs have very fine openwork panels and slender columns topped with ornate capitals and covered in twining vines. Be sure to notice the unique tower. Unusually the 15th-century extension was built across the original low lantern tower at a 45-degree angle. And don't miss the bullet holes still visible in the southwest door of the nave, leftovers from the 1640s, when Roundhead troops stayed in the village and stabled their horses in the church.

Cartmel Priory Gatehouse
LA11 6PU

Once the gatehouse to the priory, this fortified tower was built around 1330–40, a time of constant danger from across the border. Its gates opened northwards and there was once a guardhouse to the east and a porter's lodge to the west, from which food and other alms were dispensed to the poor. When the priory was dissolved in 1536 the gatehouse was saved, probably because it also served as a courthouse. It was later a prison and subsequently a school. Today, it is owned by the National Trust and houses a community-run heritage centre, where you can learn more about the history of Cartmel, its buildings and countryside.

EAT AND DRINK
Aynsome Manor Hotel ◉
aynsomemanorhotel.co.uk
LA11 6HH | 015395 36653

Once a country residence of the Pembroke family, this is an elegant little country house at the head of the Cartmel Valley, looking southwards towards the priory, the meadows and the woods. Inside, it has an old-school feel, with starched tablecloths, silverware and gleaming glasses, deep windows and portraits in oils gazing down from the walls. Pick any number of courses from the daily-changing menu, or go for the full five. Whatever you choose, it will be freshly prepared with imaginative combinations of flavours.

Cartmel Village Shop
cartmelvillageshop.co.uk
The Square, LA11 6QB
015395 36280

This is the home of probably the most moist and delicious sticky toffee pudding in the world.

The Cavendish Arms
thecavendisharms.co.uk
LA11 6QA | 015395 36240

A babbling stream flows past the tree-lined garden of this 450-year-old coaching inn situated within Cartmel's village walls, its longest-surviving hostelry. Many traces of its history remain, from the mounting block outside the main door to the bar itself, which was once the stables. Low, oak-beamed ceilings, uneven floors, antique furniture and an open fire create a traditional, cosy atmosphere. As well as Cumbrian ales, the food owes much to its local origins. The menu changes every six weeks, including lunchtime sandwiches, starters and full meals. The owners have teamed up with a local company that offers carriage tours of the village.

L'Enclume ⊛⊛⊛⊛⊛
lenclume.co.uk
Cavendish Street, LA11 6PZ
015395 36362

Perfectly in tune with the Lake District village surroundings, L'Enclume looks like the solid 700-year-old blacksmith's forge it once was (the name is French for 'anvil') – but in the hands of Simon Rogan it has morphed into a world-class culinary destination. On the inside, things aren't much different: the sparse interior is all whitewashed walls with minimal adornment, polished stone floors and unclothed tables. Most kitchens these days claim to supply their kitchens from the local larder, but few achieve the level of control over the ingredients' provenance that is achieved here: much of what's on your plate will have been picked a short while ago at Rogan's six-acre organic farm nearby, or foraged from the local countryside. What he doesn't produce himself is sourced from trusted local suppliers. The service team are on hand to

5 Cumbrian puddings

▶ **Cumberland Rum Nicky**. Try the one at **Middle Ruddings Country Inn and Restaurant** at Braithwaite (middle-ruddings.co.uk | CA12 5RY 017687 78436).

▶ **Borrowdale Sticky Banana Pudding** from **Lucy's On A Plate**, Ambleside (lucysofambleside.co.uk LA22 0BU | 015394 32288).

▶ **Cartmel Sticky Toffee Pudding**. Widely available but the best you'll find is from the **Cartmel Village Shop** (cartmelvillageshop. co.uk | LA11 6QB 015395 36280).

▶ **Bread and Butter Pudding**. This old favourite can be found in various guises throughout the region.

▶ **The World's Most Expensive Chocolate Pudding. Lindeth Howe Country House Hotel** (lindeth-howe.co.uk LA23 3JF | 015394 45759). It's made from four different types of Belgian chocolate, flavoured with whisky, peach and orange, layered with champagne jelly and glazed with edible gold leaf. Instead of being topped with a cherry there's a two-carat diamond and you get to wash it down with half a grand's worth of pudding wine. There's a couple of drawbacks to trying this. The first is the three weeks notice you need to give to order it. The second is the price tag – £22,000.

help with the multi-course menus, dealing with the inevitable queries on their more idiosyncratic contents, giving advice with charm and professionalism. With inventive cooking of this ilk, the kitchen needs its gadgets, but everything is done here for a reason rather than mere effect. Humour and technical brilliance are there from the off, and the flavour combinations are uniformly clever. Matching wine to these complex flavours is a challenge that the sommelier team approach with passion, championing lesser-seen grape varieties, biodynamic wines, and always keen to support English producers. Simon Rogan also runs Rogan & Company Restaurant (see below).

The Masons Arms

masonsarmsstrawberrybank.co.uk
Strawberry Bank, LA11 6NW
015395 68486

A charmingly atmospheric pub with low, beamed ceilings, old fireplaces and quirky furniture, and a stunning location overlooking the Winster Valley. Take a seat in the busy bar, dining rooms or heated covered terraces and try one of the popular dishes such as warm pitta bread and home-made hummus. There's plenty of choice of full hearty courses to follow. Wash it down with a pint of Thwaites Wainwright or Hawkshead Bitter. You'll find a variety of accommodation options here too.

Pig & Whistle

pigandwhistlecartmel.co.uk
Aynsome Road, LA11 6PL
015395 36482

The co-landlord here with Penny Tapsell is Simon Rogan, one of Britain's most accomplished chefs. The pub has long been his local, and he intends it to remain just that – a local. His short but perfectly formed menu offers simple but remarkably good value-for-money dishes. Real ale drinkers may run into a Dizzy Blonde in the bar – it's one of Robinsons of Stockport's seasonal brews.

Rogan & Company Restaurant ⊛⊛⊛

roganandcompany.co.uk
The Square, LA11 6QD
015395 35917

After more than a decade in Cartmel, Simon Rogan is heralded as one of the UK's finest chefs, with restaurants

▲ Castlerigg Stone Circle

in London and Manchester to spread the word. Rogan & Company may be the second-string venue in Cartmel, but it could hold its own anywhere in the country. The two-storey Lakeland house of roughcast stone and undoubted charm is surrounded by a rolling landscape divided by drystone walls, with Cartmel Priory an impressive backdrop. Its riverside location is a winner too. The à la carte menu reflects Rogan's approach – although he is not working at the stoves of course – and supremely good produce lies at the heart of every dish that comes from the kitchen.

▶ **Castlerigg Stone Circle** MAP REF 261 D4

english-heritage.org.uk

Castle Lane, CA12 4RN

Just 2 miles east of Keswick is one of the most dramatic and atmospheric stone circles in Britain. It dates from about 2000 BC, and, like many of these ancient stone sites, its original purpose remains unknown. There are 38 stones in the circle itself, with a further 10 in the centre, and the circle is dramatically situated – surrounded by high fells, with Helvellyn to the southeast. Made of volcanic Borrowdale rock, brought here by the glaciers of the Ice Age, the construction is actually oval in shape, 107 feet across at its widest point. The name of the stone circle means 'the fort on the ridge', though no evidence of any fort exists here.

▶ Cockermouth   MAP REF 260 C4

For a small country market town, Cockermouth has plenty of history behind it. The most significant event as far as most of today's visitors are concerned is that William Wordsworth was born here in 1770. If you have visited Dove Cottage in Grasmere (see page 134), where the poet later lived, you will be surprised at the grandeur of his birthplace. The Georgian town house, dating from 1745, has been faithfully restored by the National Trust and furnished in mid-18th-century style, with some of Wordsworth's own personal effects.

Other famous names associated with Cockermouth include Fletcher Christian – the mutineer on *The Bounty* – Mary, Queen of Scots and Robert the Bruce.

The town now houses a printing museum, an art gallery at Castlegate House and Jennings Brewery, which dates from 1828 and offers hour-long guided tours.

TAKE IN SOME HISTORY
Wordsworth House and Garden
nationaltrust.org.uk
Main Street, CA13 9RX
01900 824805 | Open mid-Mar to Oct Sat–Thu 11–5; closed Fri
William Wordsworth was born here on 7 April 1770, and his happy memories of the place greatly influenced his work. Imaginatively presented as the Wordsworth family home in the 1770s, the house offers a lively interactive visit with hands-on activities and costumed players.

VISIT THE GALLERY
Castlegate House Gallery
castlegatehouse.co.uk
CA13 9HA | 01900 822149
Mon and Sat 10–5, Thu–Fri 10–4, Tue–Wed and Sun by appointment only
You'll find a warm and friendly welcome here whether you go

▼ Wordsworth House

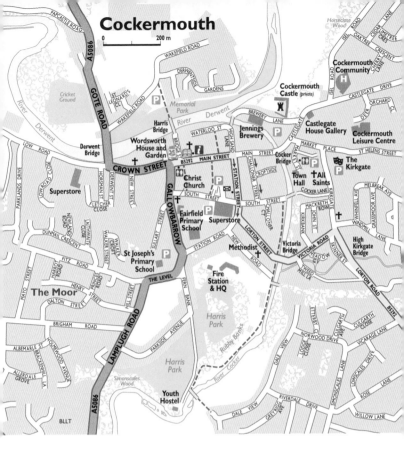

Cockermouth

0 200 m

to browse or to buy. The gallery specialises in 20th-century and contemporary British art by internationally renowned artists – such as Sheila Fell, Percy Kelly, Carel Weight, Ken Howard and many others – as well as up-and-coming artists, particularly from the north of England and southern Scotland. There's also plenty of ceramics and pottery to see.

TOUR THE BREWERY
Jennings Brewery
jenningsbrewery.co.uk
The Castle Brewery, CA13 9NE
01900 820362 | Tours: Mar–Oct
Wed–Sat 1.30, Nov–Dec and Feb
Thu–Sat 1.30

5 local ales

▶ **Catbells Pale Ale**, Hesket Newmarket Brewery

▶ **Lakeland Golden**, Bitter End Brewpub, Cockermouth

▶ **Langdale**, Old Hall Brewery, Hawkshead

▶ **T'Owd Tub**, Dent Brewery, Dent

▶ **Sneck Lifter**, Jennings Brewery, Cockermouth (see below)

Jennings Brewery was originally established as a family business in 1828 and moved to its current location in 1874. It is a traditional brewer, using Lakeland water drawn from the brewery's own well. On the brewery tour, you can see how all the beers are made and complete the tour by sampling them at the Old Cooperage bar. There is also an on-site shop if you would like to take some home.

PLAY A ROUND

Cockermouth Golf Club

cockermouthgolf.co.uk

Embleton, CA13 9SG

017687 76223 | Open daily

This fell course, rearranged by course designer James Braid, has exceptional views of the Lakeland hills and valleys and the Solway Firth. The greens are small but well-maintained. There's a hard climb on the 3rd and 11th holes and the 8th, 10th and 16th are testing too.

EAT AND DRINK

Kirkstile Inn

kirkstile.com

Loweswater, CA13 0RU

01900 85219

Stretching as far as the eye can see, the woods, fells and lakes are as much a draw today as they must have been in the inn's infancy some 400 years ago. The beck below meanders under a stone bridge, oak trees fringing its banks, with the mighty Melbreak towering impressively above. Tucked away next to an old church, this classic Cumbrian inn stands just half a mile from the Loweswater and Crummock lakes and makes an ideal base for walking, climbing, boating

and fishing. The whole place has an authentic, traditional and well-looked-after feel – whitewashed walls, low beams, solid polished tables, cushioned settles, a well-stoked fire and the odd horse harness remind you of times gone by. You can call in for afternoon tea, but better still would be to taste one of the Cumbrian Legendary Ales – Loweswater Gold, Grasmoor Dark Ale, Esthwaite Bitter - brewed by landlord Roger Humphreys in Esthwaite Water near Hawkshead. Traditional pub food is freshly prepared using the best local produce and the lunchtime menu brims with wholesome dishes that will satisfy the most hearty appetites.

The Trout Hotel ⓦ

trouthotel.co.uk

Crown Street, CA13 0EJ

01900 823591

Until he was eight, the poet William Wordsworth lived next door, although then this 17th-century building was a private house. Much remains to remind us of its heritage: stone walls, exposed beams, marble fireplaces, restored plasterwork, period stained-glass, and a carefully preserved oak staircase. At the bar ales from town brewery Jennings are joined by Carlisle-brewed guest, Corby Blonde. Fresh, locally sourced ingredients drive the menu. A drink or a meal in the gardens overlooking the River Derwent is an enjoyable way of passing time.

▶ Coniston MAP REF 257 D3

If you want to get a little off the beaten track and explore a
magnificent range of peaks, the little grey town of Coniston
is the perfect destination. Located near the northern tip of
Coniston Water and overlooked by the bulk of the Old Man
of Coniston at 2,634 feet, it offers plenty of peace and space.

It was these mountains, and the mineral wealth they yielded,
that created the village of Coniston. While copper had been
mined in this area since the Roman occupation, the industry
grew most rapidly during the 18th and 19th centuries and the
village expanded accordingly. The Ruskin Museum tells the
story of copper mining, slate quarrying and farming, as well as
the lives of celebrities such as John Ruskin, Arthur Ransome
and Donald Campbell. Don't miss Ruskin's home, Brantwood,
on the shores of the lake; you can visit both the house and the
beautiful grounds. And no visit to the Lakes is complete without
a boat trip. If you have your own boat you can launch it from the
public slipway (no powered craft) or you can hire a sailing
dinghy or rowing boat by the hour.

Take some time to drive or walk to nearby Tarn Hows, one
of the most popular beauty spots in the Lakes.

▼ Coniston Water and the Old Man of Coniston

▶ **Brantwood** MAP REF 257 D3

brantwood.org.uk
LA21 8AD | 015394 41396
Open mid-Mar to mid-Nov daily 10.30–5, mid-Nov to mid-Mar Wed–Sun, 10.30–4

Brantwood is undoubtedly one of the most beautiful houses in the Lake District, not least owing to its situation on the eastern shore of the lake with views across Coniston Water. The atmosphere is particularly special as so many of Ruskin's possessions remain; it's as if he may return at any moment. There's a brief introductory video and then you can explore the seven historical rooms – each brimming with his furniture, art and objects. There is a small printed guide to the rooms, and volunteer stewards are on hand to answer any questions. For younger visitors, there are quizzes and activity sheets to tackle.

Even if you don't visit the house, the grounds are an attraction in their own right. Brantwood has unique mountainside gardens in a 250-acre estate with spectacular views. Half of the estate is ancient woodland with a stunning diversity of flora and fauna. Elsewhere, there are lakeshore meadows and high, open fell and eight beautifully landscaped gardens. No matter what your level of fitness, you can find a walk to suit, from low-level rambles through the garden to energetic hikes to Crag Head. A trail guide is available in the shop. If you want a real insight into the stories behind the estate and Ruskin's experiments in land management go on one of the guided walks. There are also lots of special events throughout the year. Check the website for details.

▼ Brantwood

▲ John Ruskin's bedroom, Brantwood

TAKE IN SOME HISTORY
Brantwood
see highlight panel opposite

The Ruskin Cross
St Andrew's Church, Tilberthwaite
Avenue, LA21 8EN
It's worth going into St Andrew's
churchyard to find the grave of
John Ruskin, who died of
influenza at Brantwood on 20
Jan 1900. The large, carved,
green-slate cross was designed
by Ruskin's friend, W G
Collingwood, who was an expert
on Anglo-Saxon crosses, and
carved by H T Miles with
symbols depicting important
aspects of Ruskin's work and
life. Collingwood also designed
the war memorial, which stands
in the churchyard. It is a
10-foot-high, sandstone Celtic
Cross. If you want to find
Donald Campbell's grave, you'll
need to go to the New Parish
Cemetery on Old Hawkshead
Road behind the Crown Hotel.

VISIT THE MUSEUM
The Ruskin Museum
ruskinmuseum.com
Yewdale Road, LA21 8DU
015394 41164 | Open mid-Mar to
mid-Nov daily 10–4, mid-Nov to
mid-Mar Tue–Sun 10.30–2.30.
Discount vouchers available for
cruises on Steam Yacht *Gondola*,
Coniston Launch and Brantwood
(see Take a Boat Trip, overleaf)
Make sure to visit the amazing
Ruskin Museum. John Ruskin's

life is fascinating. He was an incredibly versatile and important political thinker, writer and artist. The museum contains many of his watercolours, drawings, letters, sketchbooks and other memorabilia representing his life's work.

Equally fascinating is the story of *Bluebird*, Donald Campbell's iconic hydroplane, which has been resurrected from the lake and is being rebuilt. Permission has been granted for future low-speed engineering proving trials on Coniston Water. A newly built extension with interpretation boards and displays is ready for the arrival of *Bluebird K7*, and a new online ticketing scheme will start at the same time, so do check the website for details.

The other boat on display is Arthur Ransome's *Mavis*, the *Amazon* described in his classic children's tale, *Swallows and Amazons*. Arthur Ransome based the book on both Lake Windermere and Coniston Water, and described many actual features from the landscape, but he invented his own geography. If you loved the book (or film) as a child, no doubt you'll enjoy mixing and matching the names and descriptions in the story to the actual locations.

Add to this the history of the geology, mines and quarries of the area, lace and linen, drystone walling, Herdwick sheep, John Usher's miniature village built in stone with painstaking detail and more, and you will realise that you need plenty of time for this visit. In fact you'll want to go back.

There are a number of self-guided walks available from the The Ruskin Museum, including 'In Ruskin's Footsteps', 'Coniston Village walk' and 'The *Bluebird* walk'. See opposite for more details.

TAKE A BOAT TRIP

Steam Yacht *Gondola*
nationaltrust.org.uk/gondola
Coniston Pier, Lake Road, LA21 8AN
01539 432733 | Apr–Oct daily.
Check website or call for the current timetable
Enjoy Coniston as wealthy Victorians did, by travelling in style in *Gondola*'s saloons or relaxing on the decks. The crew will give you a commentary on Coniston's history and themes, such as *Swallows and Amazons* or *Bluebird*, while you enjoy the spectacular scenery in old-fashioned comfort. You can find out all about *Gondola*'s steam engine and watch the engineer feeding the firebox. Originally launched in 1859, *Gondola* sailed Coniston Water until 1936. Having been beautifully rebuilt, she returned in 1980. You can take a full-lake cruise, a half-lake cruise or combine a part cruise with walking. There's also an afternoon tea or a picnic cruise. Check the website for details and times.

Coniston Launch

conistonlaunch.co.uk
Pier Cottage, Lake Road,
LA21 8AJ | 017687 75753
Check website for the timetable

This is a great way to enjoy the lake and explore the area. Since 2005, the boats have used electric motors instead of diesel, with solar panels helping to recharge the batteries so that they are now environmentally friendly and quieter. You can take one of the themed cruises such as *Swallows and Amazons* or *Bluebird*. Alternatively buy a hop-on, hop-off ticket for a day or a week to make the most of your Coniston experience.

GO WALKING

Self-guided walks from The Ruskin Museum (see page 107).

Tarn Hows

You can drive to Tarn Hows from Coniston along the B5285 Hawkshead road. Better still, you could walk one of the loveliest parts of the long-distance Cumbria Way (see page 94) to reach it. Once there, you can picnic at the tarn, which is studded with islands, surrounded by gorgeous conifer woodland and with the most beautiful backdrop of rolling hills.

In Ruskin's Footsteps

One of the great attractions of this guided walk is that it takes you right off the beaten track with hardly a tourist in sight. The route winds up steeply from the base of Long Crag, with rewarding views at every stage. Soon the whole of Coniston is laid out behind you, and you'll be able to see various places with Ruskin connections. Once above the impressive waterfall, White Ghyll, you follow a footpath along a marshy plateau, down to a stream and finally up to the viewpoint at the

▼ Tarn Hows

top of Yewdale Crag itself. On the way back, the route heads down the old peat road near Tilberthwaite, returning to Coniston via Whin Woods. The walk is approximately 5 miles and generally takes about four to five hours. You'll need a reasonable level of fitness and suitable boots and clothing.

Coniston Village Walk

This short, low-level walk is easy and you can take it at a leisurely pace. The leaflet explains all about Coniston's history and heritage, including its connections with Arthur Ransome and Donald Campbell – the route visits Campbell's memorial and grave, Ruskin's Cross in the churchyard (see also page 107) and the old school where he gave lessons.

You can really appreciate Coniston's past as you visit the old station, the former miners' houses up on the Banks, the 16th-century Black Bull, and the forge. There are local legends and the story of the landscape, the mountains and Mountain Rescue. The distance is just over a mile and takes approximately two hours.

EAT AND DRINK

The Black Bull Inn & Hotel
blackbullconiston.co.uk
1 Yewdale Road, LA21 8DU
015394 41335

Beside a stream stands this traditional Lakeland pub. Its bare stone walls, oak beams, log-burning stove and part-slate floor all contribute to its appeal, while of further interest, at least to beer drinkers, is its own

▼ The Coniston Launch *Campbell* on Coniston Water

microbrewery's Bluebird Bitter, commemorating Donald Campbell's attempts on the world water speed record; it also brews Old Man Ale, named for the local 2,634-foot mountain. Those out walking all morning or all day can look forward to sandwiches or filled jacket potatoes, or something heartier from the main menu.

The Bluebird Café

thebluebirdcafe.co.uk
Lake Road, LA21 8AN
015394 41649

Set in a stunning location overlooking the lake, this cafe offers a varied menu – from cakes and snacks to full main courses – all freshly cooked and moderately priced. You can combine a visit here with a cruise on the lake and they provide the picnics for the *Gondola* Picnic Cruises (see page 108).

The Green Housekeeper Cafe

16 Yewdale Road, LA21 8DU
015394 41925

The food in this friendly cafe is great. They serve freshly made sandwiches using home-made bread and fillings, hearty non-greasy breakfasts, hot soup and snacks. If you order an afternoon tea, you will be served with an enormous pot of tea accompanied by a selection of scones or cakes. Vegetarians will find a number of tasty options on the menu and they do their best here to cater for special diets too.

▶ PLACES NEARBY

The hamlet of Torver, on the old packhorse trail to the Duddon Valley, can be found just a couple of miles south of Coniston on the road to Barrow-in-Furness (see page 64). You can reach it by road, or by alighting from the Coniston Launch at the Torver jetty and walking up the village.

The church of St Luke is a reminder that the village was once more important than it is today – it had a railway line which was used for transporting stone and slate from the nearby quarries. The boat continues to the southern end of the lake, or you could simply cross the water to visit Brantwood (see page 106).

Torver is a day's walk from the start of the Cumbria Way at Ulverston (see page 225) so it's an ideal place to stop along the way.

▶ **Dalemain** MAP REF 258 B1

dalemain.com

Two miles north of Ullswater, CA11 0HB | 017684 86450 | House open Apr
to mid-Dec Sun–Thu 11.15–4 (closes at 3 in Oct); Gardens, tea room & shop,
Sun–Thu 10.30–5 (closes at 4 from Oct to mid-Dec)

Dalemain is a country house and garden that's still home to the
Hasell-McCosh family. The estate has evolved over time – at its
core there's a 12th-century pele tower with a kitchen garden,
an Elizabethan knot garden and a Stuart terrace from 1680,
while the house facade is Georgian. The gardens have a sense
of continuity with the past, as well as personal touches added
by the present family, such as the Children's Garden developed
by Mrs Hasell-McCosh when her own children were small.

The Terrace Walk, with its buttressed retaining wall, is much
as it was when Sir Edward Hasell laid it out in the 17th century,
although there are now several rambling roses attempting to
invade the gravel path and a deep herbaceous border below the
walls of the house. At the end of the terrace is a handsome
Grecian fir next to the Knot Garden, which has a marble
fountain as its central feature surrounded by low box hedges
filled to overflowing with herbs, campanulas and antirrhinums.

From here, the ground slopes upwards to the west, with a
lawn planted with old apples, plums and pears on one side of a
gravel path and a deep border with splendid shrub roses edged
with sedums, phloxes, rodgersias, meconopsis and irises at the
other. At the top of the garden, a classically proportioned
summerhouse is built into an alcove.

A door leads into Lob's Wood where a path winds between
beech and oak trees on the top of a steep bank above the Dacre

▼ Dalemain House

Beck. Further along the wall is a pavilion, with a pointed roof and mullioned windows, dating from 1550. A flight of steep steps leads down to the Wild Garden – bright with drifts of daffodils in spring and flowering trees and shrubs and the Himalayan blue poppy, *Meconopsis grandis*, in the early summer months. The latter was planted by Sylvia McCosh, the current owner's mother.

The Children's Garden features plants with 'animal' names, including bear's breeches (*acanthus*), snapdragon (*antirrhinum*) and foxglove (*digitalis*). Each plant is identified by locally handcrafted wooden animal signs; similar examples are for sale in the gift shop.

John de Morville owned the oldest surviving part of the house, the pele tower, at the time when his brother Hugh was involved in the murder of Thomas à Becket. The Layton family, who held Dalemain from the 13th to the 17th centuries, added the buildings around the courtyard. These include the medieval Great Hall, with its Tudor ceiling, and the Priest's Hiding Chamber, originally reached by climbing the kitchen chimney, but now accessed from the housekeeper's room. The haunted solar holds 'The Luck of Dalemain', a superb wine glass of about 1730, engraved with the Hasell coat of arms.

Lady Anne Clifford, a rich heiress whose portrait hangs here, left a legacy to her 'secretarie' Sir Edward Hasell, and he used it to buy Dalemain in 1679. Another Edward added the classical Georgian front that transformed the jumble of old buildings. The star of the show, however, is the Chinese Drawing Room, with its hand-painted wallpaper featuring a riot of pheasants, peonies and butterflies, Chippendale chairs and an English fireplace carved with spirited dragons.

▶ **PLACES NEARBY**

Church of St Andrew

Dacre village, CA11 0HL

The building dates from the 12th to the 19th centuries. Built in the local red sandstone, it is on a monastic site referred to by the Venerable Bede in AD 731. The existing building is Norman, with additions of the 13th and 14th centuries and then extensive alterations in the 18th and 19th centuries, but look for the remnants of an earlier age. The stone on the floor belongs to the 10th-century Viking period, and two ancient stone cross-shafts, carved with people and fantastical creatures, date from the ninth century. Don't miss the famous stone-carved Dacre Bears in the four corners of the graveyard. The first shows the bear asleep. The bear then wakes to find a cat or a lynx on its back, which it tries to remove in the third carving. In the fourth the bear appears to have eaten the animal.

▶ Dalton-in-Furness   MAP REF 257 D5

The ancient town of Dalton-in-Furness was once the principal town of Furness. You can enjoy a walk round the historic buildings at the Market Place. Look out for the unique cast-iron shopfront at No. 51 Market Place, the elegant Victorian drinking fountain, the market cross and the slabs of stone used for fish drying in the 19th century.

MEET THE ANIMALS
South Lakes Safari Zoo
southlakessafarizoo.com
Crossgates, LA12 8JR
01229 466086 | Open daily Aug
10–6, Mar–Jul and Sep–Oct 10–5,
Nov–Dec 10–4.30
Whether you want to hand feed giraffes, penguins and kangaroos or get up close to rhinos, tigers, bears, hippos, monkeys, vultures and lemurs, the whole family will love South Lakes. There are aerial walkways and viewpoints, a gift shop and the Maki restaurant, all overlooking a recreated African savannah where rhinos, giraffes and baboons wander.

EAT AND DRINK
Clarence House Country Hotel & Restaurant
clarencehouse-hotel.co.uk
Skelgate, LA15 8BQ | 01229 462508
The white-fronted hotel is perfectly positioned between sandy beaches and the lush green acres of Lakeland. A dining room designed like an orangery affords covetable views over the St Thomas Valley, and terrace tables make the best of the sun. The seasonal menu reflects a versatile blend of British and international cuisine; there's a grill, too, and Friday night is carvery night.

▶ Dent MAP REF 259 D5

If there were a vote for the most attractive village in the Dales, it would hardly be surprising if Dent won first prize. It consists of a beautiful cluster of pretty whitewashed cottages and cobbled streets in the lush green valley that is Dentdale. This does, of course, mean that it's extremely busy in the holiday season, and you would be best to visit at other times if possible.

Dent Station is on the Settle–Carlisle railway line, a scenic 72-mile railway route, and is the highest mainline station in Britain, at 1,150 feet. However, if you're planning to travel by train, be warned that the station is 5 miles from the village itself. The connecting bus service only runs on Saturdays so you'll need to arrange a lift or a taxi. Apparently, when one local was asked why they built the station so far from the village, he replied bluntly, "Appen they wanted t'put it near t'track.'

Dent has a flourishing artistic community with knitters, musicians, authors and photographers among its diverse population, and you can see much of the craft they produce for sale in the area. The local Dent Brewery ales are also very popular. The brewery began life at the Sun Inn (see Eat and Drink, page 117) at the centre of the village but grew so successfully that it had to seek new premises at Cowgill, further up the valley.

Adam Sedgwick was born in Dent in the Old Parsonage in 1785, attended the local grammar school and then went on to become Woodwardian Professor of Geology at Cambridge. The pink Shap granite memorial fountain in the main street marks his distinguished career as a geologist. In 1985, to commemorate the 200th anniversary of his birth, the National Park Authority created the Adam Sedgwick Geology Trail, near Sedbergh. Leaflets are available at National Park Centres and Tourist Information Centres.

Both black and grey marble was quarried near here in the past. The Stone House Marble Works flourished in the 18th and 19th centuries at Arten Gill, southeast of Dent Station, where you will also find Dent Head Viaduct, one of the most amazing constructions on the Settle–Carlisle railway line. Many of the stations contain marble quarried at Dent. In the days when the quarries were working, the knitters were busy knitting and the mills were humming with weaving, Dentdale's population reached almost 2,000 – about three times what it is today.

◀ South Lakes Safari Zoo

VISIT THE HERITAGE CENTRE
Dent Village Heritage Centre
museumsintheyorkshiredales.co.uk

LA10 5QJ | 01539 625800

Open daily 11–4

The best place to start exploring Dent is at this centre, on the western edge of the village. Here you will find out the story of the valley, its people, industry and wildlife. Many of the exhibits are of genuine Dales provenance, with a large number from the collection of Jim and Margaret Taylor of High Laning Farm – the centre's founders, who have spent many years rescuing and refurbishing the artefacts. You can see a kitchen with a range, the pantry where the butter was churned and the pig salted, and the parlour dressed in its best for entertaining visitors. There is also a wealth of information on the farm animals in the area and Adam Sedgwick, Dent's most famous son.

EAT AND DRINK
Stone Close Tea Room
stoneclose.co.uk

Main Street, LA10 5QL

01539 625231

It's hard not to enjoy the convivial atmosphere conjured up at this lovely whitewashed tea room, where you'll find an amiable combination of locals, writers, artists, talkers and walkers. The 17th-century cottage, with its cast-iron range, flagstone floor, exposed beams and original fittings, has a well-earned reputation for serving wholesome food, including dishes that are suitable for a vegetarian or vegan diet. Everything is freshly cooked on the premises, using local, seasonal, organic and Fair Trade produce as far as possible.

Sun Inn
suninndent.co.uk

Main Street, LA10 5QL

01539 625208

Dent may feel like a village where time has stood still, but the Sun Inn was a true pioneer in the home-brewing and fine-dining revolution that has revitalised many country pubs. The Dent Brewery was established behind the pub in 1990, although it has since moved up the road to larger premises. You can enjoy its excellent output here, particularly when accompanied by no-nonsense pub grub – the tasty sausages and pies are truly excellent. Charming public rooms, original coin-studded beams, an open coal fire and a fascinating collection of local photos will all add to your enjoyment. It's also worth following the website links to www.dentdale.com, a community site that will let you know what's on in and around the village.

◀ Dent Head Viaduct

▶ Derwentwater MAP REF 261 D5

At 1.25 miles, this is the Lakeland's widest lake and it's attractively dotted with islands. These include, in the very centre, St Herbert's Island, named after the saint who lived here as a hermit in the seventh century. Derwent Isle was once home to German miners who came to work around Keswick (see page 161) and the Newlands Valley in the 16th century.

With Borrowdale closing in to the south, and crags on either side of the lake's southern half, Derwentwater is a popular favourite. You can explore the lake and its surroundings using the ferries. They run between the seven landing stages located all around the lake, so passengers can get off and walk the many footpaths through the woods and climb up to the various

viewpoints. There are also good views from the high narrow road on the lake's western edge. You'll find the visitor information centre in Keswick.

The eastern side of Derwentwater is rich in waterfalls, such as the spectacular Lodore Falls in the southeastern corner, which is one of the stops for the ferries. The National Trust owns much of the land, mainly due to the efforts of Canon Hardwicke Rawnsley, vicar of Crosthwaite and Secretary of the National Trust from its formation in 1895 until his death in 1920. The beautiful Friar's Crag, on the northern shore of Derwentwater close to the Keswick boat landings, was given to the National Trust (along with Lords Island and Calf Close Bay) to be his memorial. Ruskin declared that this view was 'one of the finest in Europe'.

▼ Derwentwater

GET ON THE WATER

Derwentwater Marina

derwentwatermarina.co.uk

Portinscale, CA12 5RE

01768 772912

Open daily 9.30–5.30

To explore Derwentwater, you can hire canoes, kayaks, rowing boats, dinghies and windsurfers here. It is also the place if you want to learn to sail or brush up your skills – they have a range of courses to suit all abilities. Check the website for details. There are 58 berths afloat and ashore, and storage for dinghies, kayaks and canoes, should you have your own boat. There's also a small chandlery shop and boat repair services.

Nichol End Marine

nicholend.co.uk

Portinscale, CA12 5TY

01768 773082 | Open daily from 9 (until 5–8 depending on season). Check website for details

You can hire motor cruisers here as well as canoes, kayaks, sailing dinghies, windsurfers and rowing boats. There's a range of courses on offer here too. Check the website to find one that matches your level of skill and proficiency. If you own a boat, they have moorings for cruisers at the jetty, as well as berths afloat and storage for dinghies, kayaks and canoes. There are boat repair services and a chandlery shop.

▼ Derwentwater

Platty Plus
plattyplus.co.uk
Lodore Boat Landing, CA12 5UU
01768 776572
This small family-run business is about 3 miles from Keswick, so if you are looking for a quieter experience on the lake, this could be the place to go. Here you can hire canoes, kayaks, sailing dinghies, windsurfers and rowing boats. They also run a range of water sports and sailing courses to suit all abilities. Check the website for more details.

Keswick Launch
keswick-launch.co.uk
CA12 5DJ | 01768 772263
You can either take a 50-minute cruise right around the lake or, alternatively, hop on and off all day until you return to where you started – or just buy a ticket for any part of the journey – which is useful if you want to go walking. The launches start from Keswick boat landings and cruise around the lake stopping at seven lakeshore jetties. Check the website for the current timetable.

GO FISHING
Angling
Keswick Anglers Association
keswickanglers.co.uk
You can fish on two rivers for brown trout, sea trout, salmon, perch and pike and you can get a permit from Keswick TIC and a number of other places. See the website for details.

▶ Dunnerdale MAP REF 257 D3

Dunnerdale, or the Duddon Valley, is as delightful and unspoiled today as it was when William Wordsworth first explored the valley. The River Duddon rises in the hills by the Wrynose Pass, and reaches the sea at the estuary of Duddon Sands. In between lies 10 miles of the most delectable scenery – not the most dramatic, or the most spectacular, but those who prefer more intimate landscapes will love Dunnerdale.

The little town of Broughton-in-Furness (see page 80) stands back from the Duddon Estuary – from Duddon Bridge a minor road takes you up Dunnerdale – but you are seldom far away from the river. Rocky and fast flowing, the river is the natural habitat of dippers and wagtails. There are grassy riverbanks just perfect for spreading out a picnic blanket. Ulpha, a straggle of houses and farmsteads, is the only village of any size in the valley.

As you continue to climb, fields and woods give way to a more rugged landscape, as Harter Fell (2,139 feet) and the higher peaks of central Lakeland begin to dominate the view. When you reach a road junction at Cockley Beck, you can either travel west to Eskdale, via the tortuous Hardknott Pass, or east, along Wrynose Pass, and down into the beautiful Little Langdale Valley.

▶ Egremont MAP REF 256 B2

With the River Ehen winding past it, and a wide main street lined with trees (and with a variety of stalls on its Friday market day), Egremont is pretty famous for ugly faces. The World Gurning Championships are held here each September at the ancient Egremont Crab Fair (egremontcrabfair.com). There are athletics competitions, animal shows, hound trails and a greasy pole competition.

The crabs at the Egremont Crab Fair are crab apples not crustaceans. The fair dates from 1267, and on the third Saturday in September the Apple Cart parade passes through the town, throwing apples to people lining the route. The highlight of the fair is the famous 'Gurning through a Braffin' competition, where whoever can make the ugliest grin (gurn) while peering through a horse collar (a braffin), is declared world champion.

As old as the fair is the castle, now in ruins, on a hilltop overlooking the main street. It was largely destroyed in the 16th century but the original gatehouse is still standing.

▶ River Duddon at Dunnerdale

VISIT THE GALLERIES
Lowes Court Gallery
lowescourt.co.uk

12 Main Street, CA22 2DW

01946 820693 | Open Tue–Sat 10–2

This listed 18th-century building was a derelict coal merchant's cottage until it was renovated in the early 1970s as an exhibition centre for local and Cumbrian craftsmen and artists. There's a great variety of artwork here including prints, sculpture, jewellery and textiles. The Tourist Information Centre is also here.

Florence Arts Centre
florencemine.com

Florence Mine, CA22 2NR

01946 824946

Open Wed–Sun 10–4

Florence Mine was the last deep-working iron ore mine to survive in Western Europe. Now the former shower block of the mine has been transformed into a new kind of centre for the arts. It has a high-spec studio room, gallery space, workshops and artists' residencies. Check the website for a list of forthcoming exhibitions and events.

EXPLORE BY BIKE
Ainfield Cycles
ainfieldcycles.co.uk

Jacktrees Road, Cleator Moor, CA23 3DW | 01946 812427

This bike shop stocks a range of quality bikes to buy or hire. You can pick up a bike here and drop it off in the northeast if you are cycling coast to coast. They also stock cycling accessories and carry out repairs.

▶ Ennerdale MAP REF 260 C5
wildennerdale.co.uk

If you want to walk away from the 'madding crowd' you will appreciate Ennerdale Water in the secluded valley of Ennerdale, situated furthest west of all the lakes. Access by car is limited as the lake has no peripheral road, and the best part of its shores can only be explored on foot. Leave your car in the car park at Bowness Knott or Bleach Green, and follow the path around the lake. If you go all the way round, it is 8 miles and be warned that the going can be tough in some places.

Behind the rows of spruce and larch, the land rises steeply, to over 2,600 feet in places. Looking south, the hills are higher still, with Pillar at 2,926 feet, in front of which stands Pillar Rock – popular with climbers since its first ascent in 1826. There are biking and bridle paths to try as well as a wealth of wildlife to see. The lake's shores and surrounding land are owned either by the National Trust or the Forestry Commission. For details of all the many paths, climbs and activities visit the website.

SADDLE UP
Bradley's Riding Centre
walk-rest-ride.co.uk
Low Cock How, Kinniside,
CA23 3AQ | 01946 861354
You can go riding at this family-run riding centre for 30 minutes, half a day or all day. They have horses to suit all sizes and abilities, and the owners will find you a riding helmet and tailor your trek to suit you.

VISIT A CHURCH
St Michael and St Mary's
Main Street, Egremont, CA22 2AY
01946 820268
This fine church was built in 1881 in the Early English style on the site of a much earlier structure. The locally quarried sandstone was used for the many carvings of the interior pillars – there are over 100. The church's lovely font is a scallop shell supported by a sculpted angel, and was copied from a church in Copenhagen.

EAT AND DRINK
Shepherds Arms
shepherdsarms.com
Kirkland Road, Ennerdale Bridge
CA23 8AR | 01946 861249
Popular with coast-to-coast walkers and cyclists, the bar is usually populated by a crowd of locals and visitors. In fact, this was once a village-centre farmhouse which also dispensed beer to the local countrymen. Today, an excellent array of Cumbrian ales is served, alongside plates of good home-made food.

▶ Eskdale MAP REF 256 C3

While so many other places in Lakeland are busy with tourists, Eskdale is another beautiful valley that remains relatively quiet. The reason? Inaccessibility. To explore Eskdale you have to take the twists, turns and hairpin bends of the Hardknott and Wrynose passes, or else go the long way round, meandering through south Lakeland. All the better, then, for those who venture this far west, for Eskdale is well worth the effort.

This is excellent walking country, with plentiful rights of way and room to roam. Take the Ravenglass & Eskdale Railway into the heart of Eskdale without blocking up the narrow road with your car. This delightful narrow-gauge railway used to carry iron ore from the Eskdale mines to the coast; now the engines carry passengers up the valley. There are seven stations along the line, all offering opportunities for scenic walks with the option of taking a later train back down to Ravenglass.

The terminus, at Dalegarth, is just a short walk from Boot, a tiny village with a friendly pub. Just up the valley, the Woolpack recalls a time when this was a watering hole for the men who drove pack ponies heavily laden with fleeces down to the coast. Beyond a packhorse bridge spanning Whillan Beck is the

▲ View over Eskdale

delectable grouping of tiny buildings that comprise Eskdale Mill (see page 202). Cereals have been ground here since 1578. Milling ended during the 1920s, but it is now restored to working order. See Ravenglass (page 200) for various attractions.

▶ Furness Peninsula MAP REF 257 D4

Furness lies between the mountainous heart of the Lake District and the great sandy estuaries of Morecambe Bay. For centuries it was owned by the monks of Furness Abbey who grazed sheep on the hills, controlled fishing rights, grew crops, planted orchards, made charcoal, smelted iron, dug peat for fuel and manufactured salt.

As a young man, William Wordsworth made a number of trips on horseback to this area of low hills, old woodlands and lush meadows by rivers and reedy tarns, which extends from Ulverston (see page 225), Broughton-in-Furness (see page 80), Coniston (see page 105), Hawkshead (see page 147) and the fringes of Lake Windermere (see page 240) to Barrow-in-Furness (see page 64) and Walney Island (see page 229) on the coast. The atmospheric red sandstone ruins of Furness Abbey (see page 64) inspired Wordsworth to feature them in

The Prelude and a couple of sonnets. He knew Barrow-in-Furness too, but only as a small village as yet untouched by the shipbuilding industry that transformed the town so rapidly.

It's a place to walk, hike or cycle along stretches of unspoiled coastline, quiet country lanes or classic routes over and around the Furness Fells. Wildlife flourishes in the nesting and wintering grounds of Isle of Walney's two nature reserves and along a coastline where various species of birds, moths, butterflies, natterjack toads and grey seals thrive.

WALK THE FURNESS WAY

contours.co.uk

The 75-mile Furness Way meanders across this picturesque and tranquil corner of the Lake District – from Arnside on the eastern side of Morecambe Bay to Ravenglass on the Irish Sea. If you follow the whole route you pass through the beautiful Lyth, Winster, Duddon and Eskdale valleys; cross Whitbarrow, Hampsfell and Muncaster Fell, all with breathtaking views of the mountains of the Lake District and the Furness coastline. Along the way the route visits a succession of attractive villages, where you can find accommodation. It also takes in several magnificent stately homes including Levens Hall (see page 180) with its superb gardens, Sizergh Castle (see page 214) and Muncaster Castle (see page 190).

▶ Glenridding   MAP REF 261 E5

This small village at the southern end of Ullswater, near the foot of Kirkstone Pass, is popular with walkers, and there are routes to suit all levels of fitness and experience. Walkers come here to do the classic Helvellyn walk along Striding Edge, which, in full winter conditions, becomes the domain solely of experienced mountaineers. There are also plenty of less challenging, low-level walks to be enjoyed, including several along the lakeshore and to viewpoints such as Keldas and Silver Crag.

GET YOUR BOOTS ON
Helvellyn
see page 150

GET ON THE WATER
St Patrick's Boat Landings
stpatricksboatlandings.co.uk
CA11 0QQ | 01768 482393 | Open
Easter–Oct/early Nov daily
Motorboats, rowing boats and mountain bikes can be hired here, the speed on the water limited to a sedate 10mph. Hires are from 30 minutes to several days. The centre serves light refreshments and offers free customer parking in an area where parking spaces are at a premium.

Glenridding Sailing Centre
glenriddingsailingcentre.co.uk
The Spit, CA11 0PE | 01768 482541
Open mid-Mar to mid-Oct daily 10–5
If you want to explore Ullswater, you can hire canoes, kayaks, sailing dinghies and rowing boats here. If you want to learn to sail or brush up your skills you can take a course; they have a range of courses to suit all abilities – including a special *Swallows and Amazons* adventure, which kids will love.

Check the website for details. If you have your own boat, they have storage for dinghies, kayaks and canoes.

TAKE A BOAT TRIP
Ullswater 'Steamers'
see page 223

EAT AND DRINK
Fellbites Café
fellbitescafe.co.uk
CA11 0PD | 01768 482781
If you want a tasty snack, home-made cakes or scones by day or a simple meal in the evening, this little cafe right in the centre of Glenridding is conveniently placed, with good food, friendly staff and great views.

Inn on the Lake ◉◉
lakedistricthotels.net
CA11 0PE | 01768 482444
The hotel is a prime piece of Lakeland real estate within 15 acres of grounds surrounding Ullswater. The lake makes pretty much the perfect backdrop and there are panoramic views from just about every public space and many of the bedrooms. There are lots of refuelling options,

from lunch in the Orangery, afternoon tea and the pub-style Ramblers Bar in the grounds, but the main culinary action takes place in the Lake View Restaurant. The elegant dining room is decorated with natural shades of lilac and fawn, with decorative touches and pictures of the local landscape – it's traditional and comfortable. The kitchen makes good use of regional ingredients to produce dishes of modernity and creativity.

▸ **PLACES NEARBY**

Watermillock is a small hamlet on the western edge of Ullswater between Pooley Bridge and Glenridding.

Macdonald Leeming House ◉

macdonald-hotels.co.uk

Watermillock, CA11 0JJ

01768 486674

The 200-year-old manor is an impressive-looking property, with eye-catching cast-iron stanchions supporting a first-floor balcony. Its location is pretty impressive too, as it's in 22 acres of grounds with direct access to Ullswater, where it has a private fishing licence. For the full-on Lakeland dining experience, head for the elegant Regency Restaurant, where floor-to-ceiling windows, hung with heavy red drapes and plush pelmets, give views to the lake and fells beyond. The menus are reassuringly familiar, with some contemporary twists to established ideas.

Rampsbeck Country House Hotel

rampsbeck.co.uk

Watermillock, CA11 0LP

01768 486442

The white-painted villa sits on a hillside overlooking Ullswater, with 18 acres all to itself, including a piece of valuable shoreline. It delivers a country-house experience which combines old-world luxury with contemporary comforts. There are acres of burnished panels, antiques and ornate ceilings throughout, and smart lounges where it's easy to lose an hour or two. The dining room itself has all the period details, plus a menu with its roots in classical French cooking.

▸ **Gosforth** MAP REF 256 B2

Gosforth is situated between Wasdale and Sellafield and is the closest large village to the Eskdale and Wasdale valleys, so it makes for a good base if you're planning to explore these dales. There has been a church on this site for more than 1,000 years so it's worth having a look for the ancient stone cross and tombs. There's also a cork tree, planted in 1833.

Close to the village is Blengdale Forest, where you can walk along the River Bleng and to the ancient packhorse bridge known as 'Monks Bridge' on Cold Fell.

SEE A LOCAL CHURCH

Church of St Mary

Wasdale Road, northeast of the village, CA20 1AZ

St Mary's has been a religious site since the eighth century and there are many ancient remains to see here. The most striking is the Gosforth Cross in the churchyard. It is Norse, from around 940, and the slender red sandstone stands 14 feet tall with detailed carvings on all four sides of Viking and Christian symbols – including the crucifixion and the pagan god, Loki. Another ancient cross in the churchyard was, for some strange reason, converted into a sundial 200 years ago. Two 10th-century 'Hogback' tombstones carved with battle scenes can also be found inside the church.

GET CRAFTY

Gosforth Pottery

gosforth-pottery.co.uk
Hardingill, CA20 1AH
019467 25296

Visit to see the range of pots for sale or try one of their courses. They run short residential courses and offer opportunities for painting and sketching.

▶ PLACES NEARBY

Seascale is a small attractive seaside resort, best known for the nearby nuclear power station, Calder Hall at Sellafield (see page 21), now operating as a reprocessesing facility for spent nuclear fuel from reactors from around the world. Seacastle is rich in history and the village can trace its origins back to an early Norse settlement as well as to Roman Britain.

Mawson's Ice Cream Parlour

Seascale, CA20 1NP | 019467 29918

The Mawson family dairy farm provides the milk that goes into the huge and imaginative range of ice cream that you can enjoy here. Choose a cone or a few scoops in or outside, or pick up a carton to take away.

Seascale Golf Club

seascalegolfclub.co.uk
The Banks, CA20 1QL
019467 28202 | Open daily

A tough links course, skilled golfers will enjoy the natural terrain and undulating greens, which give a variety of holes and add considerable character to the challenge. There are far-reaching views of the western fells, the Irish Sea and the Isle of Man.

Sella Park House Hotel

penningtonhotels.com
Calderbridge, Seascale, CA20 1DW
01946 841601

This historic 16th-century manor house sits in 6 acres of lovely gardens running down to the River Calder. There's no faulting the splendid seasonal Cumbrian produce it hauls in as the basis of its up-to-date cooking. Vegetables, fruit and herbs are plucked fresh from the kitchen garden at nearby Muncaster Castle, and great care is taken in tracking down the best local meat and fish.

▶ Grange-over-Sands MAP REF 257 E5

Neat white limestone buildings, colourful gardens and a sunny aspect and disposition quickly made Grange a popular seaside resort for Victorian visitors. The 'grange' in the town's name belonged to the monks of medieval Cartmel Priory (see page 97), who had a vineyard here and a small harbour for bringing in sea coal. There was a fashionable health spa using the water from St Ann's Well at Humphrey Head, which was said to be good for gout and 'the stone'. The railway arrived in 1857 and the promenade along the front was built in 1904.

The town looks south over the alluring and treacherous sands of Morecambe Bay, once the main route to Lancashire. It's the place to bring your binoculars if you're interested in birds and wildlife, but the whole area around here is packed with fascinating places to explore.

WALK THE CISTERCIAN WAY

If you're looking for two or three days of moderate walking, try this 33-mile walk from Grange-over-Sands to Roa Island, near Barrow-in-Furness. It follows the low limestone fells that fringe the shores of Morecambe Bay and the sands of the Furness and Cartmel peninsulas. It is an ancient waymarked trail, but some waymarks are missing or not entirely obvious, so make sure that you have the relevant OS map before you set out. The route passes the historic Cartmel Priory (see page 97), the market town of Ulverston (see page 225), Dalton-in-Furness (see page 114), the ancient capital of Furness and Barrow-in-Furness (see page 64), an attractive Victorian seaside town where you can visit Furness Abbey (see page 64), and finishes at Roa Island, just beyond Barrow.

▼ Morecambe Bay, overlooked by Grange-over-Sands

PLAY A ROUND
Grange-over-Sands Golf Club
grangegolfclub.co.uk
Meathop Road, LA11 6QX
015395 33180
A fairly flat parkland course
with well-sited tree plantations,
ditches and water features, and
excellent drainage throughout.
If you are an older golfer or
have some mobility problems,
the flatness is a bonus, but
there are still some tricky
holes. The excellent drainage
makes it playable when other
courses are closed.

EAT AND DRINK
Clare House ◉
clarehousehotel.co.uk
Park Road, LA11 7HQ
015395 33026
The Read family has been
running Clare House since
the end of the 1960s, and their
care and attention is evident
at every turn. The beautiful,
immaculately tended gardens
have a feeling of seclusion from
the swirling tourist traffic of the
town, and the traditional decor
and fittings inside complement
the fine views over the bay.
Well-spaced tables dressed in
crisp linen, attended by smartly
turned-out staff, are the order
of the day, and the cooking
cleaves to an essentially
modern British style.

Hazelmere Café and Bakery
thehazelmere.co.uk
1–2 Yewbarrow Terrace, LA11 6ED
015395 32972
Taste more than 50 different
types of cuppa at this traditional
Victorian tea room. Local
specialities include
Cumberland Rum Nicky
and pheasant burgers.
You can also buy artisan breads,
cakes and pastries to take
home. It's a great place to
select a picnic – choose
from savoury pies, home-made
preserves and sandwiches.
They also do a range of
ready-to-cook meals to
take away, which are just
perfect if you are on a self-
catering holiday.

▶ Grasmere   MAP REF 257 E2

The village of Grasmere is central – geographically and historically – to the Lake District. The village is in a valley surrounded by hills, just a short stroll from Grasmere Lake. If you prefer low walks on gentler ground you'll find some round the lake here. On the other hand, if you want a challenge Grasmere is an ideal base for tackling Helvellyn and the Langdale Pikes.

William Wordsworth was on a walking tour of the Lake District with his friend Samuel Taylor Coleridge when he spotted the little house that would become his home for eight years. You can visit two of Wordsworth's homes in Grasmere – Dove Cottage (see overleaf) and Rydal Mount (see page 206).

▼ Grasmere

VISIT THE MUSEUM
Dove Cottage and The Wordsworth Museum

wordsworth.org.uk

LA22 9SH | 015394 35544

Open daily Mar–Oct 9.30, Nov–Feb 9.30. Closed 24 Dec–31 Jan

The charming Dove Cottage was the home of William Wordsworth between 1799 and 1808, and it was here that he wrote some of his best-known poetry. The cottage has been open to the public since 1891, kept in its original condition. Displays include manuscripts, works of art and items that belonged to the poet. There is a changing programme of special events; check the website for details. Although Wordsworth's home was small, there was a constant stream of visitors, many of whom belonged to the great and good of the world of art and literature. Previously home to an inn called The Dove and Olive Branch, at that time the cottage was known as Town End. An adjacent coach house has been converted into the Wordsworth Museum.

Allan Bank

nationaltrust.org.uk

LA22 9QB | 015394 35143

Open daily April to early Nov 10.30–5, Feb half-term 10.30–4, Mar & early Nov to mid-Dec Fri–Sun 10.30–4

By the time Wordsworth's wife, Mary, was expecting their fourth child, Dove Cottage was becoming too small. The family moved first to Allan Bank, a Georgian house the poet had condemned as an eyesore when it was built. They stayed for two years before moving to the Rectory, now a private home, and finally Rydal Mount (see page 206), which you can also visit. From 1917, Allan Bank was home to Canon Hardwicke Rawnsley, one of the founders of the National Trust. He died in 1920, leaving the house to the charity. Today, it makes for a simple visitor experience – a place where people can unwind with a book from the library; where families can paint and draw; or where you can make a cup of tea and just gaze out at the surrounding landscape.

SEE A LOCAL CHURCH
Church of St Oswald

Church Stile, LA22 9SN

You'll find Wordsworth's grave here in the churchyard along with those of his wife and sister and some of his friends. The tower, porch and south wall are all that remain of the 14th-century church. It was not until 1841 that the church floor was flagged – prior to that it was earthen and parishioners were simply buried beneath it. The baptistery window depicts St Oswald, and two of the south windows are by the famous Pre-Raphaelite artist Henry Holiday (1839–1927).

Every year in July, Grasmere celebrates its Rushbearing Festival, a custom dating back to the days when the earthen floor of the church was strewn with rushes, both for warmth and cleanliness.

EAT AND DRINK

Baldry's Tearoom

baldryscottage.co.uk
Red Lion Square, LA22 9SP
015394 35301

This all-day cafe is good for anything from a cup of quality coffee or loose-leaf tea to lunch or teatime treats, which might include home-made pies, soups or sandwiches. All baking is done on the premises and many of the breads, cakes and scones are gluten-free.

The Britannia Inn

thebritanniainn.com
Elterwater, LA22 9HP
015394 37210

Walks and mountain-bike trails radiate from the front door of this free house in the Langdale Valley, just a short drive from Ambleside. Built as a cobbler's and farmhouse more than 500 years ago, the whitewashed building became an inn some 200 years back. The bar area is essentially a series of small, cosy rooms with low-beamed oak ceilings and winter coal fires. The bar is well stocked with guest beers, as well as the house special – brewed by Coniston. In mid-November, the two-week beer festival brings an even wider selection. The inn offers a wide choice of fresh, home-cooked food.

The Dining Room 🏵🏵

lakedistricthotel.co.uk
Oak Bank Hotel, Broadgate,
LA22 9TA | 015394 35217

The old Victorian Oak Bank Hotel has lots of charm, with

5 places to eat

pretty gardens that run down to the River Rothay and decor that is smart and comfortable. The Dining Room restaurant – equally comfortable and refined – is perhaps surprisingly, then, among all this civilised conformity, the setting for some ambitious and creative food.

The Gingerbread Shop

grasmeregingerbread.co.uk
Church Cottage, LA22 9SW
015394 35428

Next to the churchyard is the fragrant Gingerbread Shop, where the famous Grasmere gingerbread is made and sold. It is made to the recipe of Sarah Nelson, who first made it in the mid-19th century. She kept the recipe in a bank vault and passed it on to her niece. The shop is no longer in the family, but the secret recipe has been passed down through the generations and is still made and sold today. Celebrities travel here to taste it, brides use it for wedding favours and

Jamie Oliver, among many others, swears it is the best gingerbread he ever tasted. So make some time between William Wordsworth and the scenery to sample some gingerbread – you'll probably want to take some home too.

Green's Café

greensgrasmere.com
College Street, LA22 9SZ
015394 35790

Everything is home-made and as much produce locally sourced as possible at this friendly cafe in the heart of Grasmere. Choose from soups, paninis, salads, wraps or baked potatoes at lunchtime and enjoy good home baking throughout the day. There are dishes suitable for vegans or those following a gluten-free diet.

Rothay Garden Hotel ◉◉

rothaygarden.com
Broadgate, LA22 9RJ
015394 35334

On the edge of Grasmere, this thoroughly (and expensively) refurbished Victorian hotel sits in a couple of acres of riverside gardens, with the panoramic sweep of the Lakeland fells as background. The country house chintz was chucked long ago, and dining goes on in a thoroughly modern conservatory-style room with restful views of the gardens and spa centre – a classy and bright setting that's just right for gently updated country house cooking offering comfort, interest and satisfaction.

The Travellers Rest Inn

lakedistrictinns.co.uk
Keswick Road, LA22 9RR
015394 35604

The Travellers Rest has been a pub for more than 500 years. In winter you'll find a roaring log fire to welcome you to the comfortable. beamed bar area and, in summer, you can enjoy lovely countryside views from the beer garden. There's a good choice of ales, such as Sneck Lifter, and you can choose a meal from an extensive menu of traditional home-cooked fare using the best of ingredients.

▶ PLACES NEARBY

The village and lake of Elterwater lie in the lovely valley of Great Langdale (see page 178). Nowadays most of the houses in Elterwater are holiday cottages.

Stoves at Langdale Hotel & Spa ◉

langdale.co.uk
The Langdale Estate, Elterwater, LA22 9JD | 015394 37302

An environmentally sensitive hotel to the south of Lake Windermere, the Langdale blends into its beckside surroundings with an attractive stone construction, neutral interior tones of brown and grey, and a view of a tumbling waterfall through a picture window in the bar. The action is in Purdey's dining room, and is a gently modernised version of Lakeland cooking that aims for subtle potency rather than garish innovation.

▶ Great Gable MAP REF 257 D2

Great Gable, standing at an impressive 2,949 feet (899m),
is a classic Lake District climb with rough paths and a few
scrambles – so you need to be fit to attempt it. It gets its name
from its appearance from Wast Water, through Wasdale Head;
its bulk resembles the great gable end of a house. If you are
very fit, you can take this route to the top. Alternatively, you can
approach it from the northeast, from Seathwaite Farm climbing
up past the waters of the Sourmilk Gill and passing Great
Gable's little brother, Green Gable. This is still a strenuous
climb, but the views from the top are a fitting reward for your
efforts – south to Scafell Pike (3,210 feet, 978m) and straight
down Wasdale towards the Irish Sea.

At the top, a plaque records the occasion, when the Fell
and Rock Climbing Club gave the surrounding area to the
National Trust in memory of their colleagues lost in World
War I. A memorial service is held here each year in November
on Remembrance Sunday.

It was also in these hills that modern climbing first started
to develop, late in the 19th century. The names alone are
inspiring – Needle Ridge, Eagle's Nest Ridge, Windy Gap.

▶ Great Salkeld & Little Salkeld MAP REF 263 D6

These two small villages on opposite banks of the River Eden
were linked in the Middle Ages by a bridge over the river.
St Cuthbert's Church in Great Salkeld is where the saint's
body rested in 880 when it was brought over from Holy Island.
Although it contains the remains of a Roman altar the present
building is Norman. Its defensive pele tower was added
in 1380.

▼ Yewbarrow, left, and Great Gable beside Wast Water

TAKE IN SOME HISTORY
Little Salkeld Watermill
organicmill.co.uk
Little Salkeld, CA10 INN
01768 881523 | Open Thu–Tue
10.30–4

Little Salkeld Watermill is a bit of a rarity. It is one of Britain's few working water-powered corn mills still producing stoneground flour the traditional way. Even better, perhaps, is that after finding out how it works, you can then buy some of the organic produce in the bakery and visit the organic vegetarian cafe. There's also a pleasant gallery, which has knitwear and a series of changing exhibitions.

10 great days out

GO BACK IN TIME
Long Meg & Her Daughters Stone Circle
Little Salkeld

You shouldn't miss this stone circle. Wordsworth said of it, 'Next to Stonehenge it is beyond dispute the most notable relic that this or probably any other country contains.' The circle has a diameter of about 350 feet, the second biggest in the country. The red sandstone Long Meg is the tallest of the 69 stones, at about 12 feet high, and stands around 60 feet outside the circle – its four corners facing the points of the compass and carved with three mysterious symbols. The Daughters, in the circle, are boulders of rhyolite, a form of granite. The circle dates from around 1500 BC, and was probably linked to some form of religious ritual.

TRY HORSE-RIDING
Bank House Equestrian
bankhouseequestrian.co.uk
Little Salkeld, CA10 1NN
01768 881257

Whether you want a lesson or just a ride, you can get it here either as a one-to-one session or in a group, and there are horses to suit all ages and abilities. If you have children who are pony club members, they can take part in a whole range of activities here at moderate prices. You can also stay here in one of the large caravans or bring a tent and camp; both options are offered as either self-catering or B&B.

EAT AND DRINK

The Highland Drove Inn and Kyloes Restaurant

kyloes.co.uk

CA11 9NA | 01768 898349

On an old drove road, this 300-year-old country inn recalls the long-vanished days when hardy Highland cattle were driven across open water from Scotland's Western Isles to markets in England. A reputation for high-quality food might suggest it's a destination pub, as indeed it is, but it's more than that, because locals love it too, one attraction being a cask-conditioned ale called Kyloes Kushie. The attractive brick and timber bar, where snacks are available, is furnished with old tables and settles; the more formal dining takes place upstairs in the hunting lodge-style restaurant, where a verandah offers fine country views. The kitchen depends on locally sourced game, fish and meat.

The Watermill Tearoom

organicmill.co.uk

Little Salkeld, CA10 1NN

01768 881523

This little cafe is attached to the watermill itself. Try some of the brilliant bakes and lunches, with five varieties of bread to choose from, all made from scratch on the premises. The mill sells its organic flour and other goodies, and has a classroom for various bread-making courses. The gallery displays local crafts. After tasting the wholesome vegetarian fare, you can pop next door and watch the flour being milled.

▶ Grizedale Forest   MAP REF 257 E3

forestry.gov.uk

LA22 0QJ | 0300 0674495 | Visitor Centre open daily 10–5 (Nov–Feb 10–4)

Your first stop here should be the visitor centre, where you can get a guide to the many waymarked trails in the forest. This estate, between Coniston Water and Windermere, was the first forest where the Forestry Commission actively encouraged outdoor activities. It was opened to the public in the 1960s and is now the largest forest in the Lake District. Look for the original sculptures among the trees or on hilltops. Sculptors have been sponsored over the years to create these artworks in the woods and there are now more than 80 of them.

EXPLORE BY BIKE

The North Face Trail

If you're an experienced mountain biker you will enjoy this red trail, with an optional black section. The 10-mile loop, starting and finishing at the visitor centre, takes you on rough tracks and curves, uphill and downhill, through woodland and meadows with outstanding views along the way.

▲ Sculpture, Grizedale Forest

Grizedale Mountain Bikes

grizedalemountainbikes.co.uk
LA22 0QJ | 01229 860335
You will find one of the biggest fleet of bikes in the north of England at this hire centre, including varied mountain bikes, children's bikes, tag-alongs, trailers and even electric bikes. Although you can often just roll up and hire a bike on the spot, it is worth booking in advance to avoid disappointment, particularly in summer. A shop sells bikes and related gear, and there's a workshop for repairs and custom builds.

▶ Hadrian's Wall MAP REF 263 D3

In about AD 121, the Roman soldiers stationed in the north were ordered to build a wall, from the Solway Firth to the River Tyne, to keep out the wild tribes of northern Britain. Meanwhile Rome tried to civilise those south of the wall by introducing such modern comforts as central heating, public baths and an efficient drainage system.

Working under the instructions of the Emperor Hadrian (AD 76–138), and taking advantage of a prominent natural ridge, the soldiers built a massive fortification around 73 miles long from a million cubic yards of stone, and strengthened at key points by forts, mile castles and turrets. The project took

approximately five years to complete, but succeeded in holding back the Picts for more than 200 years.

There are several examples of Roman remains of houses, forts and baths along the wall, although the finest examples – Chesters, Corbridge, Vindolanda and Housesteads – are to the east. In addition to the fort at Birdoswald (see page 70), there are the remains of turrets at Piper Sike, Leahill and Banks East, while at Hare Hill, near Lanercost, is a section of the wall that stands nine feet high. The entire structure now forms the western part of a UNESCO World Heritage Site – 'The Frontiers of the Roman Empire' – that includes large sections of wall across Germany too.

From Harrow's Scar, near Birdoswald, to its end at the Solway Firth – a distance of 30 miles – the wall was originally made of turf – and some of the turrets were free-standing to enable turf ramparts to be run up them. Although the wall was rebuilt in stone, a 2-mile stretch, west of the River Irthing from Gilsland to Bowness, did not follow the line of the original wall, and so remains of the older turf wall can still be seen running nearby.

The Hadrian's Wall Path National Trail between Bowness-on-Solway and Wallsend opened in 2004, and – given all the history, scenery and cosy pubs along the way – is now one of the most popular National Trails (see opposite).

▼ Birdoswald Roman Fort and visitor centre

EXPLORE BY BIKE

Hadrian's Cycleway

If you want to get an overview of Roman Britain this long-distance route – National Cycle Route 72 – will take you along the Cumbrian coast and right across the country, following the Roman frontier. Allow three or four days for this 160-mile trip, which passes through some glorious countryside, taking in a series of Roman sites on the way. It more or less follows the path of Hadrian's Wall, but starts on the Cumbrian coast at the ancient village of Ravenglass. Even in Roman times, Ravenglass was recognised as an important natural harbour and the Roman fort of *Glannoventa* guarded it from invaders. After following the coast to the Solway Firth, the route continues by quiet roads along the wall to Tynemouth. You will find a hybrid bike the most suitable for this route but you could manage with a road bike.

WALK THE WALL

Hadrian's Wall, National Trail

As long as you are moderately fit, you should be able to complete this walk in just over a week. It covers 84 miles, from Bowness-on-Solway to Wallsend on Tyneside, and the scenery is breathtaking – taking you through rugged moorland, rolling fields and the vibrant cities of Carlisle and Newcastle-on-Tyne, as well as following the route of Hadrian's Wall. No wonder it's one of the most popular long-distance trails in England.

▼ Hadrian's Wall, Birdoswald

▶ Hardknott Pass & Roman Fort   MAP REF 257 D2

To get to the Roman Fort here you have to drive up Hardknott Pass, which rises 1,000 feet out of Eskdale in little more than a mile. It is one of the most spectacular roads in the country, with hairpin bends as steep as 1-in-3. If the road is icy, or you are towing a caravan, don't even consider this road! For cars, it is a scary drive, if you are not used to narrow, winding, hill roads; but most problems arise at peak holiday times. So take it slowly, carefully and use your gears – the views and the experience are well worth the effort.

When you gaze down from the remains of the fort at the western end of the Hardknott Pass (1,291 feet) it's easy to see why the Romans chose this site. Hardknott Castle Roman Fort enjoys a commanding position down into the green valley of Eskdale. Attacks from three sides were impossible and a trench prevented attacks from the east.

Soldiers were garrisoned here to safeguard the road they had constructed to link the fort at Ambleside and the port of Ravenglass. Preferring to take the most direct route, they drove their road over the most difficult terrain in the Lake District,

▲ Hardknott Pass and the Roman Fort

through the Hardknott and Wrynose passes. Despite the wonderful views, the Roman soldiers must have regarded isolated, windswept *Mediobogdum* as an unglamorous posting. The ruins, however, are still impressive. The soldiers carried out their drills on a flat parade ground nearby. The bathhouse would have been one of their few home comforts.

▶ Haverthwaite   MAP REF 257 E4

Haverthwaite, beyond the southern tip of Windermere, is the southern terminus of the Lakeside and Haverthwaite Railway. There's an adventure playground by the railway station. As in the railway's heyday, you can combine the scenic journey with a leisurely cruise on Windermere.

Newby Bridge (see page 177) marks the southern limit of the lake, where it drains into the River Leven. Some 2 miles from Newby Bridge is Stott Park Bobbin Mill (see page 177), which used to produce bobbins for the local industry.

TAKE A TRAIN RIDE
Lakeside and
Haverthwaite Railway

lakesiderailway.co.uk

Haverthwaite Station, Nr Ulverston, LA12 8AL | 01539 531594 | Call or check the website for the timetable

This is one of the best days out in Windermere, particularly if you combine the scenic train journey with a cruise on the lake. Originally a branch of the Furness Railway, the line used to carry goods and passengers from Ulverston to connect with the Windermere steamers at Lakeside. Four passenger steamers began service in 1850; trains began running 20 years later. Passenger numbers peaked just before World War I, but sadly declined from then onwards and finally, in 1967, the railway closed.

A group of rail enthusiasts fought to buy the branch line and re-open it as a recreational line, using steam-hauled trains. Despite many setbacks they succeeded in taking over the 3.5-mile stretch of line between Haverthwaite and Lakeside and have maintained the service ever since.

▶ Haweswater   MAP REF 258 B2

Haweswater lies east of Ullswater and Windermere and is the most easterly of the lakes. But while it may sound like just another lovely natural lake, modern Haweswater is, in fact, a reservoir, created in the 1930s. The haunting secret beneath its surface is the village of Mardale Green and the dairy farms of the Haweswater Valley. Most of the houses were blown up, but when the water levels are low the remains of roads and

▼ Haweswater, with Carling Knott

houses can still be glimpsed and you can even walk across a long submerged bridge. You can't help but feel an eerie shiver to see this long forgotten lost place emerge from the water.

You will also see an abundance of wildlife here, with peregrine falcons, buzzards and sparrowhawks now breeding in the valley. Otters have also colonised the area, no doubt feeding on the rare char and freshwater herring that are also found here. Other mammals include both roe and red deer, and red squirrels.

On the western shores of the reservoir steep crags rise to the ridge of High Street (see page 150) – the high fell taking its name from a Roman road across the summit. In the east is the ancient Naddle Forest, where you can find wood warblers, tree pipits, redstarts and several species of woodpecker.

▶ **Hawkshead**   MAP REF 257 E3

When you visit Hawkshead you'll understand why the young William Wordsworth loved it so much. He was a pupil at the Grammar School between 1779 and 1787 and lodged with Ann Tyson, whose cottage still stands. The school also survives and you can see the desk on which he carved his name.

Wordsworth would easily recognise this intriguing maze of tiny thoroughfares, alleyways and courtyards. The whitewashed houses – many of them 17th century – possess an architectural anarchy that adds a great deal to the charm of the village. The monks of Furness Abbey once owned much of it, in the days when it was an important market town. Only one building now remains from monastic times: the sturdy little courthouse, just north of the village.

There is a large car park, leaving the narrow streets peacefully car-free, and you will enjoy just wandering around this picturesque village. However, Hawkshead is extremely popular so if you don't like crowds, avoid visiting on a busy bank holiday.

VISIT THE MUSEUM AND GALLERY

Beatrix Potter Gallery
nationaltrust.org.uk
Main Street, LA22 0NS
015394 36355
Check website for opening times.
Admission by timed ticket, including NT members

Revisit your childhood at this exhibition of Beatrix Potter's original illustrations from her storybooks. The gallery is housed in the former office of her husband, William Heelis, and the building itself dates from 17th century. There was much more to Beatrix Potter than her role as a popular children's author and artist, and here you'll find a wealth of information about her life as a farmer and a pioneer of the conservation movement. The exhibits on display here change annually.

The Old Grammar School Museum

hawksheadgrammar.org.uk
Main Street, LA22 0NT
015394 36735 | Open Apr–Sep
Mon–Sat 10.30–1, 1.30–5, Sun 1–5.
Closed Oct–Mar

Find out why boys were allowed to drink beer, smoke and carve their names on the desks at this interesting museum. William Wordsworth's time at the school is well documented and you can see his name carved into his wooden desk. The museum has a fascinating collection of artefacts relating to the old school, some of which date back to the 16th century, including the Charter signed by Elizabeth I.

WALK THE HIGH ROPES

Go Ape! Grizedale

goape.co.uk
LA22 0QJ | 0845 6439215
See website for details
(pre-booking advised)

This course is the jewel in the crown of Go Ape! Built on the side of a hill, it's seriously high. If you're brave enough, you'll fly 656 feet across the top of the Grizedale Beck and enjoy the view of the forest canopy from a platform 60 feet up a magnificent Douglas Fir.

SEE SOME LOCAL CHURCHES

Hawkshead Methodist Chapel

Flag Street, LA22 0PE

Standing at the corner of The Square, this simple whitewashed building was converted in 1862 into a Nonconformist chapel from two cottages – both possibly dating from the 17th century. The first floor juts out over Flag Street and is likely to be a remnant from these early buildings. Inside, the chapel is small and seats around 40 people. From the outside, you can see a graceful round-headed window and a handsome porch.

The Methodist founder John Wesley visited Cumbria 26 times. His last visit to Kendal was in 1788, when he was 85.

St Michael and All Angels Church

hawksheadbenefice.co.uk
LA22 0NT | 015394 36301

Take a stroll up to the parish church overlooking the village and have a look at its wall frescoes. It was built in around 1300 on the site of an older church and, as it exists today, mainly dates from the 16th and 17th centuries. Wordsworth referred to it in *The Prelude*. The church was painted white at the time:

> *I saw the snow-white church upon her hill*
> *Sit like a throned lady sending out*
> *A gracious look all over her domain*

EAT AND DRINK

Hawkshead Relish Company

hawksheadrelish.com

The Square, LA22 0NZ

015394 36614

Pop in to sample the award-winning relishes, which include some very unusual food combinations. But be warned, you are unlikely to leave without buying something even if you have a sweet tooth because they also do scrumptious puddings.

Kings Arms

kingsarmshawkshead.co.uk

The Square, LA22 0NZ

015394 36372

Set in the square, this 16th-century inn is always packed in summer. In colder weather, bag a table by the fire in the traditional carpeted bar, quaff a pint of Hawkshead Bitter and tuck into lunchtime light bites or hearty evening meals. Keep your eyes open for the carved figure of a king in the bar.

Old Hall Brewery

cumbrianlegendaryales.com

LA22 0QF

015394 36436

Established in 2003 using a small three-barrel kit, you'll find this successful brewery just south of Hawkshead village on the shores of Esthwaite Water. Their Loweswater Gold was The Champion Ale of Britain in 2011. The brewery buildings date back to the 1500s and the barn dates from the 17th century.

The Queen's Head Inn and Restaurant ◉

queensheadhawkshead.co.uk

Main Street, LA22 0NS

015394 36271

On the village's main street, the 17th-century Queen's Head is a stone's throw from Esthwaite Water. Behind the pub's flower-bedecked exterior, the low oak-beamed ceilings, wood-panelled walls, slate floors and welcoming fires combine to create a relaxed, traditional setting. You can sample real ales, an extensive wine list and a menu full of fresh, quality local produce.

The Sun Inn ◉

suninn.co.uk

Main Street, LA22 0NT

015394 36236

This listed 17th-century coaching inn, supposedly, has two resident ghosts – a giggling girl and a drunken landlord. The wood-panelled bar has low, oak-beamed ceilings. If you are hill walking you will particularly appreciate being able to warm yourself next to the log fires, while the real ales and locally sourced food can't help but appeal to all.

▶ PLACES NEARBY

Outgate is a pretty but tiny settlement north of Hawkshead and west of Windermere.

Outgate Inn

outgateinn.co.uk

LA22 0NQ | 015394 36413

Once owned by a mineral water manufacturer and now part of

Robinsons Brewery, this 17th-century Lakeland inn is full of traditional features, including oak beams and a real fire in winter. The secluded beer garden at the rear is a tranquil place to enjoy the summer warmth. There's a wide selection of home-cooked food, including salads and light bites, as well as hearty options if you're coming in ravenous from the hills. Gluten-free menu and vegetarian choices, too.

▶ Helvellyn MAP REF 261 E5

This was Wordsworth's favourite mountain and you will join thousands more if you trek to its summit at 3,116 feet (950m). It is a grand climb, but it has arduous stretches, especially on its jagged eastern edges. If you're thinking of venturing onto the hill, make sure you're prepared for sudden changes in weather. Snowfall is not unknown on the tops, even as late as June, and dense mist can envelop them at any time. If you're a novice, join one of the many organised groups.

Warnings aside, the peak is accessible by reasonably fit walkers as long as you make sure you have extra clothes for the top, sturdy boots and a map. A popular approach is from Wythburn on the southeastern shores of Thirlmere Reservoir (see page 219). This route heads up Helvellyn's steep southwestern slopes, with splendid views across Thirlmere to the west. The eastern approaches are longer but scenically more dramatic, from Glenridding (see page 128), for example.

The arduous climb may take your breath away, but the views from the top of Helvellyn will do so again – north along the valley towards Keswick, and east beyond the mountain lake, Red Tarn, to the distant high peaks of the Pennines. Just south of the summit is a memorial by Wordsworth and Sir Walter Scott. The words are a sign that you have reached the highest point in the area. Only Scafell Pike, at 3,210 feet (978m), and Scafell, at 3,162 feet (964m), are higher than Helvellyn.

▶ High Street Roman Road MAP REF 257 F2

The Troutbeck Valley was designated by the Romans to be the starting point for a remarkable road, High Street, which took an uncompromising route straight across the mountain ridges between the lakes of Ullswater and Haweswater. The road probably linked the Roman forts at Ambleside and Brougham with their port at Ravenglass on the west coast.

▶ Helvellyn towards Thirlmere

▷ Holker Hall   MAP REF 257 E5

holker.co.uk

Cark in Cartmel, Grange-over-Sands, LA11 7PL | 015395 58328 | Hall open
late Mar–Oct Wed–Sun 11–4; gardens 10.30–5). Cafe, food hall and gift shop
Mar–Oct Wed–Sun 10.30–5 and some weekends in Nov and Dec (check
website for details)

Remarkably, despite the obvious grandeur of Holker Hall, it
still has the atmosphere of a family home – not least because
the rooms are free of ropes and barriers.

Still home to Lord and Lady Cavendish, it is the sort of house
where, at every turn, you expect to see the hearty clergymen,
eager young noblemen, elderly housemaids and animated
younger daughters of the aristocracy straight from the pages of
an Anthony Trollope novel.

Holker is largely a creation of the third quarter of the 19th
century. A disastrous fire in 1871 destroyed the whole of the
west wing, including paintings and furniture. The seventh
Duke of Devonshire commissioned local architects Paley and
Austin – then among the best country-house designers in
Britain – to rebuild the wing in pale red sandstone in a grand
yet relaxed Elizabethan style, complete with large bay windows
and a copper dome.

The library has deeply comfortable armchairs, gorgeous
French furniture and a lively collection of family portraits. His
microscope and copies of his learned works remember Henry
Cavendish, the scientist who discovered nitric acid. There is a
portrait by Richmond of Lord Frederick, who was assassinated
in Phoenix Park, Dublin, in 1882.

The drawing room still has its original red silk walls, while
the chimneypiece in the dining room is constructed of local

▼ Holker Hall

marble and finely carved wood – one of several throughout the house – and incorporates a Van Dyck self-portrait.

Fine craftsmanship is everywhere. On the main staircase look at the balusters, every one of them is different. Each room retains some of that joyous sense of jewelled clutter so loved by the Victorians. One of the bedrooms has Wedgwood plaques and blue Jasper Ware on the fire surround while another has furnishings from 1937, when Queen Mary stayed at Holker. The family used to play carpet bowls down the gallery, a spacious and sunny contrast to the hall, which recalls winter evenings around a roaring fire.

The extensive gardens and woodland, some 25 acres in total, are formal and informal by turns. Here, you'll find the only surviving monkey puzzle tree planted from seeds that were brought to England in 1837, as well as a superb display of magnolias and rhododendrons and, of course, the Great Holker Lime. One of the largest trees of its kind in Britain, this one was planted in the 17th century and is 26 feet in circumference.

▶ Hutton-in-the-Forest MAP REF 262 C6

hutton-in-the-forest.co.uk

CA11 9TH | 017684 84449 | Gardens open Apr–Oct Sun–Fri 10–5. House open mid-Apr to mid-Oct Wed–Thu, Sun & BHs 11.30–4

You really can walk back through history in this house. The oldest part is the fortified pele tower, built in the 1350s by the de Hoton family as protection against the Scots and the border reivers. The house reflects centuries of history and change, and is an incredibly rich illustration of the development of the country house in northern Britain.

The legendary Sir Gawain is said to have stayed with the Green Knight at Hutton, which was then surrounded by dense woodland. In 1292, Edward I was a visitor during the heyday of the royal hunting forest of Inglewood. The Fletchers, ancestors of the family who still live here, bought the property in 1605. The Long Gallery was built in 1630, and the light classical east front in the 1680s. The Renaissance facade, with its light-coloured stonework and delicate classical features, contrasts dramatically with the rest of the building.

The final additions were made in the 1820s, when Salvin designed the dominant southeast tower, and added battlements to the pele. The impressive Stone Hall with its barrel vaulted ceiling is the oldest room, contrasting with the later rooms, which are warm with wood panelling, good furniture and family pictures. The charming Cupid Staircase, with its carved cherubs, and the Cupid Room, with its delicate plaster ceiling of 1744, testify to the romantic associations of the house. There is a more formal air about Salvin's dining room and the Long Gallery retains its distinctly Jacobean flavour.

Look out for the portrait of John Peel, who was employed here as a huntsman in the 18th century. Also 18th century is the engraving of the house, made by Kip. It is astonishing how little the house has changed since he put pen to paper.

Before you go, take a stroll around the beautiful gardens, which include a delightful walled garden, a woodland walk, terraces, topiary and three ponds with cascades.

▶ Kendal MAP REF 258 B4

As you drive from the M6, the first sight of Kendal in the valley below means that the Lakes are 'only just round the corner'. The one-way traffic system can be frustrating, so it's better to go on foot if you want to investigate Kendal's numerous 'yards' or alleyways. The castle is in ruins but the splendid view from the top is worth the climb. It is best known for being the home of the Parr family and you may hear that King Henry VIII's sixth wife Catherine Parr was born at Kendal Castle. This is very unlikely, since by the time Catherine was born, the castle was beyond repair and her father based in London.

Near the parish church is Abbot Hall. This elegant Georgian house is now an equally elegant art gallery, showing works by the many artists – including Ruskin and Constable – who were inspired by the unique Lakeland landscape. Also at Abbot Hall is the Museum of Lakeland Life and Industry, which aims to bring recent history to life. At the opposite end of town, close to the railway station, the Kendal Museum has fascinating displays of geology, archaeology and natural and social history if you want to discover more about the area.

▶ Kendal

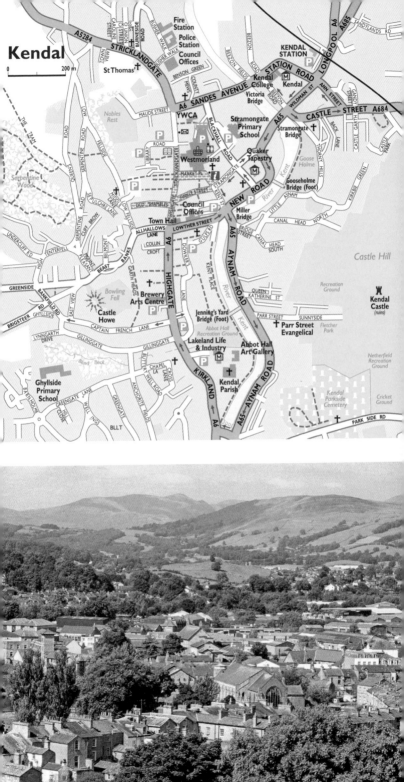

VISIT THE MUSEUMS AND GALLERIES

The Quaker Tapestry

quaker-tapestry.co.uk
Quaker Tapestry Exhibition Centre,
Stramongate, LA9 4BH
01539 722975 | Open Mar to
mid-Dec Mon–Sat 10–5
Look for this exhibition in the Friend's Meeting House. The 77 embroidered panels are the work of 4,000 men, women and children from some 15 countries. Anne Wynn-Wilson, author of *Quakers In Stitches* had the vision of a number of tapestry panels telling something of the Quaker story and beliefs. Completed in 1996, the panels, each measuring 25 by 21 inches, show factual stories from the forefront of the Industrial Revolution, developments in science and medicine, astronomy, the abolition of slavery and stages of social reform.

There is also a collection of documents, photographs and samplers associated with the making of the embroidered panels. As well as the tapestry, there are articles of clothing, embroidery and other domestic items relating to Quaker history, and interactive displays and activities for children. Here, you can also learn about Quaker events and insights, and of the considerable contribution that these quiet Nonconformists have made to the advances of the modern world.

The Exhibition Centre building itself is one of the finest Georgian buildings in Cumbria, with a beautiful, peaceful walled garden. It is a Grade II listed building that was designed by local architect Francis Webster in 1816. The tea room serves healthy lunches and snacks, and caters for vegetarians and vegans.

▼ Abbot Hall Art Gallery

Museum of Lakeland Life

lakelandmuseum.org.uk
Abbot Hall, LA9 5AL
01539 722464 | Open mid-Jan to
mid-Dec Mon–Sat 10.30–5
(10.30–4 Nov–Feb), Sun in summer
school holidays. Closed mid-Dec to
mid-Jan

Find out how people lived and
worked in bygone days as you
explore the reconstructed
shops, room settings and a
farming display. You can see the
toys that children played with,
and how different Georgian and
Victorian life was from today.
There's a farmhouse kitchen
with traditional recipes and
utensils, a bedroom full of
period furniture, including a
magnificent 16th-century
four-poster bed, and a parlour
with rare 17th-century oak
panelling. You can go into the
study of Arthur Ransome and
immerse yourself in the world
of *Swallows and Amazons* with

the author's typewriter, desk,
personal mementoes and
original illustrations. Other
displays include a traditional
chemist's shop, Lakeland
industries, and the local Arts
and Crafts Movement.

Kendal Museum

kendalmuseum.org.uk
Station Road, LA9 6BT
01539 815597 | Open Tue–Thu
10–4. Closed Christmas & New Year

This rather quirky museum is
based on the collection of
'curiosities' first exhibited by
William Todhunter in 1796. He
charged admission at the rate
of 'one shilling per person;
children and servants 6d each'.
There are displays of wildlife,
both local and global, including
a case full of iridescent
humming birds which seems
unpleasant by today's
standards. You can find out
about the archaeology and

▼ Kendal Castle

natural history of the Lakes and there's also a display devoted to author Alfred Wainwright, one of Kendal's best-known adopted sons. His seven handwritten guides to the Lakeland hills became classics in his own lifetime (see page 36). You can see Wainwright's office in Kendal Museum, where he held the post of honorary curator for many years. A hand-drawn map reveals his interests were already in place at the tender age of 10. However, it wasn't until he was 45 that he began the task of writing his *Pictorial Guides*. Other books about his beloved 'North Country' followed, until his death in 1991.

Abbot Hall Art Gallery

abbothall.org.uk
LA9 5AL | 01539 722464 | Open mid-Jan to mid-Dec Mon–Sat 10.30–5 (closes at 4 Nov–Feb). Closed mid-Dec to mid-Jan. (Also open Sun in summer school holidays)

This Grade I listed Georgian villa on the banks of the River Kent is one of Kendal's most important buildings. There are two floors of light-filled spaces, where you can see a permanent collection of works by George Romney spanning his entire career; 18th- and 19th-century paintings and watercolours; a large number of drawings and watercolours by Ruskin; and an exhibition of contemporary art. The upstairs galleries have commanding views of the River Kent and Kendal Castle and show works by major British artists, including Sean Scully, Frank Auerbach, and Ben and Winifred Nicholson. Check the website for temporary exhibitions planned throughout the year.

GET INDUSTRIAL

Greenside Lime Kiln

This scheduled Ancient Monument is all that remains of a much larger lime-burning operation. The interpretation boards provide an invaluable introduction to this once prolific industry.

TRY HORSE-RIDING

Holmescales Riding Centre

holmescalesridingcentre.co.uk
Holmescales Farm, Old Hutton, LA8 0NB | 01539 729388

Whether you're a novice or an experienced rider, this centre has horses and courses to suit all ages and abilities. You can go hacking or take lessons with one of their horses or your own.

CATCH A PERFORMANCE

The Brewery Arts Centre

breweryarts.co.uk
122a Highgate, LA9 4HE
01539 725133

If you fancy an injection of culture, popular or high-brow, you'll find it here. Housed in an old Victorian brewery, the centre stages productions from Shakespeare to edgy drama. Live music ranges across folk, rock, jazz, blues, contemporary and classical. The arts centre also commissions and presents dance, from hip hop to ballet to contemporary dance. You'll find comedy as well, from solo stand-ups to sketch shows and musical comedy. Alternatively, you might decide to take in a movie, maybe the latest big-screen blockbuster or a specialised or classic film.

PLAY A ROUND
Carus Green Golf Course & Driving Range
carusgreen.co.uk
Burneside Road, LA9 6EB
01539 721097 | Open daily
Surrounded by the rivers Kent and Mint, this pretty flat course has views of the Kentmere and Howgill fells. The holes here vary in difficulty. The rivers come into play on five holes and there are also a number of ponds and bunkers.

Kendal Golf Club
kendalgolfclub.co.uk
The Heights, LA9 4PQ
01539 733708 | Open daily
More than 100 years old, this is an elevated parkland and fell course with breathtaking views of Lakeland fells and the surrounding district. The short par 3, 17th hole is particularly memorable – the tee shot is played over a limestone outcrop ('the battleship') to a small green.

EAT AND DRINK
The 2 Sisters Cafe
plumgarths.co.uk
Crook Road, Lakeland Food Park, LA8 8LX | 01539 736300
This little cafe, next to Plumgarth's Farm Shop, serves delicious breakfasts, lunches and snacks. Monika and Magda love cooking and they produce everything fresh on the premises, using ingredients from the farm shop. If you go here once, you will definitely return for a warm welcome and great food in comfortable relaxed surroundings.

Brew Brothers
brew-brothers.co.uk
69 Highgate, LA9 4ED
01539 722237
Opened in 2014, this quirky cafe serves home-made treats, good coffee and excellent light lunches with laid-back style.

Burgundy's Wine Bar
burgundyswinebar.co.uk
19 Lowther Street, LA9 4DH
01539 733803
This wine bar has a real village 'local' atmosphere where young, old and inbetweeners get together in friendly, convivial surroundings. You will often find live music on here – Thursday night is live jazz night. Four real ales are always on, as well as speciality Belgian and German beers and a phenomenal choice of wines.

Castle Dairy
castledairy.co.uk
26 Wildman Street, LA9 6EN
01539 814756
Housed in Kendal's oldest inhabited building, this restaurant and art gallery welcomes customers with its log fires, antique furniture and historic ambience, which all

add to the unique feel of the place. It is a stunning piece of medieval architecture in excellent condition, and probably Kendal's only surviving 'true' medieval house. The name 'Dairy' is most likely the result of a historical misspelling, as its true name relates to 'Dowry', meaning a house where a Dower or a widow would have lived. There are many other stories to this ancient building; just ask one of the staff and they will tell you. Kendal College apprentices staff the place under the careful eye of the chef. The restaurant menu is short but good quality. There's also an interesting bar menu at very reasonable prices. The Dairy allows Kendal College's art students to display and sell their pieces, which makes for some very interesting exhibitions.

Castle Green Hotel ◉◉
castlegreen.co.uk
Castle Green Lane, LA9 6RG
01539 734000

This charming country house is now a luxurious spa hotel. A £250,000 splashout on the Greenhouse restaurant and bar means a stylish makeover, with a boldly patterned carpet and walls crowded with little pictures. The panoramic views over the fells are undisturbed, while innovative Cumbrian food pours forth from the kitchen. You can take afternoon tea in this delightful setting too.

▶ **PLACES NEARBY**
The Punch Bowl
thepunchbowla65.com
Barrows Green, LA8 0AA
015395 60267
If, when heading for The Lakes, your route involves leaving the M6 at junction 36, this is the first pub you'll encounter. In the inviting bar the real ales change frequently, and you can play pool, darts and dominoes. Committed to local sourcing, the kitchen has a mantra: 'Proud to serve proper pub food in decent portions'.

▶ Kentmere   MAP REF 258 B3

The valley of Kentmere begins at Staveley, just off the A591 between Kendal and Windermere. From Staveley the road meanders prettily along the valley bottom heading northwards, clinging to the River Kent before coming to a halt at the charming little village of Kentmere. The village church, St Cuthbert's, has a bronze memorial to Bernard Gilpin, who was born at Kentmere Hall in 1517 and eventually became Archdeacon of Durham Cathedral. From Kentmere, you can continue to explore the head of the valley on foot, or take footpaths 'over the top' into either the Troutbeck Valley or the remote upper reaches of Longsleddale. Be warned, parking is limited in the village.

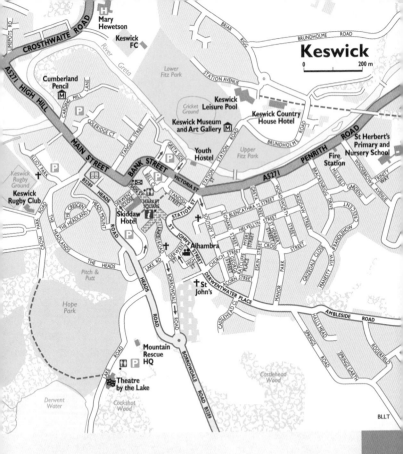

Keswick MAP REF 261 D4

Keswick is a natural centre for mountain climbers, country walkers and more leisurely tourists alike. It is small, with a population of less than 5,000, but is said, for its size, to have more beds for guests than anywhere else in the country. This gives an idea of what it can be like on a sunny bank holiday weekend, when its reliance on tourism is most obvious.

In the past, however, it was mining that kept it alive. The industry flourished in the 16th century with the formation, at the behest of Elizabeth I, of the Company of Mines Royal. Expert miners came from Germany and settled on Derwent Isle. The mining industry declined by the second half of the 19th century, but a new source of prosperity came in 1865 when the Cockermouth–Penrith railway line was built.

Graphite is the reason that the Cumberland Pencil Museum exists here today. A delightfully quirky specialist collection, it shows that even the humble pencil has a fascinating history.

Keswick also has one of the oldest museums in the county, the Keswick Museum and Art Gallery, which has a good display on Lakeland's literary connections, while the Keswick Mining Museum covers the area's geology and industrial history.

On the northern edge of Keswick at Crosthwaite is the Church of St Kentigern, whose best-known incumbent, Canon Rawnsley, was the first Secretary of the National Trust. A friend of Beatrix Potter, he was also an author, journalist, orator and educationalist. His influence pervades almost every corner of Keswick and Cumbria.

▼ Keswick

▶ Cumberland Pencil Museum

pencilmuseum.co.uk
Southey Works, Greta Bridge,
CA12 5NG | 017687 73626
Open daily 9.30–5 (except
Christmas Day, Boxing Day
and New Year's Day)
This forward-thinking
museum investigates the
history and technology of
an object most of us take
utterly for granted – the

humble pencil. Did you know that the first pencil was made locally
in the 1550s? You will find lots more well-presented information
about pencils, including details of modern production methods.
The whole thing is very much geared to keeping children
interested, with an on-site giant and other exciting innovations,
such as a replica of the Borrowdale mine, where graphite was first
discovered. You can see the world's longest coloured pencil,
manufactured in 2001, there's a children's activity area, a shop
selling artists' materials, and Sketchers Coffee Shop, where all the
food they serve is locally sourced. The coffee shop has an enviable
riverside location with views of Catbells.

Throughout the year, there are artist demonstrations and tuition
workshops showing various techniques using pencils. Family fun
days here are great on rainy days, with quiz trails around the
museum, drawing competitions and a host of things to make and
do in the Kid's Art Studio. Check the website for details.

▶ Theatre by the Lake

theatrebythelake.com

Lakeside, Lake Road, CA12 5DJ | 01768 774411 | Open all year

This theatre has been described as 'the most beautifully located and friendly theatre in Britain'. It is a short stroll from Derwentwater on the edge of Keswick and sits amid the magnificent western fells of the Lake District. You will find a huge range of presentations here and it is well worth checking their website to see what is showing while you are visiting the Lakes.

The theatre has two stages, a 400-seat main house and 100-seat studio, putting on up to nine productions of classic, modern and new plays throughout the year. The resident company of around 14 actors performs six plays in repertory from May to November, and produces a new play every year. If you are in the area at Christmas, particularly with children, go to their Christmas play if you can get a ticket.

The theatre also hosts a variety of festivals, visiting companies and musicians.

▼ Peter Macqueen and Richard Earl in *She Stoops to Conquer*

▲ Derwentwater

VISIT THE MUSEUMS AND GALLERIES

Cumberland Pencil Museum
see highlight panel on page 163

Keswick Museum and Art Gallery
keswickmuseum.org.uk
Station Road, CA12 4NF
017687 73263 | Open daily 10–4
With something for all the family, the accent at this museum is firmly on the local area, its geology, history and literature, its decorative and fine arts and the personalities that have lived here. Revamped for the 21st-century at a cost of over £2 million, the museum has a permanent collection encompassing more than 20,000 artefacts. Its changing temporary exhibitions are also a draw. These run over the summer months and have plenty of hands-on activities for kids, which might range from taking a bird's-eye journey over the Lakes in the cinema to

creating pen and ink sketches in the style of Wainwright (see page 36).

CATCH A PERFORMANCE

Theatre by the Lake
see highlight panel opposite

TAKE A BOAT TRIP

Keswick Launch
see page 121

EXPLORE BY BIKE

Keswick Mountain Bike Centre
keswickbikes.co.uk
133 Main Street, CA12 5NJ
017687 73355/75202
You can hire mountain bikes suitable for all sizes here, as well as helmets, spare parts and bike locks.

Whinlatter Bikes
whinlatterbikes.com
82 Main Street, CA12 5DX
017687 73940
Mountain bikes for men, women and children, plus tag-alongs

and buggies can be hired here. There's a workshop for repairs to your own bike as well.

PLAY A ROUND
Keswick Golf Club
keswickgolfclub.com
Threlkeld Hall, Threlkeld, CA12 4SX
017687 79324 | Open daily
This parkland course is not very long, at just over 6,200 yards, but the par of 71 shows that it is a good test for golfers of all abilities – numerous hazards, tree-lined fairways and well-protected greens testify to that. The natural landscape, with outstanding, panoramic views of Blencathra, Skiddaw and Clough Head among others, makes this an especially impressive course to play.

EAT AND DRINK
Brossen Steakhouse ◉
innonthesquare.co.uk/brossen
Main Street, CA12 5JF
01768 773333

The Inn on the Square is a revamped hotel with a contemporary edge and a restaurant that is all about prime protein cooked over coals. The dining room is light, bright and casual, with a view into the kitchen and murals depicting butchers' charts.

The George
thegeorgekeswick.co.uk
3 St John's Street, CA12 5AZ
017687 72076
This is Keswick's oldest coaching inn and it's a handsome 17th-century building in the heart of the town. Restored to its former glory, and retaining its traditional black panelling, Elizabethan beams, ancient settles and log fires, it makes a comfortable base from which to explore the fells and lakes. Expect to find local Jennings ales on tap to accompany classic pub food prepared from local ingredients.

▼ Keswick and Skiddaw

Keswick Brewery

keswickbrewery.co.uk
The Old Brewery, Brewery Lane,
CA12 5BY | 017687 80700
This small craft brewery was
established in 2006 on the site
of a much older brewery that
closed way back in 1897.

Morrels

morrels.co.uk
34 Lake Road, CA12 5DQ
017687 72666
The Victorian house situated
between the Theatre by the
Lake and Keswick Market
has been repurposed into
a combination of self-
catering apartments with
a contemporary brasserie
restaurant on hand – perfect
for when the self-catering
impulse falters.

Pheasant Inn

thepheasantinnkeswick.co.uk
Crosthwaite Road, CA12 5PP
017687 72219
This is an open-fired, traditional
Lakeland inn owned by
Jennings Brewery, so you will

find their regular range on tap,
and a monthly guest beer. The
seasonal menus, using
home-cooked, locally
sourced food, range from
Cumbrian traditional to
international favourites.

The Royal Oak at Keswick

theinnkeswick.co.uk
Main Street, CA12 5HZ
017687 74584
Located on the corner of
Keswick's vibrant market
square, this large yet friendly
18th-century coaching inn
combines contemporary
comfort with charming
reminders of its place in local
history. It is understandably
popular with walkers – it's
within a few strides of
England's three highest peaks;
dogs are permitted in the bar
and some of the bedrooms.
Lancaster Bomber is one of the
award-winning Thwaites ales
on tap. The kitchen's careful
sourcing of ingredients from
ethical suppliers ensures
sustainability as well as

freshness, and local artisans including the Thornby Moor Dairy are supported and named on the menu. The menu represents excellent value for money.

▶ PLACES NEARBY

The Horse & Farrier Inn
horseandfarrier.com
Threlkeld Village, CA12 4SQ
017687 79688

From this late 17th-century Lakeland inn at the foot of Blencathra there are views across to the Helvellyn range. Within its whitewashed stone walls you'll find slate floors, beamed ceilings and open log fires, with hunting prints decorating the bars and panelled snug. Cockermouth's Jennings and a guest brewery supply the real ales while the pub also maintains a reputation for good food due to its long-standing commitment to local, seasonal produce.

Threlkeld Quarry and Mining Museum
threlkeldquarryandminingmuseum.
co.uk
Threlkeld, CA12 4TT
017687 79747 | Open daily
Easter–Oct 10–5

Find out about all aspects of Cumbrian mining, quarrying and geology by taking a trip through a reconstructed mine and wander around the vintage excavators and machinery in the quarry. The Mining Room contains artefacts, plans and photographs of explorations of many local mines. The Quarry Room looks at the local geology, with rock samples on display.

▼ Catbells and Derwentwater

▶ Kirkby Lonsdale MAP REF 258 C6

This tiny market town in Cumbria marks the far western limit of the Yorkshire Dales. It is a delightfully unspoiled place, and its charms have been recognised by artists and authors, from Constable and Turner to Ruskin and Wordsworth, all of whom have sung its praises over the years. Even the street names such as Jingling Lane and Salt Pie Lane are quaint.

A Roman fort has been excavated at Burrow, just 2 miles south of the town, and in 1227 King Henry III granted a market charter, which allowed for a weekly market and an annual fair to be held in the town. The fair died out in the 19th century, but the market still thrives every Thursday in Market Place – the lovely butter cross here dates from the early 20th century.

Make sure you walk to the edge of town to see the medieval Devil's Bridge spanning the River Lune. It is one of the town's most notable features, with its three graceful arches striding over the water, and a very popular meeting place for bikers. Its date is not known for sure, though records from the late 14th century tell of repairs to a bridge in the town. No one knows when it first acquired its cheerful name, although a poem of 1821 tells the tale. A Yorkshire woman, known for being a cheat, one night heard her cow and pony calling from the far side of the swollen river. The devil appeared and offered to build a bridge, and his payment would be to keep the first thing that crossed over the bridge. He knew that her husband was coming home and thought he would capture him, but the canny

▼ Ruskin's View, Kirkby Lonsdale

woman tricked him by throwing a bun across the bridge, which her dog chased after. The devil grinned at the woman's trickery, and disappeared in flames. The bridge is now open for pedestrians only, to help preserve it.

A short way downriver you can see a piece of limestone, known as the Devil's Neck Collar, which has a hole worn through it by the action of the water.

SEE A LOCAL CHURCH
The Church of St Mary the Virgin
Queens Square, LA6 2AU
This impressive building probably dates from the late 11th and early 12th centuries. Look for the lovely Norman archway beneath the solid square tower. It has some fine stained glass and a delicately carved pulpit. Outside, near the north entrance, is a tower, which can be seen in J M W Turner's famous painting of 1822, *Kirkby Lonsdale Churchyard*, which serves as another reminder of the timeless and inspirational nature of this attractive little town.

PLAY A ROUND
Kirkby Lonsdale Golf Club
kirkbylonsdalegolfclub.com
Scaleber Lane, Barbon, LA6 2LJ
015242 76365
A parkland course on the east bank of the River Lune and crossed by Barbon Beck, Kirkby Lonsdale Golf Club is surrounded by the beautiful scenery of the Lune Valley and mainly follows the lie of the land. The course is gently undulating and the beck creates a number of water hazards.

EAT AND DRINK
Hipping Hall ◉◉◉
hippinghall.com
Cowan Bridge, LA6 2JJ
015242 71187
The word 'hipping' refers to an old term for stepping stones, which allowed a dry crossing of the wonderfully named Broken Beck (the wee stream running through the grounds). The hall has been on this site for centuries and has a timeless appeal, and for a place with the moniker 'hall' it is relatively modest, but charming nonetheless. Standing between the Lake District and the Yorkshire Dales within its own mature garden, Hipping Hall has a real asset in its restaurant. Oli Martin is the man in the kitchen and he's serving up impressively contemporary and considered plates of food. From the à la carte and tasting menus come dishes of refinement and creativity.

Pheasant Inn ◉
pheasantinn.co.uk
Casterton, LA6 2RX | 015242 71230
An 18th-century coaching inn with a proper bar complete with real ales and a snug, the Pheasant Inn also boasts traditional bedrooms and a

wood-panelled restaurant. It's a family-run place, operated with enthusiasm by a couple of generations of Wilsons. When it comes to eating, grab a table by the fire in the bar, or head on through to the slightly more refined restaurant – whichever you prefer, as the menu is the same throughout. Expect dishes that reflect the easy-going pub setting but don't lack ambition.

The Sun Inn ◉◉

sun-inn.info

6 Market Street, LA6 2AU

015242 71965

Kirkby Lonsdale retains immense character and charm, beautifully evidenced in the classic period building that is The Sun Inn. It burrows back from a pretty pillared frontage into a comfy mix of low-slung beams, oak and flagstone flooring and cosy alcoves focused on a feature fireplace at the heart of the pub. The enthusiastic owners are keen supporters of locally produced goods; expect beer from the town's microbrewery to accompany the uplifting bill of fare sourced from the surrounding countryside.

The Whoop Hall

whoophall.co.uk

Burrow with Barrow, LA6 2GY

015242 71284

Set in the gorgeous Lune Valley with fells rising to over 2,000-feet just up the lane, this considerately modernised 400-year-old coaching inn is a grand base for exploring the nearby Yorkshire Dales National Park. Yorkshire also provides beers such as Black Sheep, and excellent local produce used on the enticing menus in the restaurant and bistro bar.

▶ PLACES NEARBY

The Churchmouse at Barbon

churchmousecheeses.com

New Road, Barbon LA6 2LL

015242 76224

This quirky shop-cum-cafe in the charming village of Barbon in the Lune Valley is a friendly place for a quick snack. As the name suggests, they are cheese specialists selling a superb range of mainly English cheese, but they also serve excellent home baking, good coffee and act as the village bistro on Saturday evenings.

Plough Inn ◉

theploughatlupton.co.uk

Cow Brow, Lupton, LA6 1PJ

015395 67700

Enjoying a new lease of life since a recent major makeover, the Plough sports a clean-lined contemporary look without sacrificing the best of its pubby character. It's a classy act with tasteful colours, leather sofas and a Brathay slate-topped bar set against the cosiness of wooden floors, beams, real fires and the like. The place hasn't lost track of what a good, up-to-date inn should be so there are real ales alongside a wide-ranging roster of please-all British cooking to suit all tastes.

Kirkby Stephen MAP REF 259 D3

kirkby-stephen.com

This is a traditional market town of historic buildings, cobbled yards, quaint corners and interesting shops in the beautiful Upper Eden Valley. Although it is in Cumbria, it stands at the foot of Mallerstang, a dale that stretches south through the recently extended Yorkshire Dales National Park. You will find the area much quieter than the better-known parts of Cumbria, but equally appealing. You can walk through this landscape of pastoral rural scenery and wild uplands and find breathtaking views in every direction. It is remote from large towns and population centres and has a strong, self-sufficient identity and community spirit.

TAKE IN SOME HISTORY
Pendragon Castle
If you are passing, it is worth having a quick look at these atmospheric remains about 4 miles south of Kirkby Stephen, by the side of the B6259, although it's worth noting there is more myth than historical fact here. The castle was named after King Uther Pendragon, the legendary father of King Arthur, although the building dates only from the 12th century. The crumbling castle is not very big but you can wander at will, despite it being on private land.

SEE A LOCAL CHURCH
Church of St Stephen
Market Square, CA17 4QX
Go into the church from the Market Square through the handsome cloisters built in 1810, where the butter market was held. The oldest part of the present church dates from 1220. Prior to that, this was the site of a Norman church, which only survived for 50 years, and before that a Saxon church stood on this spot. You can see many ancient relics here. There are some well-preserved bread shelves, a fine Shap granite and Italian marble pulpit, and a 17th-century font. Look for the beautiful engraved panel over the entrance to the Hartley Chapel showing the Stoning of St Stephen, crafted by John Hutton. He was also responsible for the memorable glass screen in Coventry Cathedral. Inside the chapel is a tub, which was used to measure a bushel of wheat.

The best feature is at the west end. It is the 10th-century Viking Loki Stone, decorated with a carved horned figure of the Norse god Loki. It is the only example in Britain, and one of only two in Europe. There is also a hogback stone, a Viking grave marker with a curved ridge, which is thought to represent the shingled roofs of these 'houses of the dead'. The tower was built in the early 16th century and in the nave you can still see fragments of a painted weave pattern.

In the churchyard look for a flat stone table, the Trupp Stone. This is where the tenants of church properties traditionally paid their tithes. It was in use until 1836.

GO WALKING
Nine Standards
Follow Alfred Wainwright's Coast to Coast long-distance walking route east from the town for 4 miles to reach Nine Standards. Located on the high moorland of the North Pennines, these tall cairns are visible for miles around, but their origins are shrouded in mystery. One claim is that they were constructed by the Romans to look like troops from a distance; others say they are boundary markers. Major repairs on them were carried out in 2005, but they refused to give up their secrets. The view from the cairns, located at 2,132 feet or 650m above sea level, is tremendous, taking in the Lake District fells, Cross Fell – the highest point in the Pennines – and countless other hills stretching far into the distance.

EAT AND DRINK
The Pink Geranium
40 Market Street, CA17 4QW
017683 71586
The Pink Geranium loves cyclists and as well as dishing up energy-rich full English breakfasts, lunchtime soups, baked potatoes and local ham and chips, they carry a good range of cycling accessories for emergencies. There's always plenty of home baking on offer.

▶ PLACES NEARBY
Ravenstonedale is an unspoiled picturesque village lying at the foot of the Howgills.

The Black Swan
blackswanhotel.com
Ravenstonedale, CA17 4NG
015396 23204
In a pretty conservation village stands this handsome, multi-gabled Victorian hotel proudly run by enterprising owners Alan and Louise Dinnes. The building has been refurbished to its former glory, and has friendly bars and a lounge warmed by an open fire. In its tranquil riverside gardens below Wild Boar Fell and the headwaters of the River Eden you might spot a red squirrel or two. An acclaimed real ale line-up features regulars from the Black Sheep brewery and guests from local micro-breweries. Meals may be eaten in both bar areas, the lounge or in either of the two beautifully decorated restaurants. As with the beers, local produce is key.

The Fat Lamb
fatlamb.co.uk
Crossbank, CA17 4LL
015396 23242
Tables outside this 350-year-old former coaching inn come with some of the most outstanding views in England. Vast fells create an undulating patchwork that completely surrounds the stone inn. A source of the River

Lune here has been tapped to create the heart of the inn's own nature reserve, where sightings have included otters, roe deer and countless upland birds. Rambling parties can pop in for breakfast before tackling the local trails; less active travellers can explore the very traditional interior of the inn, where quirks like a huge aircraft propeller and a stuffed ram's head provoke comment. Lounge at the bar near the old Yorkshire range, quaff Yorkshire beer and peruse a menu of pub stalwarts and daily-changing tasty specials.

The King's Head
kings-head.com
CA17 4NH | 015396 23050
There are real fires in the restaurant of this whitewashed pub, where a three-course lunch or evening meal may be enjoyed. Three regularly changing real ales and eight wines by the glass are served in the open-plan bar.

▶ Kirkstone Pass

Kirkstone Pass is, at a maximum of 1,489 feet, the highest road in the Lake District, as well as one of the most spectacular. You can imagine the effort it took in days of yore for charabancs – the early form of pleasure buses – to labour up the long haul, from either Ambleside or Troutbeck. The Kirkstone Inn, where these roads converge, would have been a welcome sight for passengers. It takes its name from the nearby Kirk Stone, which resembles a church steeple.

The Kirkstone Pass continues through some magnificent mountain scenery, before dropping down, past Brothers Water, into Patterdale.

▼ Kirkstone Pass

EAT AND DRINK

Kirkstone Pass Inn

kirkstonepassinn.com

LA22 9LQ | 015394 33888

It is worth stopping here just for the view, but it is also 500 years old and the highest pub in Cumbria. It will not disappoint you with its oak beams, open fire, home-cooked meals and friendly welcome.

▼ Kirkstone Pass

5 hauntings

▶ **The Kirkstone Pass Inn** (this page) is crawling with ghosts, including a boy who was killed by a coach and a ghostly coachman who pops in for a pint.

▶ The spectre of Lord Lonsdale apparently drives a ghostly coach and horses round **St Peter's Church** in Askham.

▶ **Broughton Moor** is supposed to be haunted by a character known as Bible John who carries a Bible with a pistol inside it.

▶ **Cartmel Priory** (page 97) is the scene of ghostly apparitions of monks.

▶ **Muncaster Castle** (page 190) is one of the most haunted buildings in England and you can register to take part in one of their ghost sits or overnight ghost vigils – that's if you dare.

▶ Lake District National Park   MAP REF 261 E5

lakedistrict.gov.uk

The Lake District National Park includes the central and most visited part of Cumbria, but stops short of the towns of Carlisle (see page 88), Kendal (see page 154) and Penrith (see page 195). The Furness Peninsula, Morecambe Bay, the northern coast and the Solway are not included.

The National Park Authority's main aims are to promote conservation, public enjoyment and the well-being of the local community, and to protect the landscape by restricting change which would be detrimental to it. The biggest landowner within the Lake District National Park is the National Trust, which looks after large tracts of some of the finest Lakeland landscapes for the enjoyment of future generations. The Forestry Commission is another major landowner. United Utilities, too, owns three large areas within the National Park, including Haweswater (see page

146), Thirlmere (see page 219) and Ennerdale (see page 124). Most of the land is, however, in the hands of individual farmers and estates.

The area was the second National Park in Britain, designated in 1951, just after the Peak District and it is the most visited National Park with more than 20 million tourists visiting every year. With its offices in Kendal, the national park has a visitor centre on Windermere at Brockhole (see page 246).

▶ Lakeside MAP REF 257 E4

Lakeside started life as a steamer pier. Then it became the terminus of the Lakeside branch of the Furness Railway. A hotel was built to cater for the passengers. It's still possible to travel here by steamer from Bowness-on-Windermere and then travel on the short distance to Haverthwaite and back via the heritage railway.

MEET THE WILDLIFE
Lakes Aquarium
lakesaquarium.co.uk
LA12 8AS | 015395 30153
Open daily Apr–Sep 10–6,
Oct–Mar 10–4.30

Here you can see creatures that live in and around freshwater lakes across the globe in beautifully themed displays, making it an ideal place to come if you have children. Find out about otters in Asia, piranhas in the Americas and marmosets in the rainforest, not forgetting all your favourite creatures that live a bit closer to home. These include diving ducks and otters in spectacular underwater tunnels, and freshwater rays and seahorses in the Seashore Discover Zone. Don't miss the world's first virtual dive bell. Experience an interactive adventure and come face to face with awesome virtual creatures – including a terrifying shark, charging hippo and fierce crocodile – without getting wet. Special themed events take place throughout the year.

TAKE A TRAIN RIDE
Lakeside and Haverthwaite
see page 146

TAKE A BOAT TRIP
Windermere Lake Cruises
see page 247

EAT AND DRINK
The Knoll Country House Hotel
theknoll-lakeside.co.uk
Lakeside, LA12 8AU
015395 31347

Hidden away in woodland close to the south of Windermere, this luxurious villa bills itself as a 'tranquil country retreat'. It has eight en-suite rooms as well as a self-contained apartment with separate access. The secluded garden beckons in the summer, or, in winter, relax in front of an open fire.

Lakeside ◉◉

lakesidehotel.co.uk

LA12 8AT | 015395 30001

The Lakeside hotel and spa sits, as you might expect, right on the water's edge at the southern shore of Lake Windermere, surrounded by wooded slopes. It started out as a coaching inn in the 17th century, and is now a substantial building, with a lakeside terrace, spa and pool. There's a brasserie as well as the Lakeview restaurant which looks out over the boats bobbing on the water. Main courses on the interesting modern British menu show that the kitchen has a thoroughly modern outlook, and the bulk of ingredients are sourced locally.

▶ PLACES NEARBY

Newby Bridge

Newby Bridge marks the southern limit of Windermere, where it drains into the River Leven. There is a convenient stop here on the Lakeside–Haverthwaite Railway (see page 146), so it's possible to combine a charming steam train journey and a lake cruise with a visit here.

Stott Park Bobbin Mill

english-heritage.org.uk

LA12 8AX | 01539 531087

Open Apr–Oct Wed–Sun 10–5

Here, you can see the journey from tree to bobbin on the original belt-driven machinery. The 1835 building is an evocative reminder of a local industry that produced bobbins for the textile mills of Lancashire. Now preserved by English Heritage, at one time this extensive working mill produced millions of wooden bobbins for the Lancashire spinning and weaving industries. There's a family trail to give you an idea of what it was like to work at the mill.

Although the mill is small compared to others, some 250 men and boys worked here to produce 250,000 bobbins a week.

Fell Foot Park

nationaltrust.org.uk

Newby Bridge, LA12 8NN

015395 31273 | Open daily dawn until dusk

Fell Foot Park is one of the few sites on Lake Windermere's eastern shore where you can get access to the water. At this 18-acre park you'll find safe bathing, boats for hire, an adventure playground and enough space to spread a picnic blanket.

A ferry runs between Fell Foot Park and Lakeside, where you can see the terminus of the restored railway and steamer berth, as well as the Lakes Aquarium with its imaginative naturalistic displays of water and bird life in rivers, lakes and nearby Morecambe Bay.

EAT AND DRINK

The Boathouse Café

Newby Bridge LA12 8NN

015395 31275

The charming boathouse is home to an excellent National Trust-run tea room in the peaceful Fell Foot Park. Here you can enjoy refreshments, snacks, home baking and light lunches. There is a good shop too, selling foodstuffs, maps and other essentials for a day outdoors.

▶ The Langdales MAP REF 257 D2

The Langdales must be two of the most beautiful valleys in the Lake District. They are no secret, as you will discover if you try to make the circular drive around Great Langdale and Little Langdale on a weekend in summer. The road is very narrow, so it's best to park at Skelwith Bridge or Elterwater, and tackle the area on foot. There are climbs and scrambles here to challenge the sure-footed, as well as lowland rambles if you just want to enjoy the view.

At Skelwith Bridge, where the B5343 Langdale road branches off from the A593, is Skelwith Force. The path to the waterfall continues to Elterwater, where you can enjoy the view of the distinctive silhouette of the Langdale Pikes.

You can see the twin humps of Harrison Stickle at 2,415 feet and Pike of Stickle at 2,323 feet from many different points.

Beyond the village of Chapel Stile, the Great Langdale Valley opens up spectacularly. The valley floor is divided up by stone walls, dotted with farmsteads and surrounded by mountain

peaks. The valley road meanders past the Old Dungeon Ghyll Hotel, and after a steep climb the road drops, with views of Blea Tarn, into Little Langdale Valley. Though not as stunning as the main valley, it is delightful and has good footpaths. It is from Little Langdale that a minor road branches west, to become first Wrynose Pass and then Hardknott Pass (see page 144) – exciting driving if your brakes are good.

One of the best walks in the Great Langdale Valley begins at the New Dungeon Ghyll Hotel. The route passes Dungeon Ghyll Force before climbing steeply uphill by Stickle Ghyll waterfalls. A surprise awaits you at the top – the still waters of Stickle Tarn, with the vertiginous cliff-face of Pavey Ark behind.

EAT AND DRINK

The New Dungeon Ghyll Hotel
dungeon-ghyll.co.uk
Great Langdale, LA22 9JX
01539 437213
This charmingly traditional pub sits in a spectacular little spot at the foot of the Langdale Pikes and Pavey Ark. Once a farmhouse, it was transformed into an inn in 1832.

Old Dungeon Ghyll Hotel
odg.co.uk
Great Langdale, LA22 9JY
015394 37272
You'll find a warm welcome and good-value food in this family-run inn. The ODG has been catering for travellers for 300 years and is usually full to overflowing with outdoor types. The Hiker's Bar is deservedly popular. As well as real ales

▼ Little Langdale

there is a large selection of the finest Scotch whisky's and a large wine cellar.

Three Shires Inn

threeshiresinn.co.uk
Little Langdale, LA22 9NZ
015394 37215

Comfortably fitting into a break in the drystone walls and hedges bordering the lane leading to the Wrynose and Hard Knott passes is this slate-built pub. It's Lakeland through and through, from its Cumbrian-sourced food, and real ales from Hawkshead to Hesket Newmarket and its comfortable accommodation. Everyone – including families and dogs – is welcome in the bar for a ploughman's, a ciabatta, a sandwich, or even a lamb stew. When it's cold there's a fire; when it's warm the place to be is the garden.

▶ **PLACES NEARBY**

Langdale, with its tranquillity and away-from-it-all atmosphere, makes a good contrast to the bustle of nearby Grasmere (see page 133) and Ambleside (see page 55).

▶ Levens Hall   MAP REF 258 B5

levenshall.co.uk
LA8 0PD | 015395 60321 | Open Apr to mid-Oct Sun–Thu;
Gardens 10–5, Hall 12–4

Levens Hall, just south of Kendal, is well worth a visit. The beginnings of the hall can be traced back to a 14th-century pele tower. Typically square, with thick walls and narrow windows, the towers allowed the wealthier landowners to protect their families, livestock and servants in times of danger. The grim medieval tower at Levens was later incorporated into a more elaborate Elizabethan building to create a comfortable family home. Levens Hall has passed through many hands, but in 1688 it came into the possession of Colonel James Grahme, supposedly as a result of a card game, and was passed on to Grahme's descendants, the Bagots, who still live at Levens.

As a result of this long family connection, you'll find an atmosphere of care and comfort here. Levens is still full of furniture and possessions, brought to the house by Colonel Grahme at the end of the 17th century. One of the Bagot ancestors married the Duke of Wellington's niece, bringing into the family a number of Napoleonic relics, including his cloak clasp of two bees, taken after Waterloo, and a superb Sèvres chocolate service made for the Emperor's mother. You can also see the earliest English patchwork quilt, made by Colonel Grahme's daughters from rare Indian cottons in about 1708. The family even owns one of the bowls Sir Francis Drake was using on Plymouth Hoe when the Armada was sighted.

As fine as the house is, its most famous feature is the topiary gardens. Colonel Grahme had a passion for gardening and engaged Monsieur Beaumont to create a topiary garden, in which yew trees were clipped into a variety of shapes – resembling nothing so much as a surreal set of chess pieces. Beaumont laid out the Hampton Court Palace gardens and spent the last 40 years of his life working at Levens Hall. You can see a portrait of him in the hall with the inscription: 'Gardener to King James ll and Colonel James Grahme.' The designs seen today, probably the finest examples in the country, are much as they were designed three centuries ago. It is the finest, oldest and most extensive topiary garden in the world. There are over 100 pieces here, each clipped to an unusual and individual design. Beaumont's imagination knew no limits and he created designs representing graceful birds, elegant beasts, chess pieces and even teacups and saucers.

Levens Hall has more than its share of ghosts too. One is the Grey Lady, able to walk straight through walls, and supposed to be the ghost of a gypsy woman who was refused refreshment at the hall. It is reported that she put a curse on the house, saying that no male would inherit Levens Hall until the River Kent ceased to flow and a white deer was seen in the park. The hall did indeed pass through the female line until the birth of Alan Desmond Bagot in 1896 – an event that coincided with the river freezing over and the appearance of a white fawn.

▼ Levens Hall

▶ Little Salkeld
see **Great Salkeld & Little Salkeld**, page 137

▶ Lorton Vale   MAP REF 260 C4

Lorton Vale is the valley that sweeps south from Cockermouth – passing the village of Loweswater, Crummock Water and finally Buttermere – before ending in the lofty Honister Pass. Five miles southeast of Cockermouth is the village of Lorton, which is divided in two. High Lorton clings to the side of Kirk Fell at the start of the Whinlatter Pass, and is famous for its yew tree. Wordsworth described this magnificent tree, which stands behind the village hall, in his poem 'Yew Trees'. It was beneath its boughs that the founder of the Quaker movement, George Fox, preached to a large crowd under the watchful eyes of Cromwell's soldiers.

At Whinlatter (see page 232), there is a Forestry Commission Visitor Centre, where you can watch the local ospreys on CCTV and discover more about this vast forest.

EAT AND DRINK
The Wheatsheaf Inn
wheatsheafinnlorton.co.uk
CA13 9UW | 01900 85199
At this white-painted, 17th-century pub you'll find an open fire in the bar and panoramic views of the lush Vale of Lorton from the child-friendly beer garden. They serve real ales from Jennings Brewery and hearty pub grub.

▶ Loweswater   MAP REF 260 C5

One of the smaller lakes, Loweswater is no less delightful for it and has the added bonus of often being less crowded than those lakes that are easier to access. To reach it, drive on the B5289 down Lorton Vale from Cockermouth but instead of continuing down the main road that leads to Crummock Water and Buttermere – as many motorists do – take a turning through Brackenthwaite. This road will take you along the north shore of the lake with parking at either end.

Loweswater village is little more than a church, a village hall and a pub, with a scattering of whitewashed farm buildings surrounded by woodland and meadows, but offers plenty of great walks in the leafy footpaths through the woods, cared for by the National Trust.

GO FISHING
Water End Farm
CA13 0SU | 01946 861465
The fishing here is controlled by the National Trust and you can get a permit from Water End

Farm. You might find the odd trout but it is mainly pike fishing here. You can also hire a rowing boat at the farm, whether for fishing or just to mess about on the lake.

▶ Maryport MAP REF 260 B3

A comparatively new Cumbrian town, Maryport was founded in 1749 to serve as a port for the coal trade, and named after Mary, the wife of the Lord of the Manor, Humphrey Senhouse II. The port quickly grew and, for a short while, was the biggest in Cumberland, with trade from the coal and iron-ore mines and also a healthy shipbuilding industry.

You can find the story of its rise and subsequent decline in the Maryport Maritime Museum. Also by the quayside is the Lake District Coast Aquarium, where you can see a surprising range of native marine and freshwater fish. On the hill above the town, the Senhouse Roman Museum, begun in 1570 by the Senhouse family, has an important collection of Roman artefacts, many found locally.

VISIT THE MUSEUMS

Maryport Maritime Museum

maryportmaritimemuseum.com
1 Senhouse Street, CA15 6AB
01900 813738 | Open Apr–Oct Tue, Thu–Sun and BHs 10.30–5. Winter Fri–Sun 10.30–4

Maryport Maritime Museum is on the quayside in the building formerly known as The Queen's Head public house. This is one of the oldest buildings in the town and, in its day, entertained and boarded a great many sailors between voyages. You can see exhibits ranging from a whale's tooth to luxury china designed for the *Titanic*. The sperm whale tooth is etched with a fascinating illustration of the whaler *Eagle*. The sailors of the 19th-century whaling ships made these intricate carvings of bone and ivory, known as 'scrimshaw' work.

Senhouse Roman Museum

senhousemuseum.co.uk
The Battery, Sea Brows, CA15 6JD
01900 816168 | Open Apr–Oct daily 10–5, Nov–Mar Fri–Sun 10.30–4

This small but fascinating museum is in the Battery, an old naval building, overlooking the Solway Firth. Most of the objects in the museum come from the fort at Maryport and the Roman settlement attached to it. John Senhouse rescued some pieces from Maryport's Roman fort in the 1570s and the family continued to add to it over the centuries. You can see the largest group of Roman military altar stones and inscriptions from any site in Britain. In the grounds, you can climb the observation tower for a clear view of the full extent of the settlement – one of the largest and best preserved Roman buildings in the north.

MEET THE SEALIFE
Lake District Coast Aquarium

coastaquarium.co.uk

South Quay, CA15 8AB

01900 817760 | Open daily 10–5

You can see aquatic life, both native and exotic, seawater and freshwater in the myriad tanks and pools in this award-winning attraction. There is a rock pool to investigate, rays that can be stroked, cascading pools of trout and even a shipwreck.

If the kids have had enough of sea life, they can let off some steam in the nautical themed adventure play park.

TIE UP
Maryport Marina

maryportharbour.com

Marine Road, CA15 8AY

01900 814431

If you're cruising the west coast, this is a good place for boats of up to 60 feet to stay for a short stopover. There are 190 pontoon berthings sheltered at all points from the weather. There is a range of services and amenities, including electricity and water on pontoons, showers and toilets and boat repairs.

PLAY A ROUND
Maryport Golf Course

maryportgolfclub.co.uk

Bankend, CA15 6PA

01900 812605 | Open daily

This is a tight seaside links course exposed to Solway breezes, with fine views across Solway Firth. The course has nine links holes and nine parkland holes, and the small streams can be hazardous on several holes. The first three holes have the seashore on their left and you can easily land in the water with a badly judged tee shot. Holes 6–14 are gently undulating open parkland, with holes 15–18 reverting to links.

▷ **PLACES NEARBY**
Allonby beach

This is a superb long sand and shingle beach with views across the Solway to the hills of southern Scotland and, on a clear day, as far as the Isle of Man. It has been a popular spot for sea bathing since the 18th century but these days you're as likely to see windsurfers enjoying the water.

▷ Millom   MAP REF 256 C4

Sitting on a peninsula, overlooking the River Duddon, Millom is well off the beaten track. The town grew with the iron and steel industries in the latter years of the 19th century. The Millom Folk Museum and TIC are both in the redeveloped railway station, now called the Millom Discovery Centre.

The Hodbarrow Iron Works, which closed in the 1960s, has been encouraged to go back to nature and the resulting brackish lagoon is now an RSPB reserve, attracting breeding wildfowl, waders and the rare natterjack toad.

VISIT THE MUSEUM

Millom Discovery Centre

millomdiscoverycentre.co.uk
Station Buildings, LA18 5AA
01229 772555 | Open all year
Mon–Sat 10.30–3.30, Sun
10.30–1.30

Completely refurbished, this museum features vivid reminders of the town's iron-mining days, including a mining cage from the Hodbarrow Mine. There's a reconstructed miner's cottage and displays of clothing in the dressmaker's shop. You can also find out about Millom in the war years and its ship-building past; Norman Nicholson, Millom's own poet; and, of course, in the station building, the story of the extensive rail network of yesteryear.

SEE A LOCAL CHURCH

Holy Trinity Church

Salthouse Road, LA18 5EY
Surrounded by farmland, Holy Trinity is close to the ruined 12th-century Millom Castle. The church was built in the 12th century, extended in the 13th century with a south aisle and enlarged again in the 14th century. Inside you'll find monuments to the Huddleston family of Millom Castle – the highlight is a fine 15th-century carved alabaster tomb of rare beauty and workmanship. It consists of the reclining effigies of a man and a woman, with the representation of six angels on either side, each bearing a scroll. Although the communion

▲ Millom Castle

rail contains work from the 1630s and the box pews remain, many of its interior features are Victorian. There are several interesting stained-glass windows, one called the 'fish' window due to its shape. In the churchyard are further monuments to the Huddlestons, including a sundial.

▶ **PLACES NEARBY**

Hodbarrow Nature Reserve

rspb.org.uk
01697 351330 | Open all year daily
This is a small RSPB Nature Reserve on the site of the

Hodbarrow Mine, which ceased production in the late 1960s. It's part of the Duddon Estuary Site of Special Scientific Interest, and you'll stand a good chance of hearing natterjack toads even if you don't see them. (Cumbria is home to about 50 per cent of the country's population.) You'll also find pleasant walks in flower-rich grasslands, with marsh orchids, bee orchids and rare flora and fauna. Look out for butterflies, skylarks, peregrine falcons, terns and occasionally the sight of dancing crested grebes.

Swinside Stone Circle
see page 215

▶ Milnthorpe   MAP REF 258 B5

Seven miles south of Kendal, Milnthorpe is an ancient market town of beautiful, old, limestone buildings and narrow lanes. The Market Square is bordered on three sides by pretty cottages and shops. The fourth side opens out on to green lawns and trees leading up to the 19th-century Church of St Thomas.

WALK THE CUMBRIA COASTAL WAY
see page 94

EAT AND DRINK
The Olive Tree
49 Beetham Road, LA7 7QN
015395 63233
This friendly little cafe makes a good stopping point for anything from breakfast to high tea. The usual paninis, soups and baked potatoes are all on offer, but they also serve up a range of more substantial meals with stir fries, home-made pies and salads.

▶ PLACES NEARBY
Lakeland Wildlife Oasis
wildlifeoasis.co.uk
Hale, LA7 7FE | 015395 63027
Open daily 10–5
This is a great all-weather activity for children of all ages. There are clouds of free-flying butterflies, exotic vegetation, fish, reptiles, birds and mammals. There are a number of intriguing working models, hands-on exhibits, computer programmes and a range of live animals to demonstrate life on Earth, through 3,000 million years of evolution. The meerkats are a particular favourite with children, especially when there are babies to coo over. Check the website for special events.

Heron Corn Mill
heronmill.org
Mill Lane, Beetham, LA7 7PQ
015395 64271 | Open all year
Wed–Sun 11–4
Here you can see a working watermill grinding corn. It is a Grade II listed 18th-century mill on the banks of the beautiful River Bela. A mill existed on this site before

1096 and then in 1220 the Lord of the Manor gave the monks of St Marie's York the right to grind their grain at his mill.

**The Wheatsheaf
at Beetham**

wheatsheafbeetham.com

LA7 7AL | 015395 62123

In the 17th century, this was a charming old farmhouse and the farmer's wife would feed the hungry labourers; it later became a popular coaching inn.

Today its long history of providing refreshment for weary and budget-conscious travellers continues with an intriguing offer from owners Jean and Richard Skelton: order a main course and pay just 1p for your starter or dessert – the fare on offer is well-cooked and satisfying. The Old Tap Bar offers Thwaites Wainwright, Tirril Queen Jean and Cross Bay Nightfall real ales, as well as Kingstone Press cider.

▸ Morecambe Bay   MAP REF 257 E5

With the mountains of the Lake District to the north, and changing patterns of water and light on the largest area of inter-tidal sands and mudflats in Britain, Morecambe Bay is an impressive sight on a vast scale. Water levels can vary by up to 34 feet at spring tides – be aware, the incoming waters advance faster than anyone can run.

At low tide, in favourable weather conditions and only with an expert guide (ask at the tourist information centre if you would like to book one), it is possible to walk across the sands from Morecambe, on the south side, to Grange-over-Sands. You should never attempt this on your own, however – the shifting sands, quicksands and currents make it extremely dangerous.

Morecambe's rail link to West Yorkshire made it a popular holiday resort for people from the Bradford area, but it saw a serious decline in the 1980s and 1990s. More recently, it has turned itself around. The town's revival has included the conversion of the former promenade railway station into the Platform Arts Centre, a stylish restoration of the gracefully curved art deco Midland Hotel, and transformation of the remains of the 1850s harbour into the Stone Jetty walkway. You can walk along here and enjoy the sculptures, games and poems carved in the stone and then watch a breathtaking Morecambe Bay sunset. There's also a campaign to re-open the Winter Gardens, a gorgeous Victorian theatre.

On the 4-mile long promenade, which is perfect for an early morning or afternoon stroll, you can see a slightly larger-than-life statue of the town's favourite son, Eric Morecambe (born

▲ Morecambe Bay

Eric Bartholomew), who took his stage name from his boyhood home and became as popular as the resort in its heyday. All this is a long way from Morecambe's humble origins as the little fishing village of Poulton-le-Sands, though the boats still fish locally for whitebait, cockles and, perhaps most famously, shrimps.

INDULGE YOURSELF
**Morecambe Bay
Brown Shrimps**
Available from local
fishmongers, Morecambe Bay
Brown Shrimps are renowned
for their delicate taste and
texture; they have been caught
locally for hundreds of years.
Fishing methods may have
changed but you can still find
the shrimps made to the same
traditional recipe. Locally
caught shrimps are cooked in
butter and then sealed and
packed into pots.

▶ Muncaster Castle MAP REF 256 C3

muncaster.co.uk
CA18 1RQ | 01229 717614 | Castle open Mar–Oct Sun–Fri 12–4, closed
Nov–Feb; gardens and owl centre open daily Mar–Oct 10.30–5, Nov–Feb
11–4

Few stately homes have a view to match the panorama from the
grand terrace of Muncaster Castle. Directly below are the gardens,
with one of the largest collections of rhododendrons in the country.
In the middle distance, the River Esk meanders prettily through the
lowlands, while the horizon is a series of stark Lakeland peaks, of
which Scafell Pike (3,210 feet, 978m) is the most prominent.

In 1208, the land at Muncaster was granted to the Pennington
family, who still own it today. The pele tower still survives beneath
later stonework, but virtually everything here today dates from the
1860s. Lord Muncaster commissioned Anthony Salvin to remodel
both the medieval remains and the 18th-century house. You can
tour the house accompanied by an audio-guided tour, recorded by
the present owner, detailing the treasures and artworks on view.

Two towers on the garden front add weight and grandeur to the
outside of this solid Victorian building, while inside there are plenty
of individual touches – for example, the hall with its enclosed

staircase, and the octagonal library, with a brass-railed gallery and fine vaulted ceiling. The rooms have splendid woodwork and panelling from Britain and the Continent, and carved chimneypieces – including one by Adam – brought from other houses. The furniture includes an Elizabethan four-poster and a superb set of Charles II walnut settees and chairs. The house contains a collection of glittering silverware by Paul Storr and a series of family portraits from the 17th century to the present.

Muncaster Castle is also the headquarters of the World Owl Trust, which is dedicated to worldwide owl conservation. You can see a variety of owls, from the pygmy owl to the gigantic eagle owl, and from native species to some of the rarest owls in the world. On fine summer afternoons you get a chance to meet the birds and watch them in flight.

As Lords of the Manor, the Pennington family owned Muncaster Mill from the 15th century right up to 1961, when the mill closed. You can easily reach the present buildings, dating from about 1700, by car on the A595 or by taking a ride on the Ravenglass & Eskdale Railway (see page 200), known affectionately as La'al Ratty. Note: Muncaster Mill is a request halt. The tiny mill, with its overshot wheel turned by the River Mite, is a reminder of a time when every village had its own corn mill. Though now restored to full working order, it is currently closed and its future is again uncertain.

SEE A LOCAL CHURCH
Church of St Michael and All Angels
CA18 1RJ

In the wooded grounds of Muncaster Castle, this church dates from the 15th century or earlier: there is evidence of a 12th-century stone in the nave. It has stained-glass windows by Henry Holiday, a Pre-Raphaelite artist who had a home in Ambleside. The west window shows the Day of Judgement: Christ in Glory with Archangel Michael. In the churchyard is a cross-shaft and wheel-head believed to date from the 10th century, a reminder of the Norse Vikings who settled here.

◀ View from Muncaster Castle

▶ **Near Sawrey** MAP REF 257 E3

A picturesque village, 2 miles from Hawkshead on the eastern side of Esthwaite Water, this tiny place is world famous for the work of one rather extraordinary woman. Beatrix Potter first came here on holiday in 1896, fell in love with the place and used the royalties from her first book, *The Tale of Peter Rabbit* (1901), to buy Hill Top. It was in this unpretentious little 17th-century farmhouse that she wrote many more of the books that have delighted children throughout the world.

The success of her books allowed Beatrix Potter to focus on her other interest – conservation – and in particular, the indigenous fell Herdwick sheep. In 1923 she bought a former deer park and farm in the Troutbeck Valley – restoring its land and thousand-strong flock of Herdwick sheep. On her death in 1943, all her properties were bequeathed to the National Trust.

TAKE IN SOME HISTORY
Hill Top
see highlight panel opposite

EAT AND DRINK
Ees Wyke Country House ◉
eeswyke.co.uk
LA22 0JZ | 015394 36393
This Georgian house above Esthwaite Water, with glorious fell views, was at one time Beatrix Potter's holiday home. It's now a comfortable, country-house hotel, where dinner is served in the dining room overlooking the lake. The daily changing four-course menu has only a couple of choices per course, but the quality is always excellent.

Sawrey House Hotel
sawreyhouse.com
LA22 0LF | 015394 36387
The location is pure Lakeland, the stone-built Victorian country house looking out over its own gardens towards Esthwaite Water and the forest of Grizedale. Those luscious views are to be enjoyed from the linened dining room, where globally inspired, locally sourced cooking displays thought, imagination and technical skill.

Tower Bank Arms
towerbankarms.co.uk
LA22 0LF | 015394 36334
The National Trust owns this 17th-century village pub on the west side of Lake Windermere although it is independently run. Situated just in front of Hill Top, it was once known as 'The Blue Pig' and later 'The Albion'. It has been the Tower Bank Arms for over a century and Beatrix Potter illustrated it perfectly in her *Tale of Jemima Puddleduck*. In the low-beamed, slate-floored main bar there's an open log fire, fresh flowers and a grandfather clock, and local brews on hand pumps from the Hawkshead and Barngates breweries. The hearty country food makes good use of local produce.

▶ Hill Top

MAP REF 257 E3

nationaltrust.org.uk
LA22 0LF | 015394 36269 | Open daily mid-Feb to Nov. Opening hours vary; check website for details This small 17th-century house is where Beatrix Potter wrote many of her famous children's stories. It remains as she left it, and in each room you can find something that appears in one of her books. Her will decreed that Hill Top should remain exactly as she had known it.

You will easily recognise details from the pictures in her books and, disregarding its rather unprepossessing exterior, Hill Top is chock full of Beatrix Potter memorabilia, including her original drawings. However, the place is so popular that it's best to avoid visiting at peak holiday times.

If you love Beatrix Potter, you'll also find lots to interest you at the Beatrix Potter Gallery (see page 147) at Hawkshead and The World of Beatrix Potter (see page 245) at Bowness.

▼ Hill Top

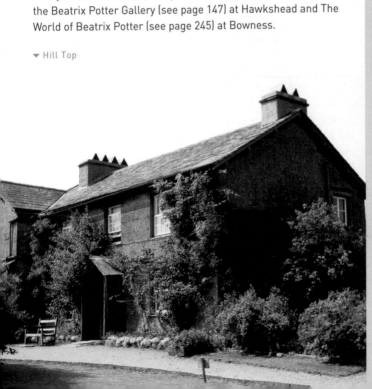

▶ Newlands   MAP REF 261 D5

Although it's close to Keswick and the busy A66, the delightful Newlands Valley is a quiet backwater. With its rolling green fields, there is little evidence left today that this was once a busy industrial mining community. In fact, you'd have to search hard to find any communities at all, as there are only a handful of farms and the two tiny hamlets of Little Town and Stair. A farmhouse at Stair has the inscription 'TF 1647'. The initials are believed to be those of Thomas Fairfax, commander of the Parliamentary forces, who stayed here after the Civil War in 1646.

Little Town's fame could hardly be more different, as its name features in Beatrix Potter's *The Tale of Mrs Tiggywinkle* – in fact Catbells, Skelgill and Little Town can all be recognised from her sketches for this book.

Copper and lead were mined on the valley's eastern slopes, and small deposits of silver and gold were also found there. Today the landscape has returned to nature, a beautiful, gentle and green landscape down in the valley, but rising up through a steep and rugged pass in the southwest before descending to Buttermere.

▶ The Pennine Way   MAP REF 263 E5

The country's premier National Trail, which follows the high Pennine ridge, has something to offer every long-distance walker. If you want to test your stamina and endurance, you could walk the whole 270 miles from the Peak District National Park along the Pennine ridge through the Yorkshire Dales, up into Northumberland and across the Cheviots. Twenty miles of the route heads through East Cumbria from Alston through Garrigill and over Cross Fell – which at 2,930 feet is the highest point on the Pennine Way – then through Great Dun Fell towards Dufton and on to High Cup Nick and Cow Green Reservoir, which are on the border between Cumbria and County Durham.

▶ Penrith MAP REF 258 B1

Another border market town that was vulnerable to Scottish raiders is Penrith and in fact it was sacked in the 14th century. Penrith Beacon on Beacon Hill at the town's northern edge was lit to warn the inhabitants of impending raids, and today it is a good viewpoint. The ruined red sandstone castle, which stands in Castle Park, dates from the early 15th century.

There are many more buildings of architectural and historical interest, including Penrith Museum and the Church of St Andrew. The graveyard here contains the reputed grave of Caesarius, the giant 10th-century Cumbrian king.

Just one mile south of Penrith at Eamont Bridge stands Mayburgh Henge. Dating from prehistoric times, its 15-foot banks surround an area of 1.5 acres, inside which is a huge and solitary stone. Close by, King Arthur's Round Table is another ancient henge monument.

Wetheriggs Pottery, also south of Penrith, has been here since 1855 and you can still see the old pottery site. When the pottery closed, its buildings were converted into an animal sanctuary, which has since moved to County Durham.

Rheged Centre, on the A66, interprets the history of the area through film and a range of innovative techniques. It has some useful shops, play areas and a cafe.

▼ Penrith Castle

TAKE IN SOME HISTORY
Penrith Castle
Opposite Penrith railway station

The castle was built in the 14th century to protect the town against border raids, and it then became a residence of Richard III in the 15th century. Although the castle is now in ruins, some of the walls stand to their full height. If you are looking for somewhere to picnic in Penrith, the park where this castle stands is an ideal spot.

VISIT THE MUSEUM
Penrith and Eden Museum
Robinson's School, Middlegate, CA11 7PT | 01768 865105 | Open Mon–Sat 10–5, also Sun Apr–Oct 11–4

You will find Penrith and Eden Museum and Tourist Information Centre in the former Robinson's School, an Elizabethan building altered in 1670 and used as a school until the early 1970s. The building is an ideal starting point if you want to explore Penrith. The museum covers the history, geology and archaeology of the area. Exhibits include some pottery from the Roman Fort near Plumpton, and 'cup and ring' stones from Maughanby. There are also displays and information relating to Lady Anne Clifford, who was a powerhouse of energy in 17th-century Cumbria. There is also a temporary gallery with changing exhibitions of local interest.

LET OFF SOME STEAM
Penrith Leisure Centre
better.org.uk
Southend Road, CA11 8JH
01768 863450 | Open Mon–Fri 6.30am–10pm, Sat 7.30am–8pm, Sun 7.30am–9pm

There are perfect wet-weather activities of every type at this excellent centre, one of a group operating across the north of England. Families can enjoy swimming or join a gym session, tackle the climbing wall, kick a ball on an Astroturf pitch or watch the younger family members enjoying the soft-play area. The sports hall offers everything from fitness classes to indoor bowls and there's an on-site cafe where you can enjoy refreshments.

▼ Mayburgh Henge

ENTERTAIN THE FAMILY
The Rheged Centre
see page 204

SEE A LOCAL CHURCH
Church of St Andrew
St Andrew's Place, CA11 7XX
Rebuilt in 1720 on an ancient site, St Andrew's is said to have been modelled on Wren's St Andrew's Church in Holborn, London. The original 13th-century tower here still stands, while the nave and chancel is built of regular sandstone blocks. The splendid and spacious Georgian internal layout is intact, with its galleries on three sides supported by two tiers of columns, and a richly decorated box-panelled ceiling. Colourful Victorian murals surround the large, vibrant stained-glass east window. In the graveyard is the Giant's Grave, a grave consisting of two tall Norse crosses between which lie four hogback stones, or grave markers. Legend has it that this is either the grave of Owen Caesarius, King of Cumbria 920–37, or his son.

GO FISHING
Blencarn Lake Stillwater Trout Fly Fishing
tuftonarmshotel.co.uk
Near Penrith | 01768 351593
The setting of Blencarn Lake is simply breathtaking, as Cross Fell and the North Pennines form a majestic backdrop to this tranquil spot. The spring-fed, 15-acre lake provides excellent stillwater fly fishing for rainbow trout. Kenny Stamper, the owner, rears the rainbow trout on site and optimum numbers are maintained. Facilities here are excellent too. There's a little bothy with toilets and an area to eat and to boil a kettle. Recommended flies when fly fishing this rainbow trout lake are Lake Olives, Buzzers, Daddies, Pheasant Tail Nymphs, Hoppers and White Lures.

PLAY A ROUND
Penrith Golf Club
penrithgolfclub.co.uk
Salkeld Road, CA11 8SG
01768 891919
This beautiful, well-balanced course is always changing direction and demanding good length from the tee. It is set on rolling moorland with occasional pine trees and splendid views of the mountains of the northern Lake District.

EAT AND DRINK
Cross Keys Inn
kyloes.co.uk
Carleton Village, CA11 8TP
01768 865588
Located on the edge of Penrith, with sweeping views to the nearby North Pennines from the upstairs restaurant, this is a much-refurbished old drovers' and coaching inn. Traditional pub meals are the order of the day with only Cumbrian meats used. You'll find appreciative locals warming their toes by the ferocious log-burner or laying a few tiles on the domino tables,

while drinking beer crafted in nearby Broughton Hall by Tirril Brewery.

The Narrowbar Café
narrowbarcafe.co.uk
13 Devonshire Street, CA11 7SR
01768 891467

The all-day breakfasts here are a real hit with visitors looking for a substantial meal. This cheerful cafe, with its outside tables and comfortable sofas, also serves a good range of lunchtime specials, with changing daily main courses, soups and vegetarian options. There's a kids' menu too, and the cafe is licensed to sell wine and beer.

The Yard Kitchen
Brunswick Road, Penrith, CA11 7LU
01768 892002

Located in a converted barn above an interesting salvage yard, this popular cafe serves tasty lunches with a continental twist and a huge range of home-made cakes. Brunswick Yard also houses Black Hand Wine, an expert wine-maker and merchant specialising in organic products.

▷ PLACES NEARBY
Lakeland Bird of Prey Centre
lbpc.co.uk
Lowther, CA10 2HH | 01931 712746
Open daily 11.30–5

There are flying demonstrations with 150 falcons, hawks, eagles, buzzards and owls from this country and abroad. The birds fly every day at 2pm and you can actually have them come to you. Children particularly like this. The bird handler is very knowledgeable and will tell you all about the birds and answer any questions. There is a small tea room serving snacks and cakes.

Church of St Andrew
Church Road, Greystoke, CA11 0TL

This church is famous for its ancient choir stalls in the chancel with carved misericords featuring Christian symbols such as a pelican and a dragon, and a fine collection of medieval glass. According to village lore, the glass was removed in haste and buried as Cromwell and his army approached, and then finally restored in 1848. But the restorers had difficulty in re-assembling the pieces in the original order and substituted fragments from other, destroyed, windows. In the East window look at the extreme left, middle height, and you will see a curious sight – a red devil beneath the feet of a bishop – but the devil was originally in another window, whispering to Eve in the Garden of Eden.

The bestiary window on the north side of the chancel is the oldest glass; other ancient glass is behind the organ and in the clear window above the Lady Chapel altar. Due to the value of the latter, fragments have been joined with lead.

Modern times have left their mark on St Andrew's too. A sculpture of the Madonna and Child was carved by two

German prisoners of war who were held at Carlisle at the end of World War II. Another, of the crucified Christ on the west wall, is by the sculptor Josefina de Vasconcellos, who lived in Cumbria.

Look for the stone by the path leading from the church to Thorpe. Known as the Plague Stone, its hollowed top, which fills with rainwater, may have once held vinegar in which coins were purified when plague victims paid their dues.

Yanwath

Yanwath is a village between the North Pennines and the hills bounding Ullswater. Yanwath Hall, on the southern side of the River Eamont, is a splendidly preserved low 14th-century pele tower and a 15th-century hall, reputed to be the finest manorial hall in England.

The Yanwath Gate Inn
yanwathgate.co.uk
Yanwath, CA10 2LF | 01768 862386
This one-time tollgate house dates from 1683, evolving into a pub several centuries later. Its favoured location between the fells and lakes, in an area of country estates and the rich pasturelands of the Eden Valley, holds the promise of great food and drink. Some of the best Cumbrian microbrewery beers from the likes of Yates and Barngates draw guests into the country-style interior with lots of beams and old pine. Lunch and evening menus vary, and content depends on seasonal or specialist availability. For lighter eaters there's an impressive tapas menu.

Upfront Gallery and Café
up-front.com
Unthank, Penrith, CA11 9TG
017684 84538
You can eat inside or on the patio at this laid-back vegetarian cafe, where everything is locally sourced and freshly prepared daily. Follow your panini, chilli or pasta with a good sticky toffee pudding before a browse in the adjoining gallery, where artists from all over Cumbria exhibit their work during the summer.

Church of St Michael
Barton, Tirril, off the B5320, CA10 2LR
In open countryside with fantastic views to the Lakeland fells, the church is on a mound in the centre of a circular graveyard. The church has a squat 12th-century central tower, with narrow windows, which may have been used for defence during the border raids. Although the church has been extended, you can clearly see the original Norman structure in the recently exposed stonework. All four corners of the Norman nave survive, and the north and south aisles were added in the 13th and early 14th centuries. Have a look at the attractive, stained-glass west window, designed by Charles Kempe in 1912.

▶ Ravenglass MAP REF 256 B3

Up to 1,000 Romans were garrisoned in Ravenglass, and the fort and harbour at Ravenglass were known to them as *Glannoventa*. Little remains of this settlement, just a short stroll to the south of the village, except for the ruins of the bathhouse. Ravenglass today comprises a short street of houses that ends abruptly at a slipway down to the beach and the estuaries of the rivers Mite and Esk. The town is now best known for the Ravenglass and Eskdale Railway, which is affectionately known as 'La'al Ratty'.

TAKE A TRAIN RIDE

Ravenglass & Eskdale Railway
ravenglass-railway.co.uk
CA18 1SW | 01229 717171 | Open mid-Mar to early Nov daily, most winter weekends daily between Christmas & New Year & Feb half-term. Call or check website for timetable

The Lake District's oldest, longest and most scenic steam railway stretches from the coast at Ravenglass, through two of Lakeland's loveliest valleys for 7 miles to Dalegarth Visitor Centre and the foot of England's highest mountains. There are at least seven trains daily from March to November, plus winter weekends and holiday periods. If you have children, this is a perfect day out for them. Check the website for all sorts of children's activities with Ratty the Water-vole Stationmaster and special event days.

Though it is now one of the most popular visitor attractions in western Lakeland, the line has had a distinctly chequered career. The railway – with a 3-foot gauge track – was built

in 1875, to carry iron ore and a few passengers from the Eskdale mines down to the coast and the main Furness line. When the mines became unprofitable, the railway closed. Then on a narrower 15-inch gauge track, it reopened in 1913 to serve Eskdale's granite quarries and to carry a few tourists until it came to a halt once again in 1953. Fortunately, a group of enthusiasts bought up the line in 1960 to run it as a tourist attraction.

Ravenglass Roman Bath House
english-heritage.org.uk
CA18 1SR | Open daily, dawn to dusk
The remains of the Roman bathhouse are among the tallest Roman structures in northern Britain: the walls stand almost 13 feet high. You can also see the earthworks of the fort nearby.

WALK THE CUMBERLAND WAY
This is an old path and no longer completely signposted. It is a tough trail and you have to be fit but it takes you through the heart of the Lake District. It is about 80 miles from Ravenglass to Appleby and takes about a week to 10 days to complete. However, you are well rewarded for your efforts as the path leads you to remote Wast Water, the most atmospheric of all the lakes, through spectacular scenery over Black Sail Pass and then below the high peaks – Great Gable, Scafell Pike, Pillar and Haystacks. There's another high-level route to the gentler Newlands Valley, the shores of Derwentwater and Keswick. From here you climb again to the Castlerigg Stone Circle (see page 101), with views back to Derwentwater and Bassenthwaite Lake. You continue through high moorland and farmland and come in sight of the Pennines before finally reaching Appleby.

5 top fells

▶ Scafell Pike 3,210 feet/978m

▶ Scafell, 3,162 feet/964m

▶ Helvellyn, 3116 feet/950m, page 150

▶ Skiddaw, 3,054 feet/931m, page 215

▶ Great Gable, 2,949 feet/899m, page 137

◀ Ravenglass and Eskdale Railway

EXPLORE BY BIKE

The Eskdale Trail

Have a cycling day out with a difference. Take your bike on a converted carriage on the Ravenglass and Eskdale Railway (see page 200) then ride from the foot of the Scafell range via riverside pastures, meadows and historic oak woods of the Eskdale Valley back down to Ravenglass. The train ride from Ravenglass to Dalegarth takes 40 minutes, biking down around two hours, depending on how often you stop. It's easy biking most of the way on country lanes, rough tracks and fields, though it can be muddy at times. On the way look out for red squirrels, roe deer and buzzards or you could visit Muncaster Castle (see page 190) or St Bega's Church (see page 205).

EAT AND DRINK

The Pennington Hotel ◉

penningtonhotels.com

CA18 1SD | 01229 717222

The venerable black and white hotel wears its age on its sleeve, having started out as a coaching inn in the Tudor era. A latter-day wash and brush-up has put it once more at the centre of life in its picturesque village, with Muncaster Castle for company. Culinary modernism is the order of the day in the light, relaxing dining room.

▶ PLACES NEARBY

Tiny Boot, with a population of less than 100, can be found along the Ravenglass and Eskdale Railway. Eskdale is another popular stop and a good base for walking. The hamlet of Santon Bridge in the Wasdale Valley is laid out around the bridge over the River Irt. It's famous for its World's Biggest Liar contest, held each November at the Bridge Inn.

Arriving here from the east, you will have crossed the dramatic Hardknott Pass with its Roman fort (see page 144), possibly one of the least welcome postings any Roman soldier could ever have had. The road continues towards the coast to join the A595, where you could turn north to Hallsenna Moor, a lowland heath and peat nature reserve. It's never been cut for peat so still retains a wide variety of plants, insects and birds – follow the boardwalks across the springy, wet moor to hunt for sundew, an insect-devouring plant.

Further south down the main road from here is Muncaster Castle (see page 190), a stately pile with lovely gardens that's home to a huge collection of many species of owl.

Eskdale Mill

eskdalemill.co.uk

CA19 1TG | 01946 723335

Check website or call for details on opening times

Eskdale Mill promises a fascinating day out, as here you can take a tour of the historic machinery of one of the oldest water-powered corn mills in England. The setting on the leafy banks of Whillan Beck, cascading down from the flanks of Scafell is truly stunning. The miller's tour is a mixture of tales of historic characters, demonstrations of the workings of the mill and the answers to any questions you care to fire at him.

Brook House Inn

brookhouseinn.co.uk
Boot, CA19 1TG | 019467 23288
Lakeland fells rise behind the inn to England's highest peak, while footpaths wind to nearby Stanley Ghyll's wooded gorge with its pretty falls, red squirrels and the charming La'al Ratty narrow-gauge railway which steams to and from the coast. There's a small drying room for walkers' or cyclists' wet gear. Up to seven real ales are kept, an amazing selection of 175 malt whiskies and there are excellent wines available by the glass. They serve lunch and dinner and the food is home-made, simply prepared from Cumbria's finest produce. This is a great community pub and it participates in the Boot Beer Festival each June.

Fellbites

ravenglass-railway.co.uk
Dalegarth Station, CA19 1TF
01229 717171
At the valley terminus of 'La'al Ratty' the Fellbites cafe serves a trainload of passengers at a time with freshly cooked, locally sourced food. It is also very handily placed for the train back to Ravenglass.

Bower House Inn

bowerhouseinn.com
Eskdale Green, CA19 1TD
019467 23244
Walkers, families and dogs are all welcome, and you'll find good pub grub at this traditional Lake District hotel, which has been serving locals and walkers since the 17th century. Inside, oak beams, ticking clocks and crackling log fires create an inviting and relaxing atmosphere in which to enjoy a pint of Bower House bitter. The comfortable bar opens out on to the garden.

Bridge Inn

santonbridgeinn.com
Santon Bridge, CA19 1UX
019467 26221
The Lake District was formed, not by ice or volcanic action but by large moles and eels. Actually, that's a lie, one of the many incredible lies told in this comfortable old inn at the annual World's Biggest Liar competition, held every November. No doubt pints of local real ales help to inspire such outrageous fibbing. With the new owners come new set menus and the chef's specials chalked up on the board. The inn is licensed for civil marriages, when, hopefully, 'I do' is not a lie.

Woodlands

santonbridge.co.uk

Santon Bridge, Near Holmrook

CA19 1UY | 019467 26281

With a great view of the local red squirrels, Woodlands tea room is attached to the Santon Bridge Craft Shop and concentrates on providing wholesome home-made food. It's handy for visiting Muncaster Castle and Eskdale, as well as Wasdale. Browse through the pretty craft shop while you are here. You will find a range of china, ceramics, leather goods, sheepskins and much more to take home with you.

▶ **Rheged**   MAP REF 258 B1

rheged.com

Redhills, CA11 0DQ | 01768 868000 | Open all year daily 10–5.30

Rheged was the name of an ancient Celtic kingdom that dominated northwest England and southern Scotland in the sixth century AD. Today it is Cumbria's largest visitor complex, and Europe's largest grass-covered building. You could happily spend a rainy day or two rattling around in here. As well as the cinema, cafes, specialist food shops and shops selling outdoor gear, books and toys, there is a large exhibition space, which hosts touring exhibitions from time to time. You can watch a changing selection of movies suitable for all the family on a giant screen and there are both indoor and outdoor play areas for children.

▶ **Rydal Mount & Gardens**

see page 206

▶ **St Bees**   MAP REF 260 A5

St Bees is the start of Lake District walking writer Alfred Wainwright's most celebrated route, the 190-mile Coast-to-Coast walk to Robin Hood's Bay in North Yorkshire. The impressive sandstone cliffs of St Bees Head rise to 300 feet.

Out to sea are views across the Irish Sea to the Isle of Man and over the Solway Firth to the hills of Galloway in Scotland. This part of the coast is Cumbria's only Heritage Coast, with land on the cliffs forming the St Bees Head RSPB Reserve. From the viewing areas, maintained by a seasonal warden, you can watch the noisy birdlife nesting on the cliffs below. Many thousands of birds return here each spring to lay their eggs and hatch their chicks before returning to the sea, where they spend three-quarters of their lives. Most prolific are the guillemots, which resemble dumpy little penguins; some 5,000 squeeze precariously onto the narrow open ledges. Razorbills, not so common, can also be seen here along with fulmars, gulls and some 1,600 pairs of kittiwakes.

The first St Bees Lighthouse consisted of a round tower of some 30 feet in height, supporting a large metal coal grate. It was the last coal-fired lighthouse in use in Great Britain when it burned down in 1822. The present lighthouse was automated in 1987 and is now monitored by Trinity House Operations Control Centre at Harwich in Essex.

In the village is the Church of St Mary and St Bega, once the nave of a priory that was partly demolished after the Reformation. St Bega is said to have been an Irish princess who fled across the sea in the ninth century to escape an enforced marriage.

SEE A LOCAL CHURCH
Priory Church of St Mary and St Bega
Abbey Road, off the B5345, CA27 0DR

The splendid 12th-century Priory Church of St Mary and St Bega has a magnificent tower, which is a significant landmark in the village. The south transept, the base of the tower and the west door remain from the original 12th-century building. Have a good look at the west door with its five semicircular arches decorated with beaked heads of men and serpents. In the wall opposite the door is the Dragon Stone, which has a carving of St Michael killing a dragon.

The priory has had a number of restorations. In 1855–68, the outstanding decorative chancel screen was installed, together with bright tiles and patterns designed to take the place of an east window. Before the restoration, the priory had a flat ceiling with box pews in the nave; in the 1960s, a central aisle was created. Within the church there are a number of carved stones, medieval slabs and effigies dating from the 10th century onwards, as well as part of the shroud of St Bees Man, one of England's best-preserved medieval bodies, which was found in the priory during an archaeological dig in 1981.

A ninth-century carved Celtic cross stands in the graveyard, a reminder of the pre-Norman church that once stood here.

HIT THE BEACH
St Bees

St Bees Bay extends in a long sweep from the promenade to Seamill Lane about a mile away. At low tide it is a vast expanse of red sand and rock pools. At the foot of the cliffs there is a shingle bank composed of dozens of types of rock sloping down to the sand. For two to three hours on either side of high tide only the shingle is clear of the water.

▶ Rydal Mount & Gardens

MAP REF 257 E2

rydalmount.co.uk

LA22 9LU | 015394 33002 | Open Mar–Oct daily 9.30–5, Nov & Feb Wed–
Sun 11–4. Closed Dec & Jan

Rydal Mount was William Wordsworth's home from 1813 until his
death in 1850. He came to this lime-washed yeoman's house on
May Day. 'The weather is delightful and the place a Paradise,'
wrote his sister Dorothy. His was a large household – it included
not only the poet and his wife Mary, but his three surviving children
and Mary's sister Sarah Hutchinson, as well as Dorothy. The move
was partly financed by Wordsworth's appointment as Distributor of
Stamps for Westmorland, which brought him his first and only
steady income, and earned Browning's scorn: 'Just for a handful
of silver he left us,' he wrote in *The Lost Leader*, 'Just for a riband
to stick in his coat.'

More than half of Wordsworth's published poetry was written
at Rydal Mount. The house was originally a farm built in 1550;
the dining room still has its early timbers and slate floor and
was enlarged about the middle of the 18th century. Wordsworth
himself was particularly attracted to the traditional style of the

house and its spectacular views over Rydal Water and Windermere. He never owned the house but leased it from the le Flemings of nearby Rydal Hall.

Wordsworth believed that a house and its garden should harmonise with each other and with their locality, and the garden here is still much as he left it, with terraces stretching across the hillside. The highest was already there when he took over the house, but he added two others – one so that Dorothy could be pushed in her invalid chair to enjoy the view. Wordsworth would pace along behind, booming new poems to himself. If you visit on a spring day Dora's Field – bought for, and named after, the poet's daughter – is crowded with wild daffodils. Even those who cannot recall another line of his poetry will know about the 'host of golden daffodils'. A walk that his sister Dorothy took along the shores of Ullswater, recorded in her diary, inspired the poem.

While living in Rydal Mount, William Wordsworth accepted the post of Poet Laureate at the age of 73, but on the strict condition that he would not be expected to compose verses on demand, the bane of most Poet Laureates.

The house was bought in 1969 by Mary Henderson, the poet's great, great-granddaughter, and opened to the public the following year, displaying mementoes of a life devoted to literature and the Romantic movement.

Fleswick Bay

This bay has one of the grandest situations of any beach in Britain, between the North Head and the South Head of St Bees. You can only reach it on foot or by boat, as towering red sandstone cliffs enclose the shingle beach. If you want to walk here, you can cross the footbridge at the north end of the promenade and walk up the South Head and along the cliff path. There is a footpath down to Fleswick Bay. At one time the shingle had many semi-precious stones, such as agates, but years of collection by visitors have made these rare. But it's worth having a look though, as you might find one along with the odd pretty pebble or two.

GO WALKING

Coast-to-Coast Walk

This 190-mile coastal walk from St Bees Head to Robin Hood's Bay, North Yorkshire, was created by Alfred Wainwright (see page 36). It passes through some of the most beautiful and varied scenery in the country, the rugged mountains and beautiful lakes of the Lake District, the rolling hills and pretty valleys of the Yorkshire Dales and the expansive heather moorland of the North York Moors, with some dramatic coastal scenery at each end. Wainwright suggested a way of breaking the walk into stages, each of which could be completed in a day. With one or two rest days, this makes the route fit into a

▼ The coastline of St Bees

two-week holiday. However, Wainwright explicitly stated that he did not intend people to necessarily stick to these stages or even to his route: for example, by reducing day-lengths to 10 or 12 miles, the walk becomes a much easier three-week trip with time to 'stand and stare'.

Although unofficial, the Coast-to-Coast Walk uses public rights of way, public footpaths, tracks and minor roads and is one of the most popular of all the long-distance footpaths in the UK. Much of it is now waymarked, but you still need your map and compass for this walk and a copy of Alfred Wainwright's book will add even more to your enjoyment. Wainwright recommended dipping your toes in the Irish Sea at St Bees at the start of the walk and dipping your toes in the North Sea at Robin Hood's Bay at the end. In between, as well as the scenery, you will enjoy the welcoming inns with cosy nooks and open fires and the satisfaction of achievement at the end.

PLAY A ROUND
St Bees Golf Club
stbeesgolfclub.co.uk
Peckmill Lane, St Bees, CA27 0EJ
01946 824300 | Open daily
Overlooking St Bees beach, this picturesque 10-hole layout on the cliffs was originally designed as a golf course for St Bees School. It has glorious views of the Solway Firth and the Isle of Man. There are some testing hazards for all golfers.

▶ Sedbergh MAP REF 258 C4

Thanks to the quirks of local government boundary changes, the largest town in the Yorkshire Dales National Park is actually in Cumbria. Even so, Sedbergh's population is still under 3,000. To the north are the high Howgill Fells. To the south the green fields fall away, across the River Rawthey to the River Dee, which runs through Dentdale. Take some time to explore this delightful and historic little town.

The old buildings of Sedbergh are its main attraction. Much of the Main Street has been designated a Conservation Area. As well as narrow alleys and tucked-away yards, Main Street contains many fine dwellings. The Sleepy Elephant outdoor gear shop dates from the first half of the 17th century, and behind it is Weaver's Yard, where the first weaving looms in Sedbergh were set up. From here, just at the back of the shop, a 17th-century chimney breast can be seen – one of the many places around Britain in which Bonnie Prince Charlie is said to have hidden at one time or another. You'll also find lots of bookshops because Sedbergh is a 'Book Town' and holds a Book Festival each September and many other book events.

Little remains of the Norman castle save a few grassy mounds, but the Church of St Andrew is worth seeing, with its ancient pews and alms boxes. Close by is the minuscule Market Place, where a market was held for almost 750 years – it now takes place on Wednesdays at Joss Lane. The Market Cross was removed in 1897 when Finkle Street was widened and other alterations made to the town as part of Queen Victoria's Diamond Jubilee celebrations. The top of the cross now stands in the garden of the Quaker Meeting House in Brigflatts, a tiny village just over one mile away. The Meeting House, built in 1675, can still be visited. It is the oldest in the north of England and retains many of its original furnishings.

ENTERTAIN THE FAMILY
Holme Open Farm
holmeopenfarm.co.uk
Off A683, LA10 5ET
015396 20654 | Open Mar–Aug
Sat–Sun 10–5, Mon & Wed–Fri 11–4;
Sep Sat–Sun 10–5

Holme Open Farm is a traditional dales working farm. You can take a tour of the farm, giving children the chance to touch, hold and feed as many different types of animal as possible. Holding and bottle-feeding baby lambs is really exciting; stroking the goats and kids is fun; sometimes being nibbled by them produces shrieks of laughter. And even the most timid children love feeding the tiny chicks. There are also ducks, geese, pigs, ponies and kittens.

Take a wander with the kids on the nature trail through the 120-acre farm, where you'll see a variety of birds, plants and other wildlife. There's even a badger hide where you can sit in the evening and watch quietly for these nocturnal beasts. The cafe offers refreshment after all the excitement.

GO FISHING
Rawthey, also Clough and Dee
Permits available from Sedbergh Mini Market, 73 Main Street LA10 5AB | 015396 20913

The Rawthey, which flows south from the Howgill Fells behind Sedbergh, is open and is easy to fish it but it doesn't hold as many trout as the Dee, which flows down Dentdale. The Rawthey has sea trout and salmon later in the season.

EXPLORE THE WORKING PAST
Farfield Mill
farfieldmill.org
Garsdale Road, LA10 5LW
015396 21958 | Open daily 10.30–5 (closes 4pm in winter)

Until the early 1990s Farfield was a functioning woollen mill, and it's now a great heritage and arts and crafts centre. Sprawling over four floors, there's lots to see, from the old mill machinery on the ground floor, to workshops, galleries, studios and changing exhibitions. Weekends see master weavers working the old machines, or you could watch

▲ The confluence of the rivers Rawthey and Dee near Sedbergh

a video about the mill's story and browse in the gallery and bookshop. Children's craft workshops run throughout the summer, and in September the people of Sedbergh join the mill in celebrating their history by creating a 'sheep trail' throughout the town – you'll see woolly wonders everywhere.

EAT AND DRINK
Dalesman Country Inn
thedalesman.co.uk
Main Street, LA10 5BN
015396 21183
This family-run 16th-century coaching inn in the pretty market town of Sedbergh is an ideal base for walkers. A range of ales from local breweries such as Coniston and Hawkshead is served in the character bar with its warming log-burner. Once home to the village smithy, the restaurant serves seasonal food showcasing local producers. The home-made gourmet pizzas are a popular choice, as are the 'native breed' steaks.

Duo Café, Bar & Bistro
smattsduo.co.uk
32 Main Street, LA10 5BL
015396 20552
At this friendly little cafe you will find a selection of drinks and light bites, main meals, snacks and cakes using fresh local produce. You can have a Yorkshire tea with your full English in the morning or a glass of wine or beer with your lunch.

Ewe Tree Café
holmeopenfarm.co.uk
Off A683, LA10 5ET | 015396 20654
You can get a range of snacks and baking at this little tea room, which also sells gifts.

▶ Silecroft MAP REF 256 C4

Silecroft is a relaxed coastal village and beach a few miles to
the north of Millom on the A5093. It is a small pleasant resort,
overlooked by the 1,800-foot-high Black Combe from where, on
a clear day, you can see Scotland, Wales, the Isle of Man and
14 counties of England.

HIT THE BEACH

Silecroft and Haverigg are both
award-winning sandy beaches.
There's plenty of space for
children to play as well as other
activities such as angling,
kiting, dog walking and
horse-riding. Silecroft has a
Quality Coast Award for its
clean waters and facilities,
while Haverigg is a Blue Flag
beach with a lighthouse.

PLAY A ROUND

Silecroft Golf Club
silecroftgolfclub.co.uk
Millom, LA18 4NX | 01229 774250
Parallel to the coast of the Irish
Sea, this seaside links course
has spectacular views inland
of Lakeland hills. It looks
deceptively easy but you
will find that an ever-present
sea breeze ensures a
sporting challenge.

▶ Silloth MAP REF 260 C2

Silloth is a small town on the shores of the Solway Firth, facing
the hills of Southern Galloway and backed by the Lake District
Fells. Turner, the famous landscape artist, painted some of
Silloth's glorious sea views and sunsets. Economically it relies
heavily on the number of caravan parks in the surrounding
countryside. It is also the venue for Silloth Beer Festival every
September (sillothbeerfestival.co.uk) and the annual Solfest
music and arts and crafts festival (solfest.org.uk) which is held
on August bank holiday weekend at Tarnside Farm, Northern
Lake and attracts thousands of visitors.

VISIT THE MUSEUM

Solway Coast Discovery Centre
solwaycoastaonb.org.uk
Liddell Street, CA7 4DD | 01697
333055 | Open Mon, Wed, Fri 10–5,
Sat 10–1
There's something to keep the
whole family interested here, as
this exhibition interprets 10,000
years of the Solway's history. It
describes the wildlife, heritage,
landscape and communities. It
shows a historic timeline from

the last ice age, through the
spread of forests that were
home to wolves and giant deer,
the clearing of the forests for
farming, the Romans and later
the Vikings and then to the
Norman Conquest. Place
names, field sizes, drainage
ditches and saltmarsh ponds
are all explained. The Industrial
Revolution exhibit describes
ports, canals and railways until
we reach the present day. The

new art exhibition includes the work of local artists and has a bi-monthly featured artist. The Tourist Information Centre is also here, with exhibitions about the history of Silloth Airfield and the Carlisle to Silloth railway.

Soldiers in Silloth

soldiersinsilloth.co.uk
Criffell Street, CA7 4BZ | 016973 31246 | Open Jun–Sep & school holidays Tue–Fri 1–4, Sat–Sun 10–4; Oct–May Sat–Sun 10–3
This quirky, all-weather attraction is home to more than 10,000 toy soldiers and their associated paraphernalia, such as tanks, castles, cannons, forts and chariots. The items, from all around the world, depict a range of historical periods. You'll find Vikings and Romans as well as cowboys, native Americans and knights in armour. Table-top exhibits include the Battle of Waterloo and Gettysburg, and there is a special section devoted to Hadrian's Wall. Based on a private collection, the museum is run by local volunteers on behalf of the community.

HIT THE BEACH
Grune Point
North of Silloth, Grune Point is a sandy, raised shingle beach approximately one mile long. You'll find a variety of interesting plants here including sea sandwort, sea holly and sand couch-grass. Note that bathing is not safe when the tide is ebbing.

PLAY A ROUND
Silloth on Solway Golf Club
sillothgolfclub.co.uk
The Clubhouse, Silloth, CA7 4AE
016973 31304 | Open daily
A championship links course with stunning views to the Lake District and across the Solway to Scotland. You'll find that the dunes, narrow fairways and heather and gorse make these superb links on the Solway an exhilarating and searching test.

EAT AND DRINK
The Gincase Tearoom
gincase.co.uk
Mawbray Hayrigg, CA7 4LL
016973 32020
Located in a converted farm building, this tea room is housed where once horses would have powered a grinding stone. There is also a shop, art gallery and rare breed animal park, so you can browse away an hour or two over a leisurely lunch or home baking.

▶ PLACES NEARBY
Beckfoot Beach
A flat sandy beach, south of Silloth, popular for fishing, this area is designated as an area of Historic and Scientific Interest and an Area of Outstanding Natural Beauty. There are spectacular views across the Solway Firth.

Heading inland on the B5302 you could stop off to glimpse the ancient abbey of Holme Cultram, whose 12th-century remains are now the parish church, before continuing to Morecambe (see page 187).

▶ Sizergh Castle & Gardens   MAP REF 258 B5

nationaltrust.org.uk

LA8 8DZ | 015395 60951 | House open Mar–Oct Tue–Sun 12. Garden, cafe & shop open 4 Jan–9 Feb & 1–8 Mar Sat–Sun 11–4, 10–23 Feb & 3 Nov–Dec daily 10–5. Timed tickets apply Sun, BHs and school holidays

Just a mile north of Levens Hall (see page 180) is Sizergh Castle, now owned by the National Trust, although the Strickland family still live here. In 1239, the heiress of Sizergh Castle married into the Strickland family, and their occupancy of the castle has been unbroken except for a short time when the family accompanied King James II into exile.

The fact that it has been lived in by the same family since 1239 makes the story of its history more immediate. Portraits of their ancestors hang on the walls along with the Stuarts that they supported. You can see the furniture that they acquired over the centuries and most of the house is their Tudor additions to the original pele tower. The pele tower dates from the Scottish border raids of the 14th century.

You can still see parts of the intricate panelling of the Inlaid Chamber, which was sold in 1891 to the V&A in London. The museum has loaned two panels back to Sizergh so that you can imagine how the room would have looked in its heyday. They also loaned the inlaid bed, which was made to match the room.

▼ Sizergh Castle

EAT AND DRINK

Low Sizergh Barn
Farm Shop and Tearoom
lowsizerghbarn.co.uk
LA8 8AE | 015395 60426
This working farm is a good stopping place for breakfast, cakes and pastries, soups, quiches and snacks, as well as a children's menu. You will also find a farm trail that leads you through ancient woodland and countryside.

▶ PLACES NEARBY

It makes sense to combine visiting the castle with taking in Levens Hall (see page 180). From here you could then take the scenic A5074 to Winster, with its church, through Row and on to Lake Windermere.

▲ View of Skiddaw across Bassenthwaite Lake

▶ Skiddaw   MAP REF 261 D4

When the Lakes first began to attract tourists in numbers in the 19th century, it was to Keswick that many of them came, and the one peak they would all walk to was Skiddaw. It is not the most attractive ascent lower down, but even though it rises to 3,054 feet (931m) it is a safe climb that most can manage in little more than two hours. You can even avoid the first 1,000 feet by parking above the village of Applethwaite, north of Keswick off the A591, and starting the climb from there. Wherever you start from, the path to Skiddaw is clearly signed. At peak times walkers will be going up in droves, so don't attempt it then if you want solitude.

However, even if you do have to share them with fellow walkers, the views are spectacular. To the north are the Scottish mountains, and in the far west is the Isle of Man. The Pennine peaks rise to the east, while all around you can identify Lakeland's many other significant hills and dales. If you want to escape the crowds, take the Cumbria Way (see page 94), which circles behind the main peak into the area known as 'Back o' Skiddaw'.

▶ Swinside Stone Circle   MAP REF 256 C4

The Swinside Stone Circle is on a spur of Black Combe, a little-explored fell, off the A596 between Millom and Broughton-in-Furness. Though it is on private land, you can see the circle of 57 standing stones from the adjacent right of way. The circle is similar in size to Castlerigg Stone Circle, near Keswick, though the setting is somewhat bleaker.

▶ Talkin Tarn MAP REF 263 D4

carlisle.gov.uk

CA8 1HN | 01697 73129

Ideal for boating, fishing and swimming, this 65-acre lake lies just north of Talkin at the heart of Talkin Tarn Country Park. There are sandy bays around the tarn and you can follow a signposted nature trail through attractive woodland, which opens to lovely views over the surrounding countryside.

GO FISHING

Talkin Tarn Country Park

carlisle.gov.uk

CA8 1HN | 01697 73129

You can fish here for pike and perch, but all fish must be thrown back. You'll need an Environment Agency rod licence; day permits can be bought on arrival.

EAT AND DRINK

Blacksmiths Arms

blacksmithstalkin.co.uk

Talkin, CA8 1LE | 01697 73452

Facing the picturesque green in Talkin village, the Blacksmiths Arms serves à la carte meals in a small restaurant or simpler fare in the comfortable lounge bars. There is also a range of cask ales.

The Boathouse Café

CA8 1HN | 01697 741050

Upstairs from one of the tarn's boathouses, this welcoming little cafe is the perfect place to enjoy the watery view while partaking of scrumptious home-made cakes and hot chocolate. There's also a little gift shop where you can buy Lakes-inspired souvenirs.

▲ Swinside Stone Circle, near Duddon Bridge

▶ Temple Sowerby   MAP REF 258 C1

The houses in this pretty village, between Penrith and Appleby, cluster around the village green. The village gets its name from the Knights Templar, who as long ago as 1228 had a religious house here. The oldest parts of the present buildings date back to the 16th century and the remainder are mainly 18th and 19th century. This is the place to go to see and be inspired by a true host of golden daffodils. In spring you can see whole swathes of yellow bobbing in the wind beneath the grand oak trees in the gardens at Acorn Bank on the edge of the village.

Near Acorn Bank you can follow the Crowdundle Beck to the River Eden and one of the largest bridges in the Eden Valley, spanning the river on four arches of red sandstone.

TAKE IN SOME HISTORY
Acorn Bank Garden and Watermill
nationaltrust.org.uk
CA10 1SP | 017683 61893
Open daily mid-Mar to Oct 10–5,
Nov to mid-Mar weekends 10–5
Particularly noted for its walled herb garden, this is a delightful garden, of some 2.5 acres. It contains the largest collection of medicinal, culinary and even narcotic herbs in northern Britain, which includes some 250 species. Some are poisonous, so you are warned not to try nibbling them. There are traditional orchards, too, and fine collections of roses, shrubs and herbaceous

borders. If you are a gardener, you can stock up with plants from the small shop. The garden is not just of interest to gardeners, though. You can follow the circular woodland walk through the woods alongside Crowdundle Beck to the restored watermill.

EAT AND DRINK
Acorn Bank
nationaltrust.org
CA10 1SP | 017683 61893
A visit to Acorn Bank's tea room is the only chance you'll get to see inside this interesting 17th-century mansion. You can get excellent home-made cakes, lunches and a children's menu along with Fair Trade teas and coffees.

The Kings Arms
kingsarmstemplesowerby.co.uk
CA10 1SB | 017683 62944
In 1799, William Wordsworth and Samuel Coleridge set off from this 400-year-old coaching inn for their exploration of the Lake District. Today the kitchen serves a mix of pub favourites and modern dishes. There's also a good vegetarian choice and a children's menu.

Temple Sowerby House Hotel & Restaurant 🏵🏵
templesowerby.com
CA10 1RZ | 017683 61578
This small-scale 18th-century country-house hotel overlooks the village green and makes a great base for exploring the area. With sandstone columns framing the view over the walled garden, high-backed patterned chairs and bundles of fresh flowers, the place has all the charm of a smart family-run country hotel. The kitchen specialises in a boldly modern British style, with influences from Europe and around the world.

▶ PLACES NEARBY
Church of St Lawrence
Church Lane, Morland, CA10 3AZ
You'll find a wonderful mix of styles here, spanning 1,000 years. The tower is 11th century but its height was raised in 1588, and the small spire was added later. The nave and aisles are 12th century and include some Norman features. The chancel and transepts were added in the next century. The chancel was rebuilt in 1600, the north aisle in the 18th century and the church was restored in both the 19th and 20th centuries.

◀ Acorn Bank

▶ Thirlmere   MAP REF 261 D5

The A591, from Grasmere to Keswick, runs along the eastern side of the long thin lake of Thirlmere. There's a car park at the southern end, near the 17th-century Wythburn chapel. From here a track leads up to Helvellyn (see page 150), and before 1879 many paths would have led downwards, too. The chapel is all that remains of Wythburn village, flooded in the 1890s when Thirlmere was dammed at the northern end and turned into Manchester's first Lakeland reservoir. Armboth in the northwest is also now beneath the waters, along with several farms on the shores of the original lake.

Thirlmere, an attractive, tree-fringed expanse, is one of the few lakes that you can drive round, as well as walk around. There's a lovely drive down the western edge through the lakeside woods with several car parks, each with forest trails leading off from them. You can walk up one of the trails to the summit of Raven Crag, but you also get good views halfway down the western edge at Hause Point, where the lake was once narrow enough to have had a bridge running across to the other side.

▶ Townend   MAP REF 257 E2

nationaltrust.org.uk

Troutbeck, Windermere, LA23 1LB | 01539 432628 | Open mid-Mar to Oct Wed–Sun & BHs 1–5

Come here to see how Lakeland farmhouses used to look. This mainly 17th-century house has no electricity, and epitomises the remoteness of the Lake District in centuries past. The fascinating house belonged to the farming Browne family for more than 300 years until it was taken over by the National Trust in 1943. You can see domestic implements, the down house for washing, cooking, pickling and brewing, and a firehouse with living quarters. You can also see the Brownes' hand-carved furniture. George Browne added his own designs to older pieces of furniture, copying older patterns – so that you sometimes can't tell which decorations were done by George, and which by his ancestors. He even added older dates and initials to his designs to make them look more antiquated. He carved the date 1687, together with the initials of his ancestors, into a bookcase he made in 1887.

George had a quirky sense of humour too. Look for the row of tiny, smiling faces in the fireplace in the main bedroom or the feet sticking out of a long case clock. His sense of humour and indeed his work was not appreciated by Beatrix Potter, who described him as 'the tiresome Mr Browne', who added 'copied patterns to a splendid old bedstead'. Don't miss the library with its unique collection of books, complete with turned-down corners and finger-marks. These amusing and often slightly bawdy storybooks were meant for the lower orders of society and were beneath the attention of serious libraries, so they haven't survived elsewhere. You'll get a real sense of the ordinary people of the past, laughing and passing round passages from their favourite books.

▶ **Troutbeck** MAP REF 257 E2

Troutbeck is a Conservation Area. The houses here are spread out along narrow country lanes, around a number of wells and springs, without a recognisable centre. However, you will find a superb collection of buildings, dating from the 16th to the 19th centuries, with original features such as mullioned windows, heavy cylindrical chimneys and a rare example of an exposed spinning gallery. The best-preserved building in the Troutbeck Valley is Townend (see page 219) – a fine example of a yeoman farmer's house. Townend offers a fascinating glimpse into what domestic life was like for Lakeland's wealthier farmers, with its low ceilings, original home-carved oak panelling and furniture, and stone-flagged floors.

SEE A LOCAL CHURCH
Jesus Church
A592, LA23 1PB

A church has stood here since the 16th century. In 1736, however, the entire church was dismantled and rebuilt. The only remnants of this structure are the massive beams, the tiny three-light window in the tower and the coat of arms of George II, painted on wood in the gallery. Dating from the time of its 1861 restoration, the colourful east window was designed by Sir Edward Burne-Jones in collaboration with William Morris and Ford Madox Brown. According to local tradition, Morris and Madox Brown came to Troutbeck on a fishing holiday at the time when Burne-Jones was working on the window, and they stayed on in the Lake District to assist him.

TRY HORSE-RIDING
Rookin House Equestrian and Activity Centre
rookinhouse.co.uk
CA11 0SS | 01768 483561

The centre caters for all levels of ability – from total beginners to experienced riders – and there's a choice of over 35 well-mannered horses and ponies of all shapes, sizes and temperaments. The rides, led by experienced instructors, go along bridleways and quiet country lanes, across open fells and through shady forests, offering glorious views of the Ullswater and Matterdale valleys along the way.

Lakeland Pony Trekking
lakesriding.co.uk
Limefitt Park, LA23 1PA
015394 31999

You can take rides or treks here combining some of the finest views and stunning scenery that the Lake District has to offer. With direct access to the tracks and bridleways of the fells, the majority of rides have no road work. You can choose from a variety of fully supervised treks, from half-an-hour to full-day rides, catering for all ages and levels of experience.

◀ Troutbeck

EAT AND DRINK
The Old Post Office
Troutbeck, LA23 1PF
015394 34713
This lovingly converted old building now houses a simple village shop and tea room. The shop sells a few basics, and the cafe puts the emphasis firmly on high-quality food and plenty of home cooking. Daily lunchtime snacks include sandwiches and paninis, while the bakes feature scones, flapjacks, lemon drizzle cakes and rich chocolate brownies.

▶ Ullswater   MAP REF 261 E5

This is the second largest lake in the Lake District, at around 9 miles long, 0.75 miles wide and just less than 200 feet deep at its deepest point – and for many, it is the most beautiful of all the lakes. On the western shores, you can follow the trail to see the splendid waterfalls that cascade down through the wooded gorge of Aira Beck and into the lake. The largest and most powerful is the 70-foot drop of Aira Force.

Near the falls you can find an arboretum, a cafe where you can enjoy snacks and refreshments, and a landscaped Victorian park. Back in 1802, William and Dorothy Wordsworth were walking near here, when Dorothy observed the 'daffodils so beautiful... they tossed and reeled and danced.' Her brother transformed her words into one of the best-known and best-loved of English poems, *Daffodils*. Aira Force itself inspired another of Wordsworth's much-loved poems, *The Somnambulist*.

The southern tip of the lake, below the shoulders of Helvellyn, is reached via the dramatic and high Kirkstone Pass, which rises to 1,489 feet. On the lake's northern tip, at Pooley Bridge, there used to be a fish market in the main square, and this area is still rich in trout and salmon.

If you take a short walk up to Dunmallard Hill you can see Iron Age remains. Below here from the pier near the 16th-century bridge, two 19th-century steamers, *Lady of the Lake* and *Raven*, take visitors down the lake. Combine a cruise with a walk to enjoy the lake and the land at their best. Near Howtown the lake narrows to about 400 yards at the strangely named Skelly Nab. The name comes from the freshwater herring, the schelly, found only here, in Haweswater and high up in the Red Tarn on Helvellyn. The silvery foot-long fish were once caught in nets strung between Skelly Nab and the opposite shore.

▶ **Ullswater 'Steamers'**

MAP REF 257 D5

ullswater-steamers.co.uk
The Pier House, CA11 0US
01768 482229 | Open all year daily

Could there be a better way to see some of England's most
magnificent mountain scenery than from one of the Ullswater
'steamers'? These boats, diesel-powered since the 1930s, call at
Pooley Bridge at the northern end of this sinuous lake, then remote
Howtown, roughly halfway along the eastern shore, before
travelling on to Glenridding (see page 128), at the foot of the craggy
Helvellyn range at the southern end. Some boats also stop at the
National Trust's Aira Force pier. Flexible tickets allow you to cruise
just one section of the route, do the whole thing in one go or hop
on and off all day. The open deck is perfect on a summer's day; in
winter, head for the covered deck or go downstairs to warm up
in the bar.

10 top walks

- From Rosthwaite to Watendlath, via Stonethwaite and Dock Tarn
- Up Penrith Beacon
- From Patterdale, along the shores of Ullswater, to Silver Point
- Coniston village to Tarn Hows
- Around Rydal Water
- Derwentwater to Walla Crag and Keswick
- From Bassenthwaite, via Great Cockup, and back through Trusmadoor
- Above Derwentwater to Cat Bells and High Spy
- Whinlatter Forest Park
- Over Muncaster Fell from Ravenglass to Eskdale Green (return on La'al Ratty, see page 200)

GET YOUR BOOTS ON
Ullswater Way

ullswaterway.co.uk

The Ullswater Way is a fully waymarked 20-mile circuit of England's second largest natural lake. It covers a variety of terrain – from picturesque farm and woodland paths to low hills and trails skirting the base of high, rugged fells. It calls in at Pooley Bridge, Watermillock, Glenridding, Patterdale and Howtown, and also pays a visit to Aira Force, one of the Lake District's most impressive waterfalls. Fit walkers might want to attempt it all in one go; most will break it down into

three or four shorter sections, hopping on and off local buses or the 'steamers' to get to and from the start of their walks. Local craftspeople and artists have created several heritage-themed installations along the route.

GO FISHING

Fishing here is free; a rod licence is all that you need. There are perch, perhaps an odd pike and schelly – an endangered and protected whitefish relic from the last ice age. However the only serious fishing is of wild brown trout. Boats are available for hire from St Patrick's Boat Landings at Glenridding (see page 128). There are only a couple, so book well in advance.

EXPLORE BY BIKE
Park Foot Caravan Site

parkfootullswater.co.uk
Pooley Bridge, CA10 2NA
017684 86309 | Open all year

You can hire mountain bikes and adult electric bikes here with helmets and accessories for a day or a half-day. There are sizes to suit all. No need to book in advance, except for large groups or a bike with a child seat.

▶ PLACES NEARBY

Howtown is a hamlet and small harbour on the east shore of Ullswater. It is about 3.5 miles from Pooley Bridge and the Ullswater 'steamers' regularly stop here.

Granny Dowbekin's Tearoom

grannydowbekins.co.uk

Pooley Bridge, CA10 2NP

017684 86453

There's been a tea room on the picturesque riverbank here since 1904, and it would take more than the dreadful floods of late 2015 to close it down.

Food and service are great, with generous portions and friendly staff. Lunches, teas and suppers are all served, with a good choice of main courses and sweet things, and it's particularly nice on a fine day when you can sit outside in the pretty waterside garden.

▶ Ulverston   MAP REF 257 D4

If you want to get off the beaten track then Ulverston, on the fringe of Morecambe Bay, generally has a tranquil, unhurried air, although on Thursdays and Saturdays you'll find the market square thronged with stalls. On top of Hoad Hill, overlooking the town, is a 90-foot copy of the Eddystone Lighthouse, which is a monument to Sir John Barrow, born in Ulverston in 1764.

He was a founder member of the Royal Geographical Society and his story is told in the town's heritage centre. Another famous son of Ulverston, Stan Laurel of the world-famous duo Laurel and Hardy, was born in Ulverston in 1890. Not surprisingly, therefore, one of the main attractions of the town is the tiny, quirky Laurel and Hardy Museum.

Ulverston has the shortest canal in Britain. At just one mile long it links the town to the sea. Built by the engineer John Rennie in 1794, it represents the high point of Ulverston's iron ore industrial history; nearby were the town's foundry and blast furnace. Ships could navigate along the canal into the town where they would be loaded with cargoes of iron and slate. The canal had a short working life of just 50 years, before the railway took over. Ulverston also went into decline as the iron ore industry gradually moved to Barrow. Today, the canal towpath provides a pleasant walk down to the sea.

TAKE IN SOME HISTORY
Swarthmoor Hall

swarthmoorhall.co.uk

LA12 0JQ | 01229 583204

See website for opening times

A 16th-century country house set in beautiful gardens and grounds amid 130 acres of farmland, Swarthmoor Hall has a real sense of place and of the people who have lived here. A new courtyard garden features a Living Quilt, a copy of a quilt in one of the bedrooms. The history of the hall is fascinating too. In the 17th century, it was the home of Judge Thomas Fell and his wife Margaret. They provided protection and hospitality for early Quakers and allowed the hall to be used as the headquarters for the movement. Fell was able to serve the Quaker Movement again, when he had charges of blasphemy against its founder, George Fox, dismissed. Years later, after the death of Thomas Fell, Margaret married George Fox. In the six historic rooms here, you can see a fine selection of 17th-century furniture as well as finding out more about early Quaker history. There is a pleasant cafe featuring local produce and you can stay in one of the en-suite rooms.

VISIT THE MUSEUMS
Ulverston Heritage Centre
visitoruk.com/Ulverston
Lower Brook Street, LA12 7EE
01229 580820 | Open Mon–Sat
9.30–4.30
Located in one of Ulverston's fascinating ginnels, the Heritage Centre is staffed by highly knowledgeable volunteers and is bursting at the seams with useful information about the local area. The centre also contains a set of records, dating from the 18th century, a museum, bookshop and gift shop.

▼ Swarthmoor Hall, near Ulverston

Laurel and Hardy Museum
laurel-and-hardy.co.uk
The Roxy, Brogden Street, LA12 7AH
01229 582292
Open daily 10–5
Bill Cubin started the museum with his collection of memorabilia, gathered from his lifelong love of 'the boys'. Starting out as a few scrapbooks of photos, the collection grew over time until it filled one small room, with pictures covering all the walls and even the ceiling. There was also a tiny viewing room for the movies. With encouragement from friends, he opened the museum. After many years at this cramped site, however, the museum had become overcrowded and, due to the hobbyist way the collection had been started, some of the pictures were beginning to look past their best. Bill's daughter and grandson, who still run it, decided to move everything to the Roxy cinema complex. In this light and spacious area, you can see the collection much more easily but it has lost that quirky feeling created by the muddle of memorabilia.

WALK THE CUMBRIA WAY
This 70-mile route will take you from Carlisle to Ulverston through the heart of the Lakes (see page 94).

CATCH A PERFORMANCE
Coronation Hall
corohall.co.uk
LA12 7LZ | 01229 588994

Coronation Hall has the largest capacity of any hall in south Cumbria. You can see a whole range of events here, including performances by touring companies in the fields of music, theatre, ballet and opera, as well as lively local presentations. It was built on the site of the famous County Hotel, which burned down in 1911. The building was completed during World War I and named to commemorate the coronation of King George V.

PLAY A ROUND
Ulverston Golf Club
ulverstongolf.co.uk
Bardsea Park, LA12 9QJ
01229 582824 | Open daily
Between 1923 and 1924, H S Colt, the highly respected golf course architect designed this course – and today it still looks almost as it did then. You'll find this undulating parkland course overlooking Morecambe Bay testing but fair and at the same time you can enjoy the glorious panoramic views of the Lakeland fells and mountains.

EAT AND DRINK
The Farmers
thefarmers-ulverston.co.uk
Market Street, LA12 7BA
01229 584469
This is one of the oldest inns in the Lake District, set opposite the Market Cross in the middle of town. Here, you'll find a hospitable welcome, whether in the traditionally decorated restaurant, with its oak beams

and impressive views of the Crake Valley, or in the 14th-century stable bar complete with a log fire and original slate floors. You can drink local ales, including Hawkshead Bitter, and enjoy a wide range of hearty pub grub.

Old Farmhouse

theoldfarmhouseulverston.co.uk
Priory Road, LA12 9HR
01229 480324

Just south of the town, and a short distance from Morecambe Bay, this is a busy pub housed within a beautifully converted barn. Its very popular restaurant in the main barn area offers an extensive traditional menu, which makes the most of regional suppliers. Local Cumbrian ales, a sun-trap courtyard garden, a big screen for live sports and a function room for private hire complete the picture.

The Stan Laurel Inn

thestanlaurel.co.uk
31 The Ellers, LA12 0AB
01229 582814

When the old market town of Ulverston's most famous son – the comic actor Stan Laurel – was born in 1890, this town-centre pub was still a farmhouse with two cottages surrounded by fields and orchards. Today it serves a selection of locally brewed real ales and a full menu of traditional pub food plus a specials board, from either the cosy, traditional bar or dining room.

▶ **PLACES NEARBY**

Bouth is a small village north of Ulverston and within the National Park, and lies on a quiet road midway between Coniston and Windermere.

Old Hall Farm

Bouth, LA12 8JA
oldhallfarmbouth.com
01229 861993 | Open daily Apr–Nov 10–5

Old Hall Farm is still farmed in the traditional manner, using 19th-century methods to work the land. You can spend the day watching what goes on, or sign up to try your hand at ploughing with shire horses, tending the Gloucester Old Spot pigs or hand milking. In spring, you can watch the ploughing using old steam-driven tractors, or come during harvest to see vintage binders and threshers at work. The farm produces wonderful cream and milk, which you can enjoy in the cafe in the shape of a cream tea – the farm pork and vegetables appear on the menu too.

General Burgoyne

thegeneralburgoyne.co.uk
Church Road, Great Urswick,
LA12 0SZ | 01229 586394

Walkers, cyclists, bikers, families and dogs are always welcome here. Known as Gentleman Johnny, General Burgoyne was a British army officer, politician and dramatist, infamous for surrendering his men to the enemy during the American War of Independence. A skull – not Burgoyne's – found during renovations in 1995 is displayed in the fire-warmed bar, where you can enjoy Robinsons beers and decent pub grub. Dine in style on the modern Orangery Restaurant.

▶ Walney Island   MAP REF 256 C6

The Isle of Walney is connected to Barrow-in-Furness by Jubilee Bridge. Originally opened in 1908, it operated as a toll bridge but was renamed Jubilee Bridge in 1935. There are three towns on the island – Biggar, North Town and Vickerstown – which was once a dormitory town for many North Yorkshire steel workers.

The ends of the island are designated Sites of Special Scientific Interest, and contain an abundance of nesting seabirds as well as amphibians and rare geological features.

GET OUTDOORS
North and South Walney Nature Reserves
Barrow-in-Furness, LA14 3YQ

A road bridge links Barrow with the Isle of Walney, which shields the tip of the Furness Peninsula, and Barrow itself, from the ravages of the sea. The southern tip of the Isle of Walney is a haven for a huge variety of birds; 250 different species have been recorded here, including migrants passing through. In the northern part of the reserve, you can walk by the saltmarshes, sand dunes and mudflats, where you might hear the loud and raucous call of the rare natterjack toad.

EXPLORE BY BIKE
W2W Cycle Route
This superb 151-mile trans-Pennine route (Sustrans Regional Route 20) begins on Walney Island and passes through a variety of wonderful countryside from the Isle of Walney to Wearmouth in Sunderland. This is a classic 'coast to coast' cycling adventure, challenging in both distance and terrain, but if you are reasonably fit you should be able to do it. Thanks to the distinctive blue National Cycle Network signs and the official maps it's easy to follow in either direction. The route is mostly on country lanes, back roads and cycle paths, and you should easily manage the few off-road bits with a touring, trekking or hybrid bike.

PLAY A ROUND
Furness Golf Club
furnessgolfclub.co.uk
Central Drive, LA14 3LN
01229 471232 | Open all year, daily
This is one of the oldest golf courses in England, with beautiful views of the Lakeland hills and the Irish Sea. Enjoy the views with six outward holes, six inward holes along the beach and six alternating in each direction.

▶ **Wasdale & Wast Water** MAP REF 256 C2

You need to approach this bleakly beautiful valley from the west, which means a long drive for most people. The reward is that Wasdale will be spectacularly empty at times when the more accessible Lakeland places are crowded with visitors. If the view up to the head of the valley seems oddly familiar, that's because the National Park Authority created their logo from this view of Wast Water and the three peaks – Yewbarrow, Great Gable and Lingmell. Scafell Pike, near the head of the valley, is the highest peak in England at 3,210 feet (978m) and although it is just 3 miles long, Wast Water is the deepest lake. The huge screes that dominate the southern shore continue their descent fully 250 feet into the cool clear waters. If you're tired of the busy Windermere waters, you will relish the tranquillity and awesome landscape at Wasdale.

The road hugs the water's edge until you reach Wasdale Head, and communities don't come much smaller than this. St Olaf's, at Wasdale Head (CA20 1AZ), is at least as old as 16th century and is one of the smallest churches in England. It is set amid yew trees, which are often found in graveyards. Some of the roof beams are believed to have been made from Viking longships. It is open during daylight hours.

▲ Wast Water

EAT AND DRINK
Wasdale Head Inn
wasdale.com

CA20 1EX | 019467 26229

Dramatically situated at the foot of England's highest mountain, adjacent to England's smallest church and also not far from the country's deepest lake, this Victorian inn is reputedly the birthplace of British climbing. The many photographs decorating the oak-panelled walls reflect the passion for this activity. Ritson's Bar is named after Will Ritson, who was awarded the very first title of 'The World's Biggest Liar'. Expect local ales and hearty food here. The annual

5 top views

▶ Ashness Bridge looking over Derwentwater

▶ Tarn Hows

▶ Rydal Water from any angle

▶ Wast Water looking towards Wasdale Head

▶ King's How on Grange Fell looking over Borrowdale and across Derwentwater

Wasdale Show takes place on the second Saturday in October and is a great reason to hang up the climbing boots for a day and maybe stay over in one of the inn's comfortable bedrooms.

▶ **Wetheral** MAP REF 262 C4

Nestling on the banks of the River Eden, conveniently located
close to Carlisle (see page 88), is the attractive village of
Wetheral. Centred around a large triangular green and edged
with gracious houses, built from the distinctive local red
sandstone, this is a lovely place to stop and explore. Two
buildings stand out from the rest: Eden Bank, a grandiose
mock château of the 19th century, which has millstones set in
its garden wall; and the elegant Crown Hotel, with a columned
porch. Look for the early five-arched railway bridge spanning
the wide River Eden, and if you take one of the footpaths into
Wetheral Woods to the south of the village, you will find
charming views of the picturesque ruins of Corby Castle on the
opposite bank. Nearby, a 15th-century gatehouse is all that
survives of the local Benedictine priory. Also overlooking the
river is Holy Trinity Church, with an unusual octagonal tower
and some splendid effigies. The quiet village of Faugh can be
found nearby.

▶ **Whinlatter Forest** MAP REF 261 D4

Whinlatter Forest is a mixed plantation of trees ranging
from Sitka and Norway spruce to Scots pine, Douglas fir and
Lawson cypress. Look out also for native broadleaves such as
birch and oak, and the more exotic western hemlock and
Japanese larch. The forest provides a habitat for a wide range
of wildlife, and on this walk you may see roe deer, foxes, red
squirrels, frogs and toads.

Overhead you may be lucky enough to spot buzzards,
peregrines and many other species of birdlife. One species you
do have a good chance of seeing, depending on the time of the
year, is the osprey. A breeding pair of ospreys has been nesting
close to Bassenthwaite Lake since 2001, the species previously

▼ River Eden

having been persecuted to extinction in England more than 150 years ago. The huge nest, built by the Forestry Commission and the Lake District National Park Authority, is located in Dodd Wood and is subject to a round-the-clock guard once the female lays her eggs. Ospreys have a wingspan of nearly 5.5 feet, and are rich brown in colour with a white head and underside. They're fish eaters and you are most likely to see one hovering over the lake, its sharp eyes scanning the water for a fish, before streaking down unerringly to snag its prey.

Ospreys winter in Africa, but return to the Lake District in the spring to breed. The lower viewing point in Dodd Wood is staffed from April through to the end of August, from 10am to 5pm. High-powered telescopes and binoculars are available during the breeding period. Cameras are also trained on the nest, so that visitors can view live footage of the birds on a video screen at the Whinlatter Visitor Centre.

Cumbria's conifer plantations were planted during the early part of the 20th century. Woodland resources were severely depleted by the end of World War I, particularly by the need for wood to build the trenches, so there was a need to rebuild and maintain a strategic timber reserve. The Forestry Act came into force in September 1919, and the new commission's first planting in the Lake District was at Hospital Plantation, Whinlatter, in the same year.

The village of Braithwaite, which has several pubs, can be found nearby.

GET INDUSTRIAL
Force Crag Mine
nationaltrust.org.uk
Whinlatter Pass, CA12 5UP
Nearest parking Braithwaite Methodist Church, CA12 5TL. Check website for open days
This was the last working metal mine in Cumbria but closed in 1991. The National Trust runs guided tours of the former mine buildings on five days each year.

ENTERTAIN THE FAMILY
Whinlatter Forest Visitor Centre
forestry.gov.uk
Whinlatter Forest Park, CA12 5TW
01768 778469 | Open daily 10–4

England's only true Mountain Forest has stunning views, fantastic walks, exhilarating mountain biking and rare wildlife. WildPlay is a 1,968-foot children's trail with climbing frames, Archimedes Screws, a log swing, pulleys and more.

WALK THE HIGH ROPES
Go Ape!
goape.co.uk
Whinlatter Pass, CA12 5TW
0845 6439215 | See website for availability (pre-booking advised)
For a day out with adventure Go Ape! This is the highest course in the country, at 1,180 feet above sea level, with views as

far as Scotland. Ride a thrilling zip slide over water and through a real mountain forest.

EAT AND DRINK
Coledale Inn
coledale-inn.co.uk
Braithwaite, CA12 5TN
017687 78272

Originally a woollen mill, the Coledale Inn dates from around 1824 and had stints as a pencil mill, a guesthouse and a private house before becoming an inn. The interior is attractively designed, and footpaths leading off from the large gardens make it ideal for exploring the nearby fells. Two homely bars serve a selection of local ales while traditional lunch and dinner menus are served in the dining room.

The Cottage in the Wood ❀❀❀
thecottageinthewood.co.uk
Whinlatter Pass, CA12 5TW
017687 78409

The Lakeland writer A W Wainwright reckoned that the northwestern fells were the most delectable in the whole district, and there they are, right before your eyes in the view from this 17th-century coaching inn. Despite its faintly fairy-tale name, it's a distinctively contemporary place, with spacious, airy rooms and a restaurant called Mountain View for its majestic prospect. The kitchen maintains an established commitment to sound regional produce in modern British dishes full of sharply honed flavours.

The Old Sawmill Tearoom
theoldsawmill.co.uk
Dodd Wood, CA12 4QE
017687 74317

This is a great place to pause if you've been visiting the osprey viewing area in Dodd Wood – look out for red squirrels too. The cafe serves food all day, so you could have home-made soup, a baked potato, or a hot- or cold-filled roll at lunch or something indulgent from the wonderful array of home-baked goodies.

The Royal Oak
royaloak-braithwaite.co.uk
Braithwaite, CA12 5SY
017687 78533

Surrounded by high fells and beautiful scenery, the Royal Oak is right in the centre of the village and is the perfect base for walkers. The interior is all oak beams and log fires, and the menu offers hearty pub food and local ales. Visitors can extend the experience by staying over in the comfortable en-suite bedrooms.

Siskins Café
forestry.gov.uk
Whinlatter Forest Visitor Centre,
CA12 5TW | 017687 78410

High on the Whinlatter Pass, Siskins Café is a great place to start and finish your exploration of the surrounding woodland. From the balcony you can watch the never-ending stream of birds on strategically placed feeders, in the trees in front of you. The food is good too.

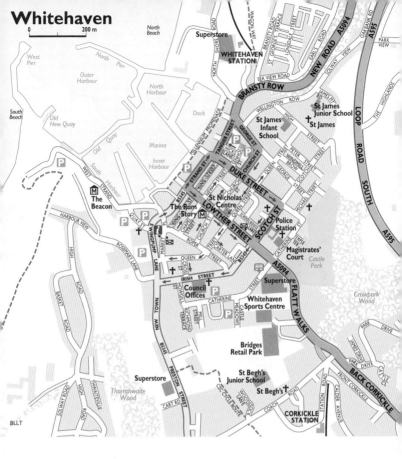

▶ **Whitehaven** MAP REF 260 A5

Your first stop in Whitehaven should be The Beacon, on West Strand, which will give you a fascinating insight into the rich history of the town and harbour with its audio-visual presentations and displays.

In the middle of the 18th century, Whitehaven was the third largest port in Britain after London and Bristol, shipping coal to Ireland and the Continent and importing tobacco from America. It was developed during the 17th century by three generations of the Lowther family, who became the Earls of Lonsdale. Until then it was a simple fishing hamlet, but the Lowthers built a harbour and a new town and it developed into a mining centre with shafts excavated far out beneath the sea.

Today, the handsome Georgian and Victorian buildings that you can still see testify to the town's prosperity. Whitehaven has a small fishing fleet and its harbour is a conservation area, with several monuments to its past mining history, which finally died out in 1986. At night, the bridge across the marina is lit up to dramatic effect. The town has two churches that are worth seeking out. St Begh's dates from around 1868 and is visually

▲ Whitehaven Harbour

quite striking, as it was built from white stone with a red-stone dressing. St James' is slightly older, from 1752, with Italian ceiling designs and a very atmospheric and moving Memorial Chapel.

For book lovers, Whitehaven has the largest antiquarian bookshop in Cumbria, (one of the largest in northern Britain), Michael Moon's Antiquarian Bookshop in Lowther Street.

VISIT THE MUSEUMS
The Beacon
thebeacon-whitehaven.co.uk
West Strand, CA28 7LY
01946 592302 | Open Tue–Sun and BHs 10–4.30
The Beacon is a museum telling the story of this fascinating corner of the Western Lake District using interactive displays and activities. It allows you to go back in time to experience the lifestyle differences between rich and poor, the hardships of working life and the dangers of disease.

The Rum Story

rumstory.co.uk
27 Lowther Street, CA28 7DN
01946 592933 | Open Mon–Sat
10–4.30. Closed 1 week in Jan

You won't want to miss this fascinating museum in the original shop, courtyards, cellars and bonded warehouses of the Jefferson family, who have the distinction of being the oldest rum trading family in Britain. The exhibitions take you back in time to the early days of the rum trade, its links with the slave trade, sugar plantations, the Royal Navy, barrel-making and more. You can explore a tropical rainforest, an African village, a slave ship and a cooper's workshop.

SEE A LOCAL CHURCH

Church of St James

High Street, opposite Queen Street, CA28 7PZ

Built in 1752, St James' has an outstanding Georgian interior and fittings; it is like being inside a vast piece of pottery decorated by Josiah Wedgwood. In the west end porch are fine Georgian staircases leading to the three-sided gallery, which is supported by columns. Look for the roundels of decorative plasterwork on the ceiling, depicting the Annunciation and the Ascension. The apse has a top-lit dome and a striking central painting of the *Transfiguration* by Giulio Cesare Procaccini (1548–1626). A memorial chapel is dedicated to the dead of both World Wars and to local people killed in

You can play bar skittles and hopscotch, while discovering the many ways in which folks had fun in days gone by.

Look out for the early industries, such as salt making, farming and fishing; join the crew aboard the *Maria Lowther* ship; survive shipwrecks with the Rocket Brigade; and then relive the decline and revival of Whitehaven Harbour. On the top floor is the Weather Gallery, full of high-tech equipment that monitors and records the weather, and you can also enjoy panoramic views of the town and coast.

mining accidents. It features a large piece of coal and uses a miner's lamp as the sanctuary lamp. All of the ground-floor windows are stained glass and include work by the renowned Victorian firms Shrigley and Hunt and William Wailes, as well as a modern window (1976) by L C Evetts.

GO SHOPPING
Michael Moon's Antiquarian Bookshop
19 Lowther Street, CA28 7AL
01946 599010

If you love books, you could lose yourself for hours in this amazing bookshop. There are 13 rooms full of 100,000 books, covering every subject known to man, on its mile of shelving, with room for at least a hundred contented book browsers.

CATCH A PERFORMANCE
Rosehill Theatre
rosehilltheatre.co.uk
Moresby, CA28 6SE
01946 692422

Oliver Messel (1904–1978), the stage, costume and film designer, designed this gorgeous little theatre. It opened on the hills above Whitehaven in 1959 and was described as a 'rose-red silk lined jewel box'. It is still one of Britain's most intimate theatres and here you'll find a diverse range of arts and entertainment from music, theatre, film, talks, comedy, shows for young people and more. Check the website for the current programme.

EXPLORE BY BIKE
Coast-to-Coast (C2C) Cycle Route
c2c-guide.co.uk

Britain's most popular long-distance cycle route follows a web of well-chosen minor roads, disused railway lines, off-road tracks and specially constructed cycle paths. As long as you are reasonably fit, you can complete at least part of this 140-mile-long route which links Whitehaven and Workington to Sunderland. Although there are some seriously hard climbs – the highest point being over 2,000 feet – the route is designed for everyone, from families to club riders. There are a number of off-road sections, but you always have the option of taking the surfaced alternative.

The route starts in the former coal mining and industrial lands of West Cumbria, travels through the stunning scenery of the northern Lake District and heads into Keswick before passing through Penrith and the lush Eden Valley with its sandstone villages. It then starts the climb up to Hartside and onto the Northern Pennines. Meandering through old lead-mining villages, such as Nenthead and Rookhope, the route heads down into the Durham Dales before entering the old steel town of Consett on the edge of the Pennines. From here, it's an easy ride through one of Britain's old industrial heartlands to the North Sea and Sunderland.

The Reivers Cycle Route

reivers-route.co.uk

The Reivers Route is also known as the 'Return C2C' as it takes you from the end of the west-to-east route, 173 miles all the way back to the start of the C2C. Part of the National Cycle Network, the route winds its way through some of the wildest and most untouched countryside in Britain. Starting at the mouth of the River Tyne, the route finishes here on the Cumbrian coast. Along the way, you follow the shores of Kielder Water, take a brief foray into Scotland and cross the rugged countryside of the Northumberland National Park. Then, after the Borders and Carlisle, you head down through the Lake District to Cockermouth and Bassenthwaite. There are alternative options you can take along the way.

Haven Cycles

havencycles-c2cservices.co.uk
Preston Street, CA28 9DL
01946 63263

You can hire all sorts of bikes here, including hybrids and mountain bikes. Each cycle comes with a rear pannier rack, mudguards, stand, gel seat, speed computer, bottle holder, lock, tool kit, puncture outfit, pump, spare tube and helmet.

ENTERTAIN THE FAMILY

Whitehaven Sports Centre

better.org.uk
Flatt Walks, CA27 7RJ
01946 695666 | Open Mon–Fri 6.30am–10pm, Sat 8.30–6, Sun 8.30am–10pm

This family-friendly sports centre offers squash and badminton, an indoor cycling studio and a well-equipped gym. They have a soft play area for children, and run activities for adults and children throughout the summer as well as year-round fitness courses. They are affiliated with the Copeland Pool, an indoor 25m pool on Cleator Road (tel 01946 696049).

EAT AND DRINK

Café West

westhouse.org.uk
56 King Street, CA28 7JH
01946 598969

All the ingredients used at this all-day cafe are locally sourced and you'll find plenty of it too. The cafe is run by West House, a charity that helps people with learning disabilities. The food's great and the efficient service comes with a smile.

Wellington Bistro

thebeacon-whitehaven.co.uk
The Beacon, West Strand, CA28 7LY
01946 592302

After exploring Whitehaven's historic waterfront, unwind in the peaceful Wellington Bistro, with freshly made sandwiches, snacks or an excellent cream tea, surrounded by the artwork of local and community groups.

▶ Windermere & Bowness-on-Windermere MAP REF 257 E3

To many visitors, a visit to the Lakes implies nothing more strenuous than mooching around the shops of Windermere and Bowness, and perhaps a relaxing boat trip on the lake. These twin towns – almost joined into one these days – attract a disproportionate number of holidaymakers. If you do want to shop, you'll find lots of quirky and interesting shops here and a buzz of activity. On the other hand, if you're looking for the National Park's ethos of 'quiet recreation', you should look elsewhere. Be aware, traffic congestion is a perennial problem, particularly in the summer months and on bank holidays.

The popularity of Windermere and Bowness is largely historical. Windermere is as far into the heart of the Lake District as the railway ever went. William Wordsworth lamented the coming of the railway; he foresaw that his beloved Lakeland would be spoiled by an influx of visitors. Certainly the railway opened up the Lakeland landscape to working people, instead of just well-heeled travellers with time on their hands. Wordsworth was right, of course – the Lake District did change.

▼ Lake Windermere with Ambleside in the distance

Bowness-on-Windermere

0 — 200 m

Fallbarrow Park
(Caravan and Holiday Park)

RAYRIGG ROAD

RAYRIGG RISE

LONGLANDS ROAD

LAKE ROAD

BERESFORD ROAD

SOUTH CRAIG

CRAIG WALK

ELM GROVE

BISKEY HOWE ROAD

NORTH TER

SOUTH TER

BANK TER

CRAG

Royalty

A5074

QUARRY BROW

QUARRY RIGG

FALLBARROW ROAD

The World of Beatrix Potter

The Old Laundry

LOW FOLD

St Martin's PDE

A592

CRAG BROW

HELM ROAD

HELM CLOSE

HELM ROAD

Bistey Howe

Windermere

Bowness Bay

To Ambleside

Curlew Crag

Royal Windermere Yacht Club

FALLBARROW ROAD

† St Martin's

PROMENADE

LAKE ROAD

FISH STREET

BELLE ISLE VIEW

LANGRIGGE HOWE

LANGRIGGE PARK

LANGRIGGE DRIVE

BEECHWOOD CLOSE

BRANTFELL ROAD

FELL WALK

BRAN

Pier 1

Pier 2

To Ferry House & Lakeside

Pier 3

GLEBE ROAD

The Belsfield Hotel

BELSFIELD ROAD

A5074

BRANTFELL ROAD

FAIRFIELD

BRACKENFIELD

Postknott Plantation

The Glebe

RECTORY ROAD

LAKE GARDENS

BACK BELSFIELD ROAD

A592

KENDAL ROAD

Post Knott

Brant Fell

Bowness Pitch & Putt

GLEBE ROAD

The Burnside Hotel & Spa

BLLT

On the other hand, millions of people are now able to enjoy its unrivalled scenery.

It may seem a bit odd that it is Windermere, rather than Bowness at the water's edge, which takes its name from the lake. But in fact, before the coming of the railway in 1847, Windermere was called Birthwaite; the station was called Windermere to attract visitors.

At Bowness Bay, the water of England's longest lake laps gently on the beach and sleek clinker-built dinghies can be hired by the hour. If you don't feel so energetic, you can enjoy a lake-long cruise, via Waterhead and Lakeside, on the cruise ships *Tern*, *Teal* and *Swan*. *Tern* is more than 100 years old and was once steam-powered. Since 2005, when the National Park Authority's 10mph water speed limit took effect, Windermere has become a more peaceful lake.

Opposite Bowness Bay is Belle Isle, the largest of Windermere's islands. You can still see the roundhouse built there in 1774, when notions of the 'romantic' and 'picturesque' were at their height. The design was much mocked at the time; Wordsworth called it 'a pepperpot'. Before that, there was a manor house on the island, which was besieged by troops of Roundheads, while the Royalist owner was busy fighting in Carlisle, and archaeological finds reveal that Belle Isle was occupied during Roman times. It was bought in 1781 as a present for Mrs Isabella Curwen, and renamed in the lady's honour. While the National Trust owns most of Windermere's little islands, Belle Isle is still privately owned.

A couple of minutes' walk from the lake, at the bottom of Bowness Hill, is The Old Laundry Theatre, which caters for visitors and locals alike. As well as a theatre, there is a regular programme of exhibitions and events. Here, too, you'll find The World of Beatrix Potter, which uses the latest technology to bring the stories of Peter Rabbit, Jemima Puddleduck and many other characters to life.

Just a mile and a half from the centre of Bowness is a house of exquisite beauty. Completed in 1900 for the Manchester brewing mogul Sir Edward Holt, Blackwell (see page 70) was designed by Mackay Hugh Baillie Scott as an astounding expression of the Arts and Crafts Movement. Today it has been restored after decades of neglect and astonishingly almost all of the distinctive decorative features have remained intact.

A further 2.5 miles north along the Ambleside road brings you to Brockhole, a fine house in gardens that shelve down to the lake shore. Built for a Manchester businessman, the house

▲ Lake Windermere

has, since the late 1960s, been the National Park Visitor Centre. Brockhole is an excellent first stop, if you are new to the Lake District. There are gardens, displays, exhibitions, an adventure playground and a full calendar of events.

The eastern shore of Windermere is, for much of its length, in private hands. Mill owners who prospered from the trade in wool and cotton eagerly bought up plots of land to create tranquil oases with views of the lake. The drive along the lake on the A592 can be disappointing since there are few public access points to the water's edge, however you will find plenty of lakeside walking on the less-populated western shore, much of which belongs to the National Trust.

For an elevated view of the lake, take a path to the left of the Windermere Hotel, at the top of the town. Within a few minutes you will be able to enjoy a glorious view of the lake and the southern Lakeland fells from the vantage point of Orrest Head. Another excellent viewpoint is the rounded hill called Gummer's How, which you can approach via a minor road just north of Newby Bridge. From the top – half-an-hour's walk from the car park – you will be able to see almost the length of Windermere, with the yachts and motorboats looking like tiny toys.

▶ The World of Beatrix Potter

MAP REF 257 E3

hop-skip-jump.com
The Old Laundry, LA23 3BX | 01539
488444 | Open daily 10–5.30, last entry
4.30 (closes at 3 on 24 & 31 Dec, at 4 on
26 Dec & 1 Jan)

If you're a Beatrix Potter fan, then
The World of Beatrix Potter will transport you straight back to your childhood, and for children it is just like stepping into the books and meeting old friends. It begins with a four-minute film presentation introducing Beatrix Potter and her stories. As you go through the exhibition you'll see 3D scenes from the stories, atmospheric lighting and real sounds and smells straight from the books – you can smell the laundry in Mrs Tiggy-Winkle's kitchen and the tomatoes in Mr McGregor's greenhouse. You can walk through Jemima's woodland glade and through the trees to see Mr Tod. You can wander through the Peter Rabbit Garden, with the cos lettuces that Benjamin Bunny nibbled and the gooseberry bush where Peter got caught in a net as he tried to escape Mr McGregor.

Using computer projection, you can take a journey to the places that inspired Beatrix Potter. And don't miss the interactive timeline, which tells the fascinating story of the author's life.

▶ Lake District Visitor Centre at Brockhole MAP REF 257 E2

brockhole.co.uk

LA23 1LJ | 015394 46601 | Open all year daily

You couldn't do better than to start your visit to the Lake District at this interesting and informative establishment designed to help you get the most out of the area. Set in 32 acres of grounds, landscaped by Thomas Mawson, on the shore of the lake, it became England's first National Park Visitor Centre in 1969. You'll find something for everyone and all the information on the Lake District you could want. It has permanent and temporary exhibitions, lake cruises, an adventure playground, an indoor play area and an extensive events programme. The kids will love Tree Top Trek – an outdoor high-ropes experience – where they can swing, climb, balance and fly their way through 250-year-old oak trees, discovering views previously reserved for the squirrels and bats. Contact the Centre for a copy of their free events guide. Canoe and sailing tuition is available in school holidays and you can hire boats in summer, weekends and school holidays.

▼ Lake District National Park Visitor Centre, Brockhole

TAKE IN SOME HISTORY
Townend
see page 219

ENTERTAIN THE FAMILY
The World of Beatrix Potter
see highlight panel on page 245

GO ROUND THE GARDENS
Holehird Gardens
holehirdgardens.org.uk
Lakeland Horticultural Society,
Patterdale Road, LA23 1NP | 015394
46008 | Gardens open all year daily
dawn–dusk, reception desk: Apr–Oct
10–4

If you're a gardener you will
love the Lakeland Horticultural
Society's 17-acre garden,
maintained completely by
volunteer members of the LHS.
You'll find plenty of like-minded
gardeners to chat to in this
splendid hillside site with
stream gardens and rocky
outcrops looking to Windermere
and the Langdale Pikes. The
garden includes specimen trees
and flowering shrubs for all
seasons. Among the highlights
are autumn heather and
shrubs, spring bulbs and
alpines. There are also national
collections of astilbe,
hydrangea and polystichum,
as well as fine herbaceous
borders, herbs and climbers.
The Lakeland Horticultural
Society was founded in 1969,
and there are a number of LHS
events throughout the year.

GET OUTDOORS
**Lake District Visitor Centre
at Brockhole**
see highlight panel opposite

SEE A LOCAL CHURCH
Church of St Martin
Junction of Church Street and
St Martin's Parade, LA23 3DE

Although built onto a 13th-
century church, most of what
you can see today dates from
the 1870 restoration. Look out
for the different roof beams,
where the chancel was
extended to the east. The tower
was heightened and all the
seating renewed. Most of the
fine murals, including two large
wall paintings in the chancel,
date from this time as well. The
1870 restoration also skilfully
restored the 15th-century
stained-glass east window,
which survived the vandalism of
Cromwell's soldiers. Looking
towards this great window from
the font is another stunning
feature: eight black-letter
inscriptions from the 16th
century, high up on the beams
between the arches.

TAKE A BOAT TRIP
Windermere Lake Cruises
windermere-lakecruises.co.uk
Bowness, LA23 3HQ; Ambleside
LA22 0EY | Lakeside, LA12 8AS
015394 43360

A cruise on Windermere is a
must. No matter where you
start your journey, be it
Bowness, Ambleside or
Lakeside, the voyage gives you
magnificent views of mountain
scenery, secluded bays and
wooded islands. You can break
your journey at any of the stops
and there is a range of ticket
options. The Freedom of the
Lake ticket from any pier is

good value, allowing you to hop on and off as many times as you want for a period of 24 hours. Or in summer take the 75-minute cruise to watch the sun set over Lake Windermere. There are lots of activities that you can combine with a cruise on the lake to make a great day out. In summer, you can take a trip on the Lakeside & Haverthwaite Steam Railway (see page 146). At any time you can visit the Lakeland Motor Museum (see page 63), the Aquarium at Lakeside (see page 176) or of course you can cruise and walk. Check the website for special events.

CATCH A PERFORMANCE
The Old Laundry Theatre
oldlaundrytheatre.co.uk
Crag Brow, LA23 3BX | 01539 488444

In this interesting Edwardian laundry building, only three minutes' walk from Lake Windermere, you'll find an intimate theatre presenting performances ranging from touring theatre companies to comedy to music and film.

EXPLORE BY BIKE
Country Lanes
countrylaneslakedistrict.co.uk
Windermere Railway Station
LA23 1AH | 015394 44544

You can hire all sorts of bikes here: trek bikes, road, hybrid and tandems; child bikes, trailers and tag-alongs are available too. Safety equipment and accessories are supplied. They also offer self-guided tours, with accommodation, meals, baggage transfers, routes and mechanical back-up all included.

PLAY A ROUND
Windermere Golf Club
windermeregolfclub.co.uk
Cleabarrow, LA23 3NB
015394 43123 | Open daily

Just 2 miles from Windermere, this is not a long course but offers heather, tight undulating fairways and fabulous views. The sixth hole has a nerve-racking but exhilarating blind shot over a rocky face to a humpy fairway, with a lake to avoid later.

EAT AND DRINK
Beech Hill Hotel & Spa ◉
beechhillhotel.co.uk
Newby Bridge Road, LA23 3LR
015394 42137

After canapés and pre-dinner drinks you can soak up the dramatic views over Lake Windermere to the fells beyond from Burlington's Restaurant. The menu's altogether more catholic than that usually found in such a context – local produce is used to good effect, and the kitchen clearly has a good solid grounding in the French classics.

Cedar Manor Hotel & Restaurant ◉
cedarmanor.co.uk
Ambleside Road, LA23 1AX
015394 43192

Built of grey stone in 1854, the manor occupies a peaceful spot in attractive gardens on the outskirts of Windermere. The restaurant is well appointed, with leather-look chairs at neatly set tables; well-trained but unbuttoned staff keep the ball rolling. Seasonality leads the kitchen, with its reliance on Lakeland produce, and the cooking is marked out by its technical precision.

Gilpin Hotel & Lake House ⍟⍟⍟

thegilpin.co.uk

Crook Road, LA23 3NE

015394 88818

This Edwardian house in 22 acres of peaceful gardens, moors and woodland is the very essence of a tranquil and luxurious getaway. Its original features (built in 1901) remain, but the impression within is of timeless contemporary luxury and comfort. Eating here remains, as ever, a highlight of a stay. The cooking is thrillingly contemporary, but clearly focused at the same time.

Holbeck Ghyll Country House Hotel ⍟⍟⍟

holbeckghyll.com

Holbeck Lane, LA23 1LU

015394 32375

Sitting proud above the shimmering expanse of Lake Windermere, Holbeck Ghyll enjoys panoramic views of the pikes and fells in the distance, and the long drive up to the front door emphasises the feeling that you are entering another world. Inside, the house is consummately stylish, its art nouveau signature decor

beautifully maintained, and an air of a peaceable retreat reigns supreme. The oak-panelled main restaurant has bundles of charm, and confident country-house cookery, with a strong classical foundation, offset with a little French-inspired modernity, is the deal here.

Lindeth Howe Country House Hotel & Restaurant ⍟⍟

lindeth-howe.co.uk

Lindeth Drive, Longtail Hill, LA23 3JF | 015394 45759

This is a classic country house with a unique pedigree – it was once home to Beatrix Potter, who wrote a couple of her tales here. So after consuming the delicious views of the lake and mountains beyond, and exploring the verdant grounds, it is back for dinner in the handsomely turned-out dining room. The kitchen team is passionate about regional produce, seeking out first-class ingredients and serving up a menu of contemporary dishes.

Miller Howe Hotel ⍟⍟

millerhowe.com

Rayrigg Road, LA23 1EY

015394 42536

Miller Howe must be the yardstick by which other country-house hotels are judged, with its emphasis on guests' comfort, luxury fixtures and fittings, 5.5 acres of landscaped grounds and stunning views over Lake Windermere to Langdale Pikes. The restaurant, spread over three rooms, with its lime-green colour scheme and wooden floor, is split-level to ensure most guests can enjoy the lake views. 'Modern British with a twist' is the self-described cooking style, and the kitchen devises relatively short but punchy menus.

The Samling ⊚⊚⊚

thesamlinghotel.co.uk
Ambleside Road, LA23 1LR
015394 31922

The immaculate white-painted house overlooking Lake Windermere provides a classic Lakeland vista. It's a gloriously peaceful spot within 67 acres of grounds, with the bucolic panorama best taken in from the terrace with a glass of something in your hand. The interior is simply smart and stylish. Country-house dining doesn't get much more modern than what's on offer in the restaurant. There's a development kitchen where dishes are created and refined, and a kitchen garden that uses progressive techniques to grow first-class produce.

Storrs Hall Hotel ⊚⊚

storrshall.com
Storrs Park, LA23 3LG
015394 47111

This sparkling-white Georgian villa stands amid 17 acres of manicured grounds, its deep windows generously taking in the classic Lakeland view of shining water and brooding fells. Inside, the decor aims for strong colour contrasts rather than bland pastels, with apple

green and aubergine the theme in the Tower Bar, so named as the bar itself was fashioned from materials salvaged from Blackpool Tower. The main dining room looks out over the gardens and makes a relaxing setting for the ingenious modern cooking.

▶ PLACES NEARBY

Claife Viewing Station

nationaltrust.org.uk
Far Sawrey, LA22 0LW | 015394 41456 | Open daily, dawn to dusk
Hop on the ferry from Bowness to the lake's west shore to visit the recently restored Claife Viewing Station. Built in the 1790s, early tourists would come here to admire the landscape through tinted windows, each colour representing different conditions – orange for autumn, for example, or dark blue for moonlight. Small strips of coloured glass have been reinstated around the edge of what were once window frames and the tower provides great views of the lake. The nearby Cafe in the Courtyard is also run by the National Trust.

The Punchbowl Inn at Crosthwaite ⊚⊚

the-punchbowl.co.uk
Crosthwaite, LA8 8HR
015395 68237

Very much a destination dining inn, The Punchbowl stands alongside the village church in the unspoilt Lyth Valley. The slates on the bar floor were found beneath the old dining room and complement the Brathay slate bar top and antique furniture. The restaurant has polished oak floorboards, comfortable leather chairs and a striking stone fireplace. Two rooms off the bar add extra space to eat or relax with a pint in front of an open fire. The menu is sourced extensively from the local area.

Hare & Hounds Inn & Restaurant

hareandhoundsbowlandbridge.co.uk

Bowland Bridge, LA11 6NN

015395 68333

In the pretty little hamlet of Bowland Bridge, not far from Bowness, the pub has gorgeous views of Cartmel Fell. Its traditional country-pub atmosphere is fostered by the flagstone floors, stacked logs, wooden tables and mis-matched chairs. Strong links with local food producers result in exclusively reared pork and lamb on the menu.

Staveley

The village of Staveley is off the A591 between Kendal and Windermere. It mainly comprises grey slate buildings, which lie between the rivers Kent and Gowan. Only the tower of its 14th-century church remains. St James was built in 1865 and it's worth going in to see the superb Arts and Crafts stained-glass east window designed by Burne-Jones and made by William Morris and Co.

Eagle & Child Inn

eaglechildinn.co.uk

Kendal Road, Staveley, LA8 9LP

01539 821320

The name of this friendly inn refers to a legend of a baby found in an eagle's nest during the time of King Alfred. The rivers Kent and Gowan meet at the pub's gardens with its picnic tables for outdoor eating and local-ale drinking. You'll find plenty of classic Cumbrian dishes on the menu, which all use ingredients from village suppliers.

Hawkshead Brewery

hawksheadbrewery.co.uk

Mill Yard, Staveley, LA8 9LR

01539 825260

This is the biggest of the Cumbrian independents, family owned and run with the aim of brewing 'traditional beers with a modern twist'.

The Brown Horse Inn

thebrownhorseinn.co.uk

Winster, LA23 3NR

015394 43443

Despite all the time-worn charm of this 1850s inn in the beautiful and tranquil Winster Valley, the decor has a subtly modern edge. The inn is virtually self-sufficient, as the vegetables and free-range meat come from the owners' surrounding land, and real ales are brewed on site. The tastily innovative cooking offers a contemporary take on traditional fare.

▸ Overleaf: Lake Windermere

▶ Workington MAP REF 260 B4

Workington is an ancient market and industrial town at the mouth of the River Derwent. Some parts of the town, north of the River Derwent, date back to Roman times. Workington became a major industrial town and port in the 18th century with the expansion of the local iron ore and coal industries and Henry Bessemer introduced his revolutionary steel-making process here. In recent years, the steel industry and coal mining have declined and the town has diversified into other forms of industry.

VISIT THE MUSEUM
Helena Thompson Museum
helenathompson.org.uk
Park End Road, CA14 4DE | 01900 64040 | Open Mon–Fri 10–4.30, Sun 1.30–4.30 (last entry 4)
Miss Helena Thompson was a local philanthropist who bequeathed her house to the people of Workington in 1940. You can see pottery, silver, glass and furniture dating from Georgian times, as well as find out about the social and industrial history of Workington. Helena had a special interest in the history of costume and needlework, and collected many examples of women's and children's dresses in the styles fashionable from the late 18th century to the beginning of the 20th century. You can see a selection of these too, along with jewellery and accessories.

CATCH A PERFORMANCE
Carnegie Theatre and Arts Centre
carnegietheatre.co.uk
Finkle Street, CA14 2BD
01900 602122
The historic Carnegie Theatre and Arts Centre started life as the Carnegie Library and Lecture Hall, built with £7,500 donated by the philanthropist Andrew Carnegie. It opened to the public in 1904 and the Lecture Hall was subsequently let as a variety show and cinema venue to earn sufficient income to pay the librarian and buy books for the library.

In 1911, the centre was extended into the adjoining house to provide an adequate variety stage. It operated as a cinema until 1958. In 1973 the Library Service moved out and the town council converted the building into an arts centre. You will now find a regular programme of events including opera, classical and popular music, as well as theatre and dance. Check the website for details.

EXPLORE BY BIKE
Coast-to-Coast (C2C) Cycle Route
see page 238

PLAY A ROUND
Workington Golf Club
workingtongolfclub.com
Branthwaite Road, CA14 4SS
01900 603460 | Open daily

This is an undulating meadowland course, with natural hazards created by a stream and trees. There are good views of Solway Firth and Lakeland Hills. The 10th, 13th and 15th holes are described as particularly testing.

EAT AND DRINK
The Old Ginn House
oldginnhouse.co.uk
Great Clifton, CA14 1TS
01900 64616
When this was a farm, ginning was the process by which horses were used to turn a grindstone that crushed the grain. This action took place in the rounded area known today as the Ginn Room and which is now the main bar, serving local ales. The dining areas – all butter yellow, bright check curtains and terracotta tiles – rather bring the tastes of the Mediterranean to mind, although the extensive menu and specials offer both the cosmopolitan and traditional. A good vegetarian choice is available, too.

▶ Yewbarrow House

yewbarrowhouse.co.uk

Grange-over-Sands, LA11 6BE | 01539 532469 | Open Jun–Sep first Sun of month or by appointment for groups of 10 or more

If you're a keen or even moderately interested gardener, don't miss this spectacular garden set high above sea level and with glorious coastal views. The use of local slate and limestone to create snaking paths, dividing walls and structural features gives the 4.5-acre garden of Yewbarrow House a fitting sense of place. The old Victorian garden has been transformed from a near-wilderness of brambles, unkempt trees and shrubs to a garden and woodland with year-round colour, a variety of moods and a number of surprises.

On an exposed, sloping site you might be surprised to see exotic plants thriving so far from their native warmer climes. And yet here at Yewbarrow House, where frost very rarely penetrates the ground, there are olive trees that bear fruitful if modest crops; mimosa that sparkles like sunlight against the neutral background of a ruined stone bridge; and myriad exciting plants that are native to Mexico, Hawaii, Africa, Australia and New Zealand.

Much of the garden is decorative and inspirational, but the Victorian Kitchen Garden also has work to do, providing fruit, vegetables and herbs not just 'for the house', as in days gone by, but for the owner's three neighbouring hotels. It is entirely organic and everything is planted using the crop rotation system. There is also a large cutting garden with row upon row of flowers that, like the produce, are sent to the sister hotels.

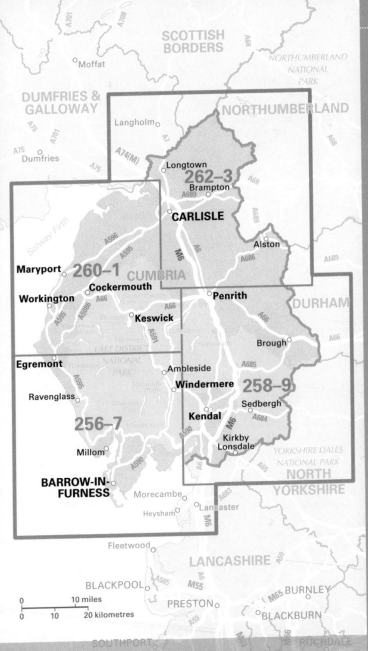

Moffat

SCOTTISH BORDERS

NORTHUMBERLAND NATIONAL PARK

DUMFRIES & GALLOWAY

NORTHUMBERLAND

Langholm

Dumfries

Longtown

262–3
Brampton

CARLISLE

Alston

Maryport

260–1 CUMBRIA
Cockermouth

Workington

Penrith

DURHAM

Keswick

Brough

LAKE DISTRICT NATIONAL PARK

Egremont

Ambleside

Windermere

258–9

Ravenglass

256–7

Kendal

Sedbergh

Kirkby
Lonsdale

YORKSHIRE DALES NATIONAL PARK

Millom

NORTH
YORKSHIRE

BARROW-IN-FURNESS

Morecambe

Lancaster

Heysham

Fleetwood

LANCASHIRE

BLACKPOOL

BURNLEY

PRESTON

BLACKBURN

0   10 miles
0   10   20 kilometres

SOUTHPORT

ROCHDALE

BURY

WIGAN   BOLTON

ATLAS

★ A-Z places listed

● Places Nearby

MANCHESTER

WARRINGTON

WIDNES   RUNCORN

Colwyn
Bay

ELLESMERE
PORT

CHESHIRE
EAST

FLINTS   CHESTER   WEST

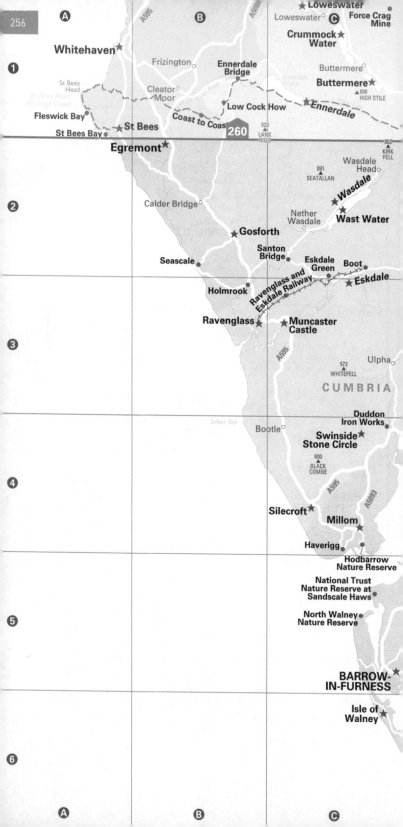

Ⓐ **Ⓑ** **Ⓒ**

①

★ **Loweswater**
Loweswater○ **Ⓒ** ★ Force Crag Mine

Whitehaven ★
★ **Crummock Water**

Frizington○
Ennerdale Bridge
Buttermere○
St Bees Head
St Bees Head Heritage Coast
Cleator○ Moor
Buttermere ★
▲ 806 HIGH STILE

Fleswick Bay ●
★ **St Bees**
Coast to Coast
Low Cock How ●
★ **Ennerdale**

St Bees Bay ●
260
533 ▲ LANK RIGG
802 ▲ KIRK FELL

Egremont ★
Wasdale Head ○

691 ▲ SEATALLAN

②
Calder Bridge○
Nether Wasdale ○
★ **Wasdale**
★ **Wast Water**

★ **Gosforth**
Santon Bridge ●
Eskdale Green ●
Boot ●

Seascale ●
Ravenglass and Eskdale Railway
★ **Eskdale**

Holmrook ●

Ravenglass ★
★ **Muncaster Castle**

③
A595
Ulpha ○

573 ▲ WHITEFELL

CUMBRIA

Duddon Iron Works ●
Solker Bay
Bootle ○
★ **Swinside Stone Circle**

600 ▲ BLACK COMBE

④
A595
A5093

Silecroft ★
Millom ★

Haverigg ●
Hodbarrow Nature Reserve

National Trust Nature Reserve at Sandscale Haws ●

⑤
North Walney Nature Reserve ●

BARROW-IN-FURNESS ★

Isle of Walney ★

⑥

Ⓐ **Ⓑ** **Ⓒ**

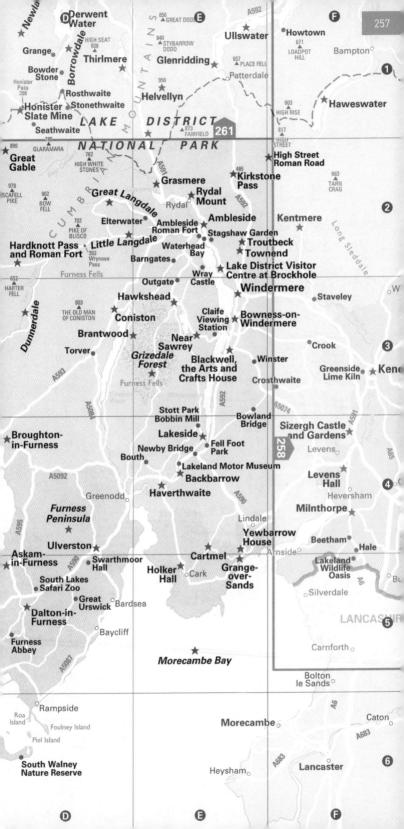

D Derwent Water
Newla...
HIGH SEAT 608 ★
★ Grange
Thirlmere
Bowder Stone ★
Henister Pass 356
Rosthwaite
★ Honister Slate Mine
Stonethwaite
Seathwaite

E 856 ▲ GREAT DODD
840 ▲ STYBARROW DODD
Glenridding
950 ★
Helvellyn
Ullswater
Howtown ●
657 ▲ PLACE FELL
671 LOADPOT HILL
Patterdale
Bampton ○

F

LAKE DISTRICT
803 ▲ HIGH RISE
★ Haweswater
817 ▲ HIGH STREET
NATIONAL PARK
873 ▲ FAIRFIELD
261

1

899 ▲ GLARAMARA
Great Gable ★
780 ▲
762 ▲ HIGH WHITE STONES
High Street Roman Road ★
663 ▲ TARN CRAG

978 ▲ SCAFELL PIKE
902 ▲ BOW FELL
★ Great Langdale
Grasmere ★
Rydal Mount ★
Kirkstone Pass ★ 485
2

702 ▲ PIKE OF BLISCO
Elterwater ●
Rydal
Ambleside ★
Kentmere ★
Hardknott Pass and Roman Fort ★
★ Little Langdale
Ambleside Roman Fort ★
Stagshaw Garden ★
Wrynose Pass
Waterhead Bay
★ Troutbeck
Townend ★
652 ▲ HARTER FELL
Barngates ●
Furness Fells
Lake District Visitor Centre at Brockhole ★

Dunnerdale
Outgate ●
Wray Castle ★
Windermere ★
Staveley ○
803 ▲ THE OLD MAN OF CONISTON
Hawkshead ★
3
★ Coniston
Claife Viewing Station ★
Bowness-on-Windermere ★
Brantwood ★
Near Sawrey ★
Crook ●
Torver ●
Grizedale Forest
Blackwell, the Arts and Crafts House ★
Winster ●
Greenside Lime Kiln ★
Ken
Crosthwaite ●
Furness Fells

Stott Park Bobbin Mill ★
Bowland Bridge ●
Sizergh Castle and Gardens ★
258
Broughton-in-Furness ★
Lakeside ★
Newby Bridge ●
Fell Foot Park ●
Levens ○
Bouth ●
Lakeland Motor Museum ●
Backbarrow ★
Levens Hall ★
4
Greenodd ○
Haverthwaite ★
Heversham ○
Furness Peninsula ★
Lindale ○
Milnthorpe ★
Yewbarrow House ★
Beetham ○
Ulverston ★
Cartmel ★
Arnside ○
Hale ●
Askam-in-Furness ★
Swarthmoor Hall ★
Holker Hall ★
Cark ○
Grange-over-Sands ★
Lakeland Wildlife Oasis ●
South Lakes Safari Zoo ●
LANCASHIR
Great Urswick ●
Bardsea ○
Silverdale ○
Dalton-in-Furness ★
5
Baycliff ○
Furness Abbey ★
Carnforth ○
Morecambe Bay

Rampside ○
Roa Island ○
Foulney Island
Piel Island
Morecambe ○
Caton ○
South Walney Nature Reserve ●
6
Heysham ○
Lancaster ●

D **E** **F**

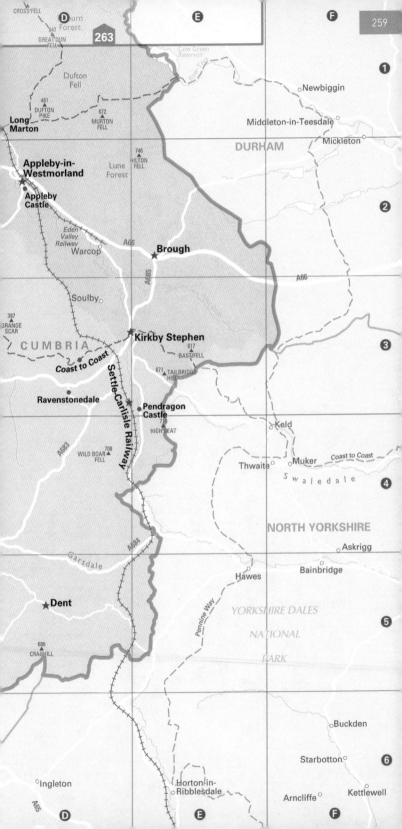

CROSS FELL

D
Dun Forest

E

F

893
GREAT DUN
FELL

263

Dufton Fell

Cow Green
Reservoir

1

Newbiggin

481
DUFTON
PIKE

672
MURTON
FELL

Middleton-in-Teesdale

Long
Marton

DURHAM

Mickleton

Appleby-in-
Westmorland

746
HILTON
FELL

Lune
Forest

2

Appleby
Castle

Eden
Valley
Railway

A66

Warcop

Brough

A685

A66

Soulby

397
GRANGE
SCAR

CUMBRIA

Kirkby Stephen

3

617
BASTIFELL

Coast to Coast

671
TAILBRIDGE
HILL

Keld

Ravenstonedale

Pendragon
Castle

710
HIGH SEAT

Coast to Coast

A683

Thwaite

Muker

708
WILD BOAR
FELL

Swaledale

4

NORTH YORKSHIRE

Askrigg

Garsdale

A684

Bainbridge

Hawes

Dent

YORKSHIRE DALES

686
CRAGHILL

NATIONAL

5

PARK

Buckden

Starbotton

6

Ingleton

A65

Horton-in-
Ribblesdale

Arncliffe

Kettlewell

D

E

F

Settle-Carlisle Railway

Pennine Way

Ⓐ

Ⓑ

Ⓒ

❶

Kirkbean ○

Mainsriddle ○

Firth

Grune
Point

Moricambe Bay

Solway

Silloth ★

❷

**Beckfoot
Beach** ●

Abbey
Town ○

A596

Westnewton ○

Allonby ●

Allonby
Bay

Prospect ○

Aspatria ○

❸

Bothel ○

A59

Maryport ★

Dearham ○

A595

**Lake District
Wildlife Park** ●

Flimby ○

Broughton
Moor ○

A596

Seaton ○

Cockermouth ★

A66

Brigham ○

Workington ★

Moss
Bay

A597

Branthwaite ○

★ **Lorton
Vale**

318
Whinlatter
Pass

❹

A5086

★ **Loweswater**

A595

Loweswater ○

**Force Crag
Mine** ●

**Crummock ★
Water**

Whitehaven ★

Frizington ○

**Ennerdale
Bridge**

Buttermere ○

Buttermere ★

❺

St Bees
Head

Cleator ○
Moor

Ennerdale Water

▲806
HIGH STILE

St Bees Heritage Coast

Low Cock How ●

★ **Ennerdale**

Fleswick Bay ●

Coast to Coast ●

533
LANK
RIGG

802
▲
KIRK
FELL

St Bees Bay ●

★ **St Bees**

Egremont ★

256

Wasdale
Head

❻

Calder Bridge ○

691
▲
SEATALLAN

★ **Wasdale**

Nether
Wasdale ○

Wast Water

★ **Gosforth**

Santon
Bridge ●

Ⓐ

Seascale **Ⓑ**

Eskdale
Green **Ⓒ** Boot

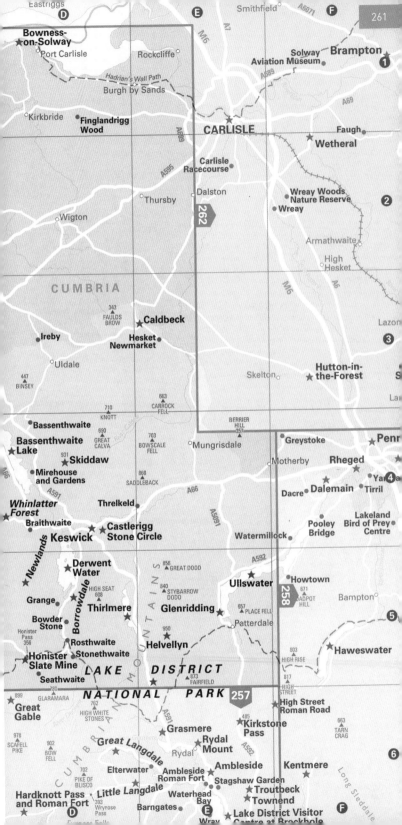

Eastriggs
Smithfield
A6071
D
E
F
1

Bowness-on-Solway
Port Carlisle
Rockcliffe
Solway
Brampton
Aviation Museum
A689

Hadrian's Wall Path
Burgh by Sands
A7

Kirkbride
Finglandrigg Wood
A595
CARLISLE
Faugh
Wetheral
A69

Carlisle Racecourse
Dalston
Thursby
262
Wreay Woods Nature Reserve
Wreay
2

Wigton
Armathwaite
High Hesket

CUMBRIA
343 FAULDS BROW
A595
M6
A6
Lazon

Ireby
Caldbeck
Hesket Newmarket
Skelton
Hutton-in-the-Forest
3

Uldale
447 BINSEY
710 KNOTT
663 CARROCK FELL
BERRIER HILL 357

Bassenthwaite
690 GREAT CALVA
703 BOWSCALE FELL
Mungrisdale
Greystoke
Penr

Bassenthwaite Lake
931
Skiddaw
868 SADDLEBACK
A66
Motherby
Rheged
4
Yar a

Mirehouse and Gardens
A591
Dacre
Dalemain
Tirril

Whinlatter Forest
Threlkeld
A5091
Lakeland Bird of Prey Centre

Braithwaite
Castlerigg Stone Circle
Watermillock
Pooley Bridge

Keswick
856 GREAT DODD
A592

Derwent Water
840 STYBARROW DODD
Ullaswater
Howtown
671 ADPOT HILL
Bampton
258
5

Grange
HIGH SEAT 608
Thirlmere
Glenridding
657 PLACE FELL
Patterdale

Bowder Stone
950
Helvellyn
803 HIGH RISE
Haweswater

Honister Pass 356
Rosthwaite
Stonethwaite
817 HIGH STREET

Honister Slate Mine
L A K E
D I S T R I C T
873 FAIRFIELD

Seathwaite
762 HIGH WHITE STONES
N A T I O N A L
P A R K
257
High Street Roman Road
663 TARN CRAG

899 GLARAMARA
Great Gable
485
Kirkstone Pass
6

978 SCAFELL PIKE
902 BOW FELL
Grasmere
Rydal Mount
A592
Kentmere

Great Langdale
Rydal
A591

702 PIKE OF BLISCO
Elterwater
Ambleside Roman Fort
Ambleside
Stagshaw Garden
Troutbeck

Hardknott Pass and Roman Fort
393 Wrynose Pass
Little Langdale
Waterhead Bay
Townend

D
Barngates
E
Lake District Visitor Centre at Brockhole
F

Wray

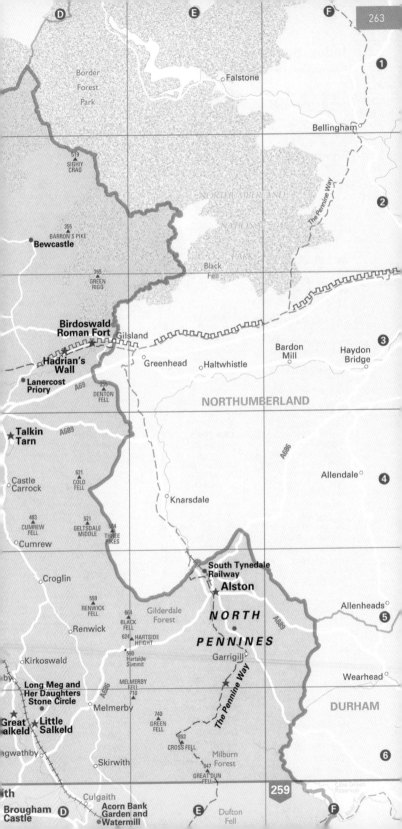

D **E** **F**

①

Border
Forest
Park

○ Falstone

Bellingham ○

②

519
▲
SIGHTY
CRAG

NORTHUMBERLAND

The Pennine Way

355
▲
BARRON'S PIKE

● Bewcastle

NATIONAL

265
▲
GREEN
RIGG

PARK

Black
Fell

③

Birdoswald
Roman Fort   Gilsland

Bardon
Mill

Haydon
Bridge ○

Hadrian's
Wall

○ Greenhead   ○ Haltwhistle

● Lanercost
Priory

A69

255
▲
DENTON
FELL

NORTHUMBERLAND

★ Talkin
Tarn

A689

A686

Allendale ○

④

Castle
Carrock ○

621
▲
COLD
FELL

○ Knarsdale

483
▲
CUMREW
FELL

521
▲
GELTSDALE
MIDDLE

584
▲
THREE
PIKES

○ Cumrew

● South Tynedale
Railway

○ Croglin

559
▲
RENWICK
FELL

664
▲
BLACK
FELL

Gilderdale
Forest

★ Alston

NORTH

Allenheads ○

⑤

○ Renwick

624
▲
HARTSIDE
HEIGHT

PENNINES

A689

○ Kirkoswald

580
▲
Hartside
Summit

Garrigill ○

The Pennine Way

Wearhead ○

★ Long Meg and
Her Daughters
Stone Circle

MELMERBY
FELL
710
▲

A686

★
Great
alkeld

★ Little
Salkeld

○ Melmerby

740
▲
GREEN
FELL

DURHAM

gwathby ○

○ Skirwith

893
▲
CROSS FELL

Milburn
Forest

⑥

847
▲
GREAT DUN
FELL

th

○ Culgaith

259

● Brougham
Castle

D

● Acorn Bank
Garden and
Watermill

E

Dufton
Fell

F

Index, themed

Page numbers in **bold** refer to main text entries

Index, places

Page numbers in **bold** refer to main entries; page numbers in *italics* refer to town plans

The Automobile Association wishes to thank the following photographers and organisations for their assistance in the preparation of this book.

Abbreviations for the picture credits are as follows – (t) top; (m) middle; (b) bottom; (l) left; (r) right; (c) centre; (AA) AA World Travel Library.

4tl AA/E Bowness; 4tr–5tl AA/T Mackie; 4b AA/T Mackie; 5bl AA/A Mockford & N Bonetti; 5r AA; 8–9 AA/T Mackie; 11 AA/T Mackie; 12t AA/T Mackie; 12b Courtesy of the Cumberland Pencil Museum; 13t Courtesy of Theatre by the Lake; 13m Courtesy of the Brantwood Trust; 13b John Morrison/Alamy; 14t AA/R Coulam; 14m itdarbs/Alamy; 14b AA/E Bowness; 15t Courtesy of The World of Beatrix Potter; 15b The National Trust Photolibrary/Alamy; 16t AA/A Mockford & N Bonetti; 16m Steve Morgan/Alamy; 16b AA/T Mackie; 17 AA/S Day; 19 AA/S Day; 20 AA/T Mackie; 22 AA/J Smith; 23 Photodisc; 24 Andrew Darrington/Alamy; 25 AA/T Mackie; 26 AA/A Mockford & N Bonetti; 29 AA/J Smith; 30 AA/A Mockford & N Bonetti; 32 AA/E Bowness; 33 AA/A Mockford & N Bonetti; 34 AA/A Mockford & N Bonetti; 36 AA/J Tims; 38 Andrew Page/Alamy; 39 numb/Alamy; 40 AA/E Bowness; 41 Courtesy of Jennings Brewery; 42 AA/J Tims; 45 AA/A Mockford & N Bonetti; 47 Courtesy of The World of Beatrix Potter/Steven Barber; 48 Mark Richardson/ Alamy; 50 AA/A Burton; 52–3 AA/T Mackie; 56 AA/E Bowness; 57 AA/E Bowness; 60 Aisle/ Alamy; 68–9 AA/A Mockford & N Bonetti; 72 Clearview/Alamy; 73 AA/A Mockford & N Bonetti; 74 AA/A Mockford & N Bonetti; 79 AA/P Sharpe; 81 shoults/Alamy; 82–3 AA/T Mackie; 85 AA/E Bowness; 87 Stan Pritchard/Alamy; 88 age fotostock/Alamy; 90 Raymond Long/Alamy; 91 AA/R Coulam; 93 UK City Images/Alamy; 100–1 AA/S Day; 102 AA/C Lees; 105 AA/A Mockford & N Bonetti; 106 Park Dale/Alamy; 107 Courtesy of the Brantwood Trust; 109 AA/P Sharpe; 110-1 John Davidson Photos/Alamy; 112 AA/T Mackie; 115 AA/P Kenward; 116 AA/D Tarn; 118–9 AA/T Mackie; 120–1 AA/A Mockford & N Bonetti; 123 AA/A Mockford & N Bonetti; 126–7 AA/J Sparks; 131 Paul White – North West England/Alamy; 132–3 steven walker/Alamy; 137 AA/E Bowness; 140 AA/T Mackie; 141 AA/R Coulam; 142 AA/R Coulam; 143 AA/R Coulam; 144–5 AA/S Day; 146 AA/S Day; 151 Stewart Smith/ Alamy; 152 AA/P Sharpe; 154–5 AA/P Bennett; 156 AA/E Bowness; 157 AA/P Bennett; 162 David Lyons/Alamy; 163 Courtesy of the Cumberland Pencil Museum; 164 Courtesy of Theatre by the Lake; 165 Barrie Neil/Alamy; 166–167 AA/T Mackie; 168 AA/T Mackie; 169 AA/D Tarn; 174 AA/S Day; 175 AA/A Mockford & N Bonetti; 178–9 AA/T Mackie; 181 John Morrison/Alamy; 185 AA/E Bowness; 188–9 Paul White Aerial views/Alamy; 190–1 AA/T Mackie; 193t WorldPhotos/Alamy; 193b AA/E Bowness; 194 AA/T Mackie; 195 AA/P Sharpe; 196 Arcaid Images/Alamy; 200–1 NDP/Alamy; 206–7 AA/E Bowness; 208 AA/A Mockford & N Bonetti; 211 AA/J Sparks; 214 AA/E Bowness; 215 AA/A Mockford & N Bonetti; 216–7 AA/T Mackie; 218 AA/E Bowness; 220–1 AA/E Bowness; 223 Steve Morgan/ Alamy; 226 AA/E Bowness; 230–1 AA/A Baker; 232 AA/R Coulam; 236–7 AA/T Mackie; 240–1 AA/A Mockford & N Bonetti; 242 AA/A Mockford & N Bonetti; 244 AA/P Sharpe; 245t Courtesy of The World of Beatrix Potter; 245b Courtesy of The World of Beatrix Potter/Ben Barden Photography Ltd; 246 John Morrison/Alamy; 252 Adam Burton/Alamy; 272 AA

Every effort has been made to trace the copyright holders, and we apologise in advance for any unintentional omissions or errors. We would be pleased to apply any corrections in any following edition of this publication.

Series editor: Rebecca Needes
Authors: Hugh Taylor and
    Moira McCrossan
Updater: Vivienne Crow
Project editor: Creative-Plus

Proofreader: Karen Kemp
Designer: Tom Whitlock
Digital imaging & repro: Ian Little
Art director: James Tims

Additional writing by other AA contributors. Lore of the Land feature by Ruth Binney. Some content may appear in other AA books and publications.

Has something changed? Email us at travelguides@theaa.com.

YOUR TRUSTED GUIDE

The AA was founded in 1905 as a body initially intended to help motorists avoid police speed traps. As motoring became more popular, so did we, and our activities have continued to expand into a great variety of areas.

The first edition of the AA Members' Handbook appeared in 1908. Due to the difficulty many motorists were having finding reasonable meals and accommodation while on the road, the AA introduced a new scheme to include listings for 'about one thousand of the leading hotels' in the second edition in 1909. As a result the AA has been recommending and assessing establishments for over a century, and each year our professional inspectors anonymously visit and rate thousands of hotels, restaurants, guest accommodations and campsites. We are relied upon for our trustworthy and objective Star, Rosette and Pennant ratings systems, which you will see used in this guide to denote AA-inspected restaurants and campsites.

In 1912 we published our first handwritten routes and our atlas of town plans, and in 1925 our classic touring guide, *The AA Road Book of England and Wales,* appeared. Together, our accurate mapping and in-depth knowledge of places to visit were to set the benchmark for British travel publishing.

Since the 1990s we have dramatically expanded our publishing activities, producing high quality atlases, maps, walking and travel guides for the UK and the rest of the world. In this new series of regional travel guides we are drawing on more than a hundred years of experience to bring you the very best of Britain.